Life Online

ETHNOGRAPHIC ALTERNATIVES BOOK SERIES

Series Editors

Carolyn Ellis   Arthur P. Bochner

About the Series

Ethnographic Alternatives will emphasize experimental forms of qualitative writing that blur the boundaries between social sciences and humanities. The editors encourage submissions that experiment with novel forms of expressing lived experience, including literary, poetic, autobiographical, multi-voiced, conversational, critical, visual, performative, and co-constructed representations. Emphasis should be on expressing concrete lived experience through narrative modes of writing.

We are interested in ethnographic alternatives that promote narration of local stories; literary modes of descriptive scene setting, dialogue, and unfolding action; and inclusion of the author's subjective reactions, involvement in the research process, and strategies for practicing reflexive fieldwork.

Please send proposals to:

Carolyn Ellis and Arthur P. Bochner
College of Arts and Sciences; Department of Communication
University of South Florida
4202 East Fowler Avenue, CIS 1040
Tampa, FL 33620-7800

Books in the Series:

Volume 1, *Composing Ethnography: Alternative Forms of Qualitative Writing*, Carolyn Ellis and Arthur P. Bochner, editors

Volume 2, *Opportunity House: Ethnographic Stories of Mental Retardation*, Michael Angrosino

Volume 3, *Kaleidoscope Notes: Writing Women's Music and Organizational Culture*, Stacy Holman Jones

Volume 4, *Fiction and Social Research: By Ice or Fire*, Anna Banks and Stephen P. Banks, editors

Volume 5, *Reading Auschwitz*, Mary Lagerwey

Volume 6, *Life Online: Researching Real Experience in Virtual Space*, Annette N. Markham

Life Online

Researching Real Experience in Virtual Space

Annette N. Markham

ALTAMIRA
PRESS

A Division of Sage Publications, Inc.
Walnut Creek • London • New Delhi

For information contact:

AltaMira Press
A Division of Sage Publications, Inc.
1630 North Main Street, Suite 367
Walnut Creek, CA 94596
explore@altamira.sagepub.com
www.altamirapress.com

SAGE Publications Ltd.
6 Bonhill Street
London EC2A 4PU
United Kingdom

SAGE Publications India Pvt. Ltd.
M-32 Market
Greater Kailash 1
New Delhi 110 048

PRINTED IN THE UNITED STATES OF AMERICA

Library of Congress Cataloging-in-Publication Data

Markham, Annette N.
Life online : researching real experience in virtual space / Annette N. Markham.
        p. cm.--(Ethnographic alternatives book series; vol. 6)
    Includes bibliographical references and index.
    ISBN 0761990305 (cloth) ISBN 0761990313 (pbk.)
    1. Communication-Social aspects. 2. Cybernetics-Social aspects. 3. Social interaction. 4. Virtual reality.
        HM258.M2623 1998
        302.2-dc21   98-25339
                                                    CIP

98 99 00 01 02 03 04 05 06 07   10 9 8 7 6 5 4 3 2 1

Production and Editorial Services: David Featherstone
Editorial Management: Jennifer R. Collier
Cover Design: Joanna Ebenstein

Contents

Series Editors' Introduction   7
Foreword, by William K. Rawlins   9
Acknowledgments   13

Introduction   15

Chapter 1   Going Online   23

Interlude   Ambivalence and the Body   59

Chapter 2   The Shifting Project, The Shifting Self   61
Setting up the Interviews   62
Conducting the Interviews   70
Everything Changes, but Should the Researcher Admit This?   77
What Am I Looking For? And Is This the Same Question as "What Am I Finding?"   79
So What Am I Really Studying?   82

Chapter 3   Themes of Life in Cyberspace   85
Online Technology as a Tool . . . or a Place . . . or a Way of Being   86
Online Experiences Are Real . . . How Could Experience Be Otherwise?   115
Control of the Text Equals Control of Self, Other, and Social Structure   120

Chapter 4   Stories of Tools and Places   127
Matthew: I'm Just Me, Really or Virtually   129
Jennifer: The Computer Is a Rather Harsh Reminder that You Aren't There   140
Mist: Online Seems Simpler, I Guess . . . It Requires Less Effort and Commitment   149
Michael: The Community Makes It a Place   156

Interlude   Drawing Boxes   165

Chapter 5   Stories of Places and Ways of Being   169
Beth: Things Seem to Be Communicated Better through My Fingers than My
    Voice   169
Sheol: Cyberspace Is My Lifeline to the World;. I Am Many Things Here   176
Terri: Mediation, and Access to It, Is Empowerment; I Physically Crave It   191
Sherie: Eloquence Makes Me Beautiful Online   200
How Does a Researcher Analyze Something She Does Not Understand?   205
In Sum . . .   210

Interlude   Silence   217

Chapter 6   Reflecting   221
Thoughts About Online Communication   221
Thoughts About My Goals   223
Thoughts About the Project   225
Thoughts About the Future   227

Afterword   231

References Cited   235
Index   241
Index of Authors Cited   245
About the Author   247

Series Editors' Introduction

Ethnographic Alternatives publishes experimental forms of qualitative writing that purposefully blur the boundaries between social sciences and the humanities. The books in this series feature concrete details of everyday life. People are presented in them as complicated and vulnerable human beings who act and feel in complex, often unpredictable ways. As social agents, constrained but not controlled by culture, the characters in these books tell stories that often show a dazzling human capacity to remake and reform cultural narratives.

We encourage authors to write ethnography reflexively, weaving details about their own lives and relationships into the stories they tell about Others. The series' authors seek to share interpretive authority by presenting layered accounts with multiple voices and by experimenting with nontraditional forms of representation, including the fictional and the poetic. They try to stay open to surprise, and during their research they encourage challenges and revisions to their own interpretations. In these books, interpretive authority ultimately lies with the community of readers who engage the text. When these texts succeed, they encourage readers to feel, think about, and compare their own worlds of experience with those of the people they meet on the pages of these stories. In addition to stimulating a dialogue among academics across disciplinary lines, the books in the *Ethnographic Alternatives* series are written in a fashion that makes them accessible to a wider public audience, including people who can influence policy and implement social change.

In *Life Online: Researching Real Experience in Virtual Space*, Annette Markham goes online to experience and examine what it feels like and what it means to spend substantial portions of one's everyday life in the chat rooms, support groups, and virtual communities of cyberspace. Interviewing heavy users online, and becoming one herself, she creates an ethnographic site for inquiring into the meanings of life online, a place where she and her readers can witness for themselves the social practices that are transforming the meanings of identity, intimacy, and community. The result is an ethnographic text that radically destabilizes the distinction between actual and virtual realities. Recognizing that computer-mediated communication is extending the horizons of human experience in new and unfamiliar ways, she raises the vexing question of what it means to have, or to be, a self in the disembodied spaces of life online. Can I have a self where my body doesn't exist? Can I be said to be "with others," when the place in which we experience ourselves as "joined" or "together" is a reality that consists only of information, a complex string of on/off switches? If I can experience the pleasures of "reality" in the dislocated and disembodied conversations that are represented by faceless texts embedded within rooms of words, then what is to become of my body? While these questions may seem abstract and philosophical, in *Life Online* they become the framework for online interviews that probe the sense-making discourses of people who have an online life.

By creating a life online in order to study online life, Annette Markham becomes one of "them." She fractures the boundaries between "subject" and "researcher" and shifts her position back and forth between autoethnographer and discourse analyst, between identifying with her participants and distancing herself from them, between the echo of theories and the call of stories, between her tenacious mind and her aching body, between belonging in the world of cyberspace and being estranged from it. As an active online participant, she engages in ethnography personally and interactively, grounding what she learns in her personal, emotional, and participatory experience. In the process, she complicates the relations between herself, her subjects, the place that they join in dialogue, and the limits and possibilities of both ethnography and technology. Going online becomes the method by which she puts herself on the line, experimenting with the various ways her participants connect to the world in order to explore the points of similarity and difference between their experience and hers. Throughout the book, she observes her own participation as well as the accounts of her participants. She notes the physical and emotional changes she goes through and interprets the diverse meanings implicated by the discourse of her participants. She treats her understanding as provisional, vulnerable, and situated—wavering between attraction and resistance to the new technologies—and holds on to an ironic attitude toward both truth and technology. The result is a refreshingly open and incisive text that encourages readers to appreciate, engage, and question life online.

Arthur P. Bochner and Carolyn Ellis

Foreword

Annette Markham wants to explore how users create, negotiate, and make sense of their social experiences in computer-mediated contexts. She investigates these dynamic processes as a user herself, by going online—to meet and engage other users and to preserve all their interactions with her in archival form. As we read, we realize that, for Annette, the project is inherently and palpably reflexive. In trying to learn about other persons' lives online, she must simultaneously make sense of her own online interactions and experiences. Through acquiring the appropriate software and exchanging texts with others, she is cocreating with them the contexts composing the object of her analysis.

This book tells the story of Annette's ethnographic adventures in cyberspace in a manner that will engage a diverse audience. Starting from square one, with no interactive capabilities, she recounts in detail her initial reluctance, as well as the programs and knowledge she had to acquire to go online, "keyboard in hand," to interview citizens of cyberspace. Some readers will find her early chapters a compelling introduction to IRCs, MUDs, MOOs, and their associated commands and customs. Old hands may feel smug about Annette's naivete when she began, while still being reminded of their early days of interactive computing and the many features of this highly technologized context they now take for granted. Regardless of your comfort with computer-mediated communication (CMC), Annette's chronicle raises numerous personal, practical, ethical, and philosophical issues concerning being with others and doing ethnography in virtual spaces.

You meet people online with Annette, you go places; maybe you come back—but not to when or where you were before you began reading. Part of her message seems to be that when we take learning and inquiry seriously, we change and are changed by our investigative efforts. We hear about the evolution of her research questions and her ways of rendering others' responses, her continual adaptation to contingencies of others' discourse, moods, schedules, and computer systems. She not only explores the everyday experiences at the heart of any ethnography, she also demonstrates the courage and insight required to acknowledge and write about them.

This book tightly and provocatively weaves first-order (the participants' naturally occurring discourse) and second-order concepts (the author's thematized reflections) in telling its tale of life online. Annette Markham uses the terms *tool*, *place*, and *way of being* to characterize how her participants describe and enact their understandings of cyberspace. She sees these concepts not as a typology but as "a continuum of ever-increasing connection of self to the Internet." Some participants tend to view CMC merely as an advanced and economical *tool* for communicating and accessing information on a global scale. Others speak of the Internet's sites, chat rooms, and communities more as *places* where they spend considerable time with valued associates. And some individuals not only describe but perform their words on the Net as a *way of being*, a profound alternative to embodied social relationships.

Keenly reflective, Annette observes how her stance toward CMC evolved during the course of this project. At first, she sees it simply as a tool to accomplish her research interests. Welcomed to interview people at Diversity University—a MOO with elaborate contextual descriptions of its campus, rooms and facilities—she begins to experience cyberspace more as a place where her ethnography is occurring. Not quite absorbed by the Web existentially, she surmises that, if she spent more time there, she could possibly grasp adopting it as a way of being. Meanwhile, she also questions her present ability to understand others who already perform their identities and live cyberspace in this comprehensive way.

This is a consummately dialogical work. Extended excerpts of online events and conversations are displayed throughout the book, sometimes in the choppy way that fragments of turns scroll by in an IRC, sometimes reworked by Annette into a more easily followed conversational form that you might see in a traditional novel. Fonts and formats from multiple computer interface programs appear at various moments—defamiliarized and animated by their juxtaposition with more standard typeface and prose. Like a postmodern Alice, Annette leaves her authorial voice behind and steps through the screen and into the text during a reproduced archive—a textual documentary—of her extended stroll through Diversity University with Beth_ANN, a friendly undergraduate she has met there. At another point, she logs onto a sex chatroom using the name Bambi and meets with bluntly aggressive sexual overtures from self-described males. In short, Annette is profoundly aware of and given over to the languages she and others exist through in this welter of texts. In rendering them, *Life Online* also invokes dialogue about meanings and practices of embodiment, feminism, social and textual performances, identity, gender, representation, authorial presence and responsibility, and, of course, ethnography.

Annette Markham seems to be saying that even though we can't discover timeless Truth, we can write and speak *truthfully* about what and how we are learning. I think you will be struck by her honesty and eye for details, even unflattering ones, about herself and others. She is a significant character in her own story about others—a significant Other if you will—who also happens to be the author. She admits limitations and cross-examines her own interview questions and motives for asking them. She continually probes her own participation in the study, her choices, revisions, and second-guesses. We are informed about dates of events and how time passed in pursuing the study, which violates the eternal and abstract "present" of most scholarly writing. We also hear descriptive specifics about the embodied and textual spaces, such as Annette's physical condition, her offices, and sites on the web, where the conversations took place. These writing practices pull you closer to the contexts of inquiry and text-based interaction. They present activities usually so thoroughly glossed that it feels humanizing and liberating to hear them discussed. Annette invites us to stand in with her, to think and feel with her. As such, the book very much resembles a novel.

I should warn you that this is not an easy book to put down. It grabs you, involves you, and intellectually engages you. It mingles words from where it's been— from aching backs and cold coffee to playing catch with virtual Frisbees. It lives. Highly nuanced and probing, at the same time it is also energetic and funny. It is written with a sense of humor and fallibility, a sense of anguish and limitation, sometimes even dread. Annette confronts the silence of the Internet, the bleakness of the screen, the shuffled, layered disarray of its endless windows and tiles. Still, for her, the Net is a discursive construction site, a work in progress frantic with activity. It is a form of life because it is a part of life.

Some people are down on the academy, cynical about our research mission, about our abilities to cultivate and teach new knowledge—and to touch and improve lives. I believe many of those concerns are well-founded, especially when we believe too deeply in our own conceits; but we are not sentenced nor destined to bore or alienate ourselves, our students, or society at large. In this book, Annette Markham questions the arrogance of any of our technological or rational powers that would substitute information for knowledge, access for wisdom, or algorithms for insight or compassion. Equally worrisome to her are instruments or programs that distract us from coming to grips or terms with the moments of our lives. Many people need permission; they need to be authorized to speak and write differently about what they are living and learning. This book contributes to the movement to do so. It incites young and experienced scholars to break the molds before they unduly constrain the forms that our writing, thinking, and feeling might take. In other words, it encourages students of social life to be *with* life—not above or beyond it.

Late in the book we learn that, as a child, Annette used to read science fiction in the stacks of a small town library. That image stays with me for several reasons in this context, because our participation in online technologies itself enacts an ongoing writing and reading of what once was science fiction but now is personal and social history. The image also lingers because I believe the child's sense of wonder, desire to learn, and openness to change are important to us as students and members of a global society. It is the spirit and duty of ethnographic writing to recognize and foster such a stance, one that permeates this fine book.

William K. Rawlins
Purdue University

Acknowledgments

for Mom and Dad

So many people helped me accomplish this project, it is difficult to know where to begin or end. The book could never have been written without the generous participation of countless computer users I met and interviewed online. In particular, my thanks go to Beth_ANN, Gargoyle, Jennifer, Lord Sheol, Mist, Michael, Matthew, Scooter, Sherie, and Terri; they taught me how to navigate their worlds, shared their experiences with me, and allowed me to use their words as the basis of this study. I may never meet them face-to-face, but I will always be thankful I knew them.

Many colleagues contributed to this project at various stages. At Purdue University, Dennis Mumby helped me see the world through a critical lens; Diane Witmer introduced me to the finer points of computer-mediated communication; Robin Clair encouraged me to write experimental ethnographies; and Ed Schiappa helped me find my own way of making good arguments.

Art Bochner and Carolyn Ellis, coeditors of the Ethnographic Alternatives Book Series, gave me the opportunity to bring this book to fruition. With each revision, Art's suggestions compelled me to write in ways I didn't think possible. He trusted me, encouraged me, and pushed me. In doing so, he helped me realize my strengths as a writer and scholar. I also want to thank Jennifer Collier, of AltaMira Press, and copyeditor David Featherstone for their discerning eyes and invaluable advice.

Throughout this project, I plagued my friends and family for support and encouragement. My mother, Virginia, and my sisters, Cathy, Julie, and Louise, listened when I needed to talk, read early versions of the manuscript, and said "It's great!" just at the right moments. Traci answered her phone at all hours of the day and night. Dave Toomey thought of titles. Kernahan listened patiently while I griped and made me laugh. Jenny, Trev, Tyler, and Anna-Banana helped me keep my balance—they fed me, took me bowling, and always held their door open for me. The girl group supported and encouraged me, even when I didn't think I needed it.

Finally, I would like to thank my mentor, colleague, and dear friend, Bill Rawlins. From the beginning, he encouraged me to follow my instincts and trust myself as a scholar and writer. He brainstormed with me, sat in on interviews, listened to my arguments, and carefully appraised draft after draft. He scrutinized every choice I made and, at the same time, gave me the motivation and faith I needed to stretch my wings. Bill inspired me to do this project, and with his help, I actually completed it. I feel very lucky to have such a teacher and friend.

In this book, I strove to be accurate, honest, and informative. If I misquoted, misrepresented, or misunderstood, I did not intend to.

Introduction

<Annette> Scooter, when did you first get connected to the Internet? What was it like?

<Scooter> I guess it was about a year ago. I swear, it has been one of the strangest years of my life. All I did was put this CD into my computer. I heard a whirring noise, and suddenly, things started happening. A message on the screen tells me to wait. So I do. After a long time, the computer TALKS to me! I didn't even know my computer could make noise! There's a guy on the screen who tells me, "Congratulations for installing your new program." God, that was weird.

<Scooter> So now, there are all these places I can go and meet people, apparently. I click on a sign to get into a bar. But the computer tells me I have to wait while it "installs the environment." It takes forever. Then, the computer tells me I can choose an avatar. I think, what's this got to do with flying? (I thought it meant "aviator." I was such a newbie!)

<Scooter> Finally, I'm really plugged into the net. I have this animated body—that's what the avatar is—and I go in these places and I can fly! I hear the sounds of a bar. I hear the clinking of glasses. I can see people. When I tell my avatar to wave, I can see it flying over the heads of people, waving!

<Scooter> Then I look up. I've just lost three hours without even thinking. The dinner dishes are not done, it's past my son's bedtime, and I've been in another world. I quickly shut off the computer and tell him, "I'm sorry Mommy has been so busy."

<Scooter> I can be whatever I want to be. I can describe myself however I want to. And I start future-tripping all the time. Instead of thinking about the present, I'm thinking about what my life is going to be like. I'm wondering what we're going to turn into.

<Scooter> I could go for years living only a virtual life, only doing the bare minimum to live my life. It's so easy to get sucked into it, because I feel physically connected to something outside myself.

<Scooter> Meanwhile, my son is lying on his bedroom floor, learning to read. He's yelling at me, "Mom! Mom!" And I'm learning how to tune it out.

<Scooter> I can feel my real life slipping away. It's a pulling sensation, as if my life is blowing away from me and I can't catch it. I picture my body breaking into pieces as my head sinks into the computer. I feel like an animation. But it feels real. So you know what I do? I go back inside the program. I know I am running away from my real responsibilities and I'm powerless against this urge in my life to run away. So I force myself to confront my helplessness and force myself to realize my life is unmanageable. Then I can finally shut the machine off and turn away, and lie on the floor with my baby and read a book with him.

<Scooter> What's happening to us, I wonder?

✳

Before I met Scooter online, I had been reading and thinking about cyberspace as an evolving cultural form; people were creating significant support groups, social networks, and even communities through the exchange of electronic messages. The stories about the meaningful consequences of these social contexts astounded me: People having strokes or severe asthma attacks were saved because they were online when the tragedy occurred and their conversational partners called for help. Others were leaving long-term relationships to establish new relationships with people they had met online—in some cases, even before they had met their new partners face-to-face.

I wanted to know why people spent so much time online. I wondered what cyberspace meant to them, how it affected or changed their lives. I wanted to know how they were making sense of their experiences as they shifted between being in the physical world and being in these textual worlds created by the exchange of messages, where they could re-create their bodies, or leave them behind.

I decided to go online to talk with some of the people who spend extensive time there. In this book, I tell the story of what it took for me to get connected and of what and whom I encountered once I was there. Through my experiences and my conversations with others, I provide an interpretation of some of the ways users (including myself) are making sense of their experiences online.

Although cyberspace is nothing more or less than a network of computer systems passing digitized strings of information back and forth through copper or fiber-optic cables, people who connect to this network often feel a *sense of presence* when they are online. Even in purely text-based online contexts, people establish and maintain intimate friendships, romantic relationships, and stable communities. This sense of presence can be quite visceral:

> So much for leaving our bodies out of this. . . . This gathering is not
> restricted to the Net, and therefore to the text on the Net, but
> extends to the flesh, the physical body. In this rare case, uncannily,
> even though online, we feel we meet in the flesh. . . . Everywhere we
> rub shoulders with each other. Everywhere users present themselves
> to each other, freely saying and doing what they choose. (Argyle,
> 1996, passim)

Online communication does seem quite extraordinary. By logging onto my computer, I (or a part of me) can seem to (or perhaps actually) exist separately from my body in "places" formed by the exchange of messages, the technical basis of which I am only beginning to understand. I can engage in activities with people of like interests around the globe using nothing but my computer, my imagination, written text, and the capacity of digital code to process and mediate aspects of my life online.

Telepresence, as this is called, is not unique to computer technologies. Indeed, a good novel, a familiar scent from the past, or a long-lost journal can transport a person to another time and place. For many of us, however, the feeling of being some*where* other than in the body with some other non-embodied yet presumably living being—particularly to the extent Argyle describes above—is a new and unfamiliar experience.

Much hype and sensationalism surrounds online technologies. I suspect a lot of us just want to know what it means to engage in virtual communication and what implications this engagement might have on our physical world. Computer-mediated communication seems to have significant consequences for what we consider to be humanness. Howard Rheingold predicts that "we *have to decide fairly soon what it is we as humans ought to become*, because we're on the brink of having the power of creating any experience we desire. . . . The power to create experience is also the power to redefine such basic concepts as identity, community, and reality" (1991, p. 386–7, italics in original).

Many people, including those I met and spoke with online, are trying to make sense of what it means to be there. How do we define or experience reality in virtual spaces? Is the body still important? Certainly the body is a host for the mind, but online I have a self where my body is not. If I can "exist" and "be" with "others" in a (non)place that is comprised only of information—a complex string of on/off switches—which is "real"? The place out here with my physical body? Or the place in there, in my mind? Does it matter? Do these distinctions make a difference in the information age? What constitutes identity in anonymous contexts? How can one have intimate relationships in purely textual domains? How does a workplace without the place work?

This book focuses on the lived experience of what it means to go and be online. It is simultaneously a description of what I encountered, an analysis of some of the texts (people) I encountered, and an analysis of the project itself. My goal was to study the organization of online communication, the way people create—primarily through textual dialogue—negotiate, and reproduce the social realities of their experiences online. Accomplishing this project required that I become involved in creating and negotiating the very context that became the object of analysis. This point is the heart of my ethnography. Every action I made that influenced the project became a text that engaged and interacted with a multiplicity of other texts. In the process of organizing and doing this study, I was taking part in the organization of that which was to be the study.

In the end, this is a study of a place I helped create, and that I continue to organize through the text here. I'm not sure how much I know, really. The structure of experience in online contexts varies widely. Since it is experienced by individuals more than by collectives, I must acknowledge that my story represents only a fragment of life in cyberspace.

I begin with an extended narrative about going online. As you read about my experiences, you should get a good sense of what it was like for me to press beyond the boundaries of my fear to experience this new context. If you have not been online much, this chapter is a good introduction to at least two online contexts, including interactive chatrooms and Multi-User Dimensions.

(I need to interrupt myself here, and this seems the most straightforward way to do it. Throughout the piece, I have set off my reflections on what I've written in this way—with italicized text enclosed in parentheses. It may be useful to consider this my self-acknowledged author's voice, similar to text that sometimes appears in footnotes. Italicized text not enclosed in parentheses indicates emphasis, as is traditional.

It occurs to me, as I try to write a preview to this book, that the book doesn't want to fit into a standard mold. I am addressing a topic I really care about, yet it has turned out to be more slippery than I ever imagined; every time I touch it, it slides a little from the center. And when I think I finally have got it, I realize it has slipped again from my grasp. I feel like I am trying to cling to a wet, slippery fish that is wriggling to return to the water. In terms of organization, the text wants to be abstract art and narrative and weaving and scholarly prose all at once. There is a delicate balance between art and garbage…or as my sister suggests, it's like knitting a sweater that fits or knitting a sweater you can only pull apart or give away.

I struggle constantly with wanting to break free of structure and tradition yet still tell a coherent tale. On the one hand, the literary form can dramatize many points that straightforward academic text cannot. On the other hand, writing an entire manuscript in narrative form is an enormously difficult task. The appealing alternative for me is to blend essay, scholarly text, and narrative; still a challenging process, but one that seems more truthful to the way I understand the connections among theory, research, and writing. In addition, writing of moments, presenting narrative fragments, speaking with the voices of others, speaking for myself, and speaking as a scholar all seem well-suited to an ethnography of this place I created with many other people, where few boundaries are heeded and most traditions and norms arise and are woven out of fragmented exchanges of texts.)

As I was saying, the first chapter describes my experiences of getting online and accomplishing the initial stages of the project. I also introduce some of the language and terminology used with certain online technologies. By describing my step-by-step discovery process, I provide novice users with a general sense of what is required to get anywhere online, as well as a narrativized image of what it might feel like to be there. (Of course, this might all be outdated by the time you read this, but at least you'll know what it used to be like.) My understanding of others is thoroughly embedded in my own experiences of going and being online. These personal experiences helped me begin to answer the overarching question: How do users make sense of their experiences in computer-mediated contexts?

In the second chapter, I discuss how the project emerged and shifted over time. I talk about how I collected information that would become data, and I address several methodological issues related to this study and to studies of online communication in general. I present a pastiche of journal entries, field notes, and email excerpts to discuss some of the dilemmas associated with studying online communication as a cultural context while simultaneously using online communication as the tool by which to study online communication. Coming to understand the project itself was integral to the process of coming to understand cyberspace, and vice versa. In many ways, I was negotiating the reality of cyberspace through my own communicative behaviors, even as I was studying how that reality gets constructed through communicative interactions. Throughout this chapter, then, you will see that the project was moving in continual loops that have not come to rest in any definitive way. Even as I write, I am constructing the context within which the ethnography took (and is taking) place.

In chapter 3, I discuss three themes that help me understand some of the ways users experience and frame online communication. In chapters 4 and 5, I present extensive excerpts of conversations with the participants and apply the themes developed in chapter three to an analysis of these interviews.

As I reflected on the ways people talked about their experiences, I first came to realize that computer-mediated communication appears to be experienced along a continuum: For some, the Internet is simply a useful communication medium, a *tool*; for others, cyberspace is a *place* to go to be with others. For still others, online communication is integral to *being* and is inseparable from the performance of self, both online and offline.

I also found reason to destabilize a traditional idea that the experience of reality is grounded in the physical, embodied world. As communication technologies allow us to exist in disembodied places and perhaps with reimagined bodies, more discussions of "What is *really* real?" emerge. To my surprise, these users told me this question was of little relevance to them; rather, *everything that is experienced is real*. Notions of reality are shifting; the words of these users reflect this shift.

Finally, these participants go online, or remain there, in part because in cyberspace the self has a high degree of perceived control. Some users enjoy the capacity to control the presentation and performance of self in online contexts. Others talk about their increased ability to control the conditions of interaction and to control the extent to which people online have access to the self. For almost every participant, control is a significant and meaningful benefit of online communication.

In the concluding chapter, I reflect on my experiences and on the participants, the project, and the future. In a sense, this ethnographic report reflects my shifting understanding of what it means to go online and be with others. I began the project knowing very little about what was required to get there and what would happen once I arrived. At the same time, I was studying a segment of the culture of

Internet users—the segment I encountered. I ended up knowing a fair amount about the technology and some of the people who are active users. I offer my conclusions about these users and communication technology in general, based on what I learned by doing this study.

In addition to these five chapters, I include other elements that are essential to the telling of the story but do not fall under the heading of "chapter." For instance, you will run into passages I call "Interludes," fragments of text I consider vital but that are not large enough to qualify as a chapter.

In general, this story is not just a study of online communication; it is also a study of how we come to know others and how we write what we think we know. As Grumet (1991) says, we speak and write because these are crucial ways to connect with others. "Our stories are the masks through which we can be seen, and with every telling we stop the flood and swirl of thought so someone can get a glimpse of us, and maybe catch us if they can" (p. 69). But what if the flood and swirl of thought itself becomes the story? It makes the story more difficult to pin down, but surely the tale is still worth telling. For as Fisher (1984) notes, "Reasoning need not be bound to argumentative prose or be expressed in clear-cut inferential or implicative structures" (p. 1). Regardless of form, the presentation of ethnographic interpretation is a (re)visionary and fragmentary result of much picking and choosing and shaping and editing.

I am not seeking to create precision and coherence in representation, but I do want to say something meaningful about how I and these participants experience online communication. I present the text in ways that might seem fragmented at times, but I do so because my experience of the entire process is in fragments and moments. In a way, I'm trying to remain true to the logic of the project as I have lived it.

A few final notes here on the format of this book. First, I use terms such as, *online communication, computer-mediated communication* (CMC), *Internet* (or *Net*), and *cyberspace*, without stipulating any notable distinctions among them. Online communication encompasses many forms of computer-mediated communication. The labels we apply to our own or others' online experiences shape the way we perceive, respond to, interact with, and define these technologies. I do not want to confuse the issue by using many different terms, but because the meanings of these terms—and the experiences they imply—are still up for debate, I do not want to stabilize them either, or to provide you with a singular meaning.

Second, to reflect more accurately what interaction actually looks like online, I occasionally use a different font, as when I present a segment of an actual conversation or email exchange. However, when I quote from the interviews to recreate parts of the conversations I had with the participants and to present my analysis, for ease and flow of reading, the appearance of those texts matches my own.

Third, I purposely left the participants' statements unedited for typing errors. Even when the conversations appear in regular typeface as dialogues, you will notice many grammar and spelling errors, as well as a significant lack of capitalization and traditional punctuation. Also, some users deliberately use nontraditional spelling and capitalization to convey a particular sentiment or identity. A person's text is vital to his or her presentation of self online, and whether these practices are intentional or not, they contribute to the reader's perception of the writer—everything about an online persona is embedded in the form and content of the written text. Therefore, you will notice many unusual typing conventions as you read these conversations, and this will undoubtedly influence your perception of the participants.

Fourth, you will notice that time does not always flow in a linear fashion when I present journal entries. I have included the dates not to confuse you, but to illustrate that the progression of reasoning through a research project is not always linear.

Finally, I have altered the names, locations, and other identifying markers of all the participants to protect their anonymity. (Theresa M. Senft is the only exception; she wanted me to use her real name.) So even when you read about "Sheol" or "Mist," these are not their real or online names.

Chapter 1

Going Online

It took three years. I had to overcome my trepidation. I feel comfortable in most online spaces now, but I suspect I will never be convinced I am truly an insider. Things change so rapidly in cyberspace—I'm constantly reminded of how little I know about what's happening on the cutting edge. In this chapter, I want to share what it took to "get connected," and talk about some of the places I've been, some of the experiences I've had, some of my thoughts about going and being online.

In general, this is a chronological ordering of my thoughts and experiences taken from the research journals I kept during the course of the project. However, critical moments of our lives do not always become relevant or "critical," until something else brings them to the foreground. In other words, I make sense of my experiences on certain dates, but the sense-making is almost always, as Karl Weick (1979) suggests, retrospective. If my story seems to loop back on itself, then it does so mostly because that is the shape of my life in (and throughout) this project. Hence, you will notice that I do not always write in a consistent tense. Maintaining a chronological consistency seemed to take some of the lived relevance out of the text, particularly the journals, so I chose to leave them in original form.

Going online took a long time and involved far more than turning on the computer, tapping out words on the keyboard, and pressing the send/enter button. It was more like entering a strange new world where the very metaphysics defied my comprehension of how worlds should work. To even begin to understand what was happening online, or to communicate with other users, I had to learn how to move, see, and talk. Until I learned these basic rules, I was paralyzed in the dark, isolated from that world as much as I would be if I were a mind without a body on the planet Earth (or so I believe).

It is crucial to emphasize this point: To be present in cyberspace is to learn how to be embodied there. To be embodied there is to participate. To participate is to know enough about the rules for interaction and movement so that movement and interaction with and within this space is possible. Although this may not be so different than what we experience whenever we enter any strange context, it seems very blatant in cyberspace, perhaps because this process cannot be ignored, and because movement and interaction *create* embodied presence, not simply accompany it.

July 1995: Logically, I know it's nothing but text appearing on the screen in front of me, but I feel like I am standing on the edge of a great clearing, unable to push my way through the remaining trees and brush to get into the open space. I don't know how to move my feet or push aside the constraints. I'm too afraid to call out for help, even though the people in the clearing look as though they are having a good time. I see other newcomers bursting into the open, having just figured out how to make themselves visible. For the most part, these other newcomers say "hi" and then just stand there, doing nothing. I hear some of them asking questions. Sometimes the response is patient and kind; perhaps that person had only recently learned to move and talk as well. But sometimes the response is brusque and very rude. From the midst of a conversation, someone might look up and shout jeeringly at the newcomer, "Go read the FAQ!" or "Haven't you been paying attention? That question was asked long ago!" (FAQ is one of hundreds of time-saving acronyms used in cyberspace; it means Frequently Asked Question(s).)

The conversations here range from inane to spirited to insulting, the latter characterized by conversationalists spitting flames at each other, vitriolic words intended to maim the other in some way. (This is known as "flaming;" if a lot of people participate, it's a "flame war.")

I come to the clearing often, but I feel too vulnerable and shy to venture forth. I know that I could participate, and I imagine the other participants would be kind and understanding. I compose contributions to conversation "threads" and deliberate over delivering them until the conversation has moved too far for my comments to be relevant. I go there less and less, knowing that I will never join in . . . will always feel locked out.

April 1997: This all began because I wanted to understand how people used and made sense of communication technology. A few months ago, I realized I would have to participate online to collect discourse toward this goal. I had successfully avoided being online during my study of people who are online by studying secondary sources or by lurking about in the online community from which I was collecting conversations. ("Lurking," in Internet lingo, means receiving messages from the group but never sending any.) I thought about the ethics of this sort of research quite a lot, and wondered if I should actually be inside the space I was studying. But I had resolved, for the span of this study, to sit comfortably behind a glass screen, acting as an anonymous, distanced observer of "Other."

I had chosen the contexts for making my observations strategically. First, I would analyze the common metaphors people use when referring to online interaction. I would look at conversations online as well as in popular magazines, television, and books to see the metaphors people prefer. After this relatively removed study was complete, I would analyze an eight-month conversation I had been listening to and archiving while I lurked in an online community (without participating, mind you). This group was quite involved in talking about fascinating issues related to the body and sexuality in cyberspace. In my study, I would analyze how this community organized its boundaries and norms through conversation. Finally, I would interview one hacker to learn how he or she made sense of identity, Other, and experience as these are connected to being online. I had lined up the interview through a colleague of mine; otherwise I might have been hard pressed to come up with one myself, unless I met one on the street.

These case studies were designed to allow me to answer one research question across three situations: "How do people make sense of the concept of reality in or through online interaction?" So it began. And after several painstaking weeks of trying to write the first analysis of metaphors, I realized something was missing from the scene. Now, three months later, I realize *I* was missing. I was surprisingly absent from my own study, which I now realize is an ethnography. I was beginning to understand that cyberspace is not simply a collection of texts to analyze; rather it is an evolving cultural context of immense magnitude and complex scope. I wanted to say something meaningful about the way people experience these new cultural contexts, but I had never really experienced them myself. Moreover, I was not talking with users, but trying to analyze their sense-making practices secondhand. Even to the extent that this somewhat tangential and abstracted approach would have been useful, I wasn't truly engaged in the project. So I changed the project.

Overcoming my fear of going online relied on two moments or revelations (which I experienced only by going online). First, I discovered that nobody really cared. And second, I learned I could be anyone, anywhere—or no one, nowhere.

The more time I spend interacting with people online, the more I realize that although other users are (probably) real persons, they do not seem as invested as I am in everything I say. For me—as humorous as it sounds—this is a great revelation.

Although I use my real last name in most settings, and I know the other users could trace this name to me, it is finally sinking in that most users don't have the time or energy to track down every person who communicates something to them

or their group. The sheer amount of information each user receives and must as-
similate means that a lot falls through the cracks. I fall through the cracks. Some
people might notice something I say or do . . . many more never will.

So now I find myself standing in the middle of the clearing, in full vocal range
of users much more acclimated than I. This does not make me conspicuous, however, because there really isn't a center stage. I know I can participate in a quiet,
unassuming way. In other words, I have the ability to wander around and listen to
various conversations taking place—some heated, some dry and dull, some over my
head, some ridiculously pretentious, some meaningless. If I want to contribute to
the conversation, or to respond to some comment that inflames or intrigues me, I
simply write my comment and send it, without waiting for a turn and without much
introduction. Then I walk away (figuratively or literally), join in or listen to another
conversation, and wander back later to see if anyone has responded to my comment. If they have, I can choose to respond, or simply listen and wander around
some more. I thus feel protected because I am just another grain of information in
an immeasurable, constantly shifting hourglass.

The second revelation that helped propel me into active participation online
was this: I feel protected by distance and/or anonymity. I realize I can adopt certain
names and acquire certain characteristics in various places. Just as I don't assume
everyone online is really what or who they say they are, I realize most people probably don't believe (or care) that I am really what or who I say I am, either. For me,
this provides a comfortable, protective facade. Of course, it wasn't that easy in the
beginning. . . .

February 13, 1997; 5:30 p.m.: I have decided to conduct "user in the net" interviews with self-described "heavy" users in various text-based online contexts. So
today, Dave (the computer guy from upstairs) was in my office for at least three
hours trying to download software that would allow me to interview people online.
For weeks I have been trying to come up with a solution to the dilemma of finding
a "place" to have a real-time textual interaction with someone online. Certain re-
quirements have to be met. I have to be able to log and archive the conversations. I
also want to be able to access and read these conversations easily, so the log has to
reflect who was talking when. Various programs can meet all of these needs; Dave
chose a software program called NetMeeting, which he said would be easy to use on
my particular computer.

"Word wrapping," "automatic scrolling," "real time." These unfamiliar words
reminded me that this entire project was unfamiliar to me. And I had this forebod-
ing feeling, as Dave was finalizing the configurations on my new NetMeeting program, that I was out of my league. Soon I would have no reason to forestall the

process any longer and I would be online, talking with other users. Whether I wanted to or not, was ready or not, I would have to reach out and actually try to touch someone through this keyboard. To be truthful, I was mortified.

Suddenly, Dave said, "Okay, try it."

I opened the program. On the screen in front of me a column listed literally hundreds of names of users currently connected to this common "area," the "dimensions" of which are actually defined by how many people are connected. It is basically a web that keeps shifting its shape as strands weave themselves into the overall structure (user connecting) and then later disappear (user disconnecting). I could see my own name on the "uls2" (user locator service #2). Three other columns gave me more information about the person, and these columns were entitled Last name, City/State, and Comments. I had carefully filled in my own columns when Dave and I were setting up my "User Preferences." I was Annette Markham, Lafayette/IN, Researcher. Here is a sample of what other people had chosen:

First Name	Last Name	City/State	Comments
0923587OT	JIKGJ9S87FN	xxxx	Japanese only
Bob	Benson	Richardson, X	Jesus is Lord
BEACH	BUNNIES	WHATEVER!	LOOKING FOR STUDS....!!!
Jacques	;-)	wants	to see naked women 'live' only
Jo D	friendlychat	Georgia	humor/honesty please!! Spring is here…
Lisa	R	Show me!	I'm video courious! Guys….couples!
Hi!	Hi!	Hi!	Hi!
John	Labonte	St.Catharine	CALL
M	Legare	Quebec	Je cherche quelqu'un qui a Minitel

John	P	NY	no cam but gays w/cams can call too
Dark	dan	SanFran	DO NOT DIS-TURB!!!
Josh	or Steve	Maine	LADIES WHO LIKE HARDCORE SEX
Jon	Tucker	Toronto	I've got voice, so let's talk.
Jon	H	Beaverton,OR	Business use only, please
miguelYjose	De Mayo	san isidro	peti aca estoy
Kim	a	24	Bi f les only
Man 32	video/sex	SEXSEX	(SEX) ladies with video only (SEX)
andrew	m	west coast	let's chat
John	L		Will ignore all but Ken L
Michel	Salinas	Santiago	Chicas bienvenidas
Pat	O'Kelley	Georgia	Private- Family only please
John	Doe	Mt. Home	CLEAN CHAT ONLY
Mary &	Dave	Us	We have VID You too pls

"Try it!" Dave said again.

Feeling most daunted, I looked at the list, then I looked at Dave. "Try what?" I said weakly, knowing full well what he meant.

"See if it works! Call someone!"

I sat there, tentative, unwilling, knowing that this was exactly what I had been afraid of, but also knowing I couldn't let Dave know I was afraid to do my own study. The only redeeming thought was that I would not have to be with a group of them. . . . I hoped. I had to select a name and click my mouse on the call button. "andrewm" looked pretty normal. At least he had put down "west coast" as his city/state, rather than "c'mon baby" or "wherever you wanna be."

I pressed the call button. And waited. A message flashed on my screen.

"andrewm is in a conference. Request to join?"

"Say yes," Dave promptly responded.
So I typed yes.

andrewm: "Hi Whats Up?"

Esra Franko: "I agree!"

andrewm: "are you a student"

Annette: "sorry to intrude. Just testing my new system."

andrewm: "that's ok. I hope it's working well"

Annette: "are you both on line much?"

Esra Franko: "oh, wellcome!"

andrewm: "Too much nyself"

andrewm: "typing is still poor though"

Annette: "I'm interviewing various users for a study I'm doing. Any interest?"

andrewm: "depends"

Annette: "good point. On what?"

andrewm: "is it about business or pleasure"

Annette: "Just want to find out about your internet experiences."

andrewm: "trust me this machine may be powerful but people are still dumb as ever"

Esra Franko: "sorry, friends, y am dealing with many things at a time . . . so let me leave for now . . . Bye to you two- and Happy early Valentine's Day!! Bye!!!!!!!"

Annette: "Perhaps about differences between real and virtual experiences."

andrewm: "the cyber sex reality that is breaking up marriages"

andrewm: "its all qualitative subjective creative imagination"

Annette: "is it real?"

andrewm: "VERY"

andrewm: "but not very at the same time"

andrewm: "its not one or the other"

andrewm: "its both"

NetMeeting is very similar to an Internet Relay Chat (another way of interacting with others online) in terms of the way the text appears. It is synchronous, or interactive. People in the know call it "real time." In other words, I type a comment, press enter, and it appears on my own screen as well as on the other participant's.

The computer is a nonjudgmental and objective mediator. It just places the comments on the screen as they come into the system; it doesn't monitor the conversation to place the pieces in their proper—which is perhaps only traditionally understood to be proper—order.

In the transcription of the conversation printed here, I cleaned up the appearance of the text somewhat, mostly the spacing and format, but I wanted to leave it as close to its original form as possible. Actually the original text looked like this:

```
MS-Chat0001
2:04:15 PM","andrewm","VERY"
2:04:26 PM","andrewm","but not very at the same time"
2:04:35 PM","andrewm","its not one or the other"
2:04:38 PM","andrewm","its both"
2:05:06 PM","andrewm","what do you want to find out"
```

I want to illustrate what this looks like as much as I can since you were not actually there to experience it firsthand. However, part of the clarity of these conversations is tied to being in the conversation. Unless you are in the conversation and following along as it develops, exact reproductions of the text can be very difficult to follow. Even with my changes to the format, this conversation is probably somewhat confusing to those not familiar with online real-time, or synchronous interactions.

It felt strange to see the text scroll up the screen so quickly, and I felt very slow and awkward. You will notice throughout this conversation with andrewm that he (at least I assume it's a male, though there's no way of knowing for sure) dominates the conversation. The questions, bantering comments, and sexual innuendoes appeared so quickly, one after the other, that I literally could not keep up.

Moreover, andrewm would not get serious, and of course, I was in a testing-the-system-for-a-serious-scholarly-study mood. He clearly felt playful. He didn't want to answer the questions and kept diverting the conversation. It surprised me at the time, but now I probably would do something similar to someone who was using this context for such serious interaction.

andrewm: "what do you want to find out"

Annette: "I'm doing a 'user on the street' sort of study."

Annette: "Just want to get users to tell stories,"

Annette: "sort of in the Studs Turkel format, if you know who that is."

andrewm: "Listen Annette: we could have a hot sexxy phone chat and whisper provocative things in each other's ear"

andrewm: "Qualitative research"

Annette: "definitely qualitative. But I'm not sure hot sexy provocations are in the interview protocol."

Annette: "And what do you mean by ear?"

Annette: "Are you interested in being interviewed at some point?"

andrewm: "What is it that you want to explore"

Annette: "discursive negotiation of reality in cyberspace, if the truth be known."

andrewm: "Are you really interested in the truth?"

Annette: "not only am i not interested in the truth, I don't really think there is any. only stories."

andrewm: "Like how I would attempt to get you to have a STEEAAAMMMY chat with me"

Annette: "yeah, yeah, whatever."

andrewm: "I mean discursive negotiation must include something of that nature"

andrewm: "Depending on . . ."

andrewm: "What you want to know or what you are affraid to find out."

andrewm: "You wanted the 'street corner' version"

Annette: "where do you spend most of your time online?"

andrewm: "cruising"

Annette: "why?"

andrewm: "the chase"

andrewm: "faster better more interactive"

Annette: "are you a student?"

andrewm: "student of life Baby"

andrewm: "read write live learn"

andrewm: "no matter what"

andrewm: "just keep doing it"

andrewm: "Call me the fish in the sea of knowledge"

andrewm: "But rember all that matrters is between the head and the heart"

andrewm: "Have a great Valentines day"

Annette: "you too"

andrewm: "Do you have a partner"

Learning this mode of communication is a process of error and practice. For instance, I would write a long sentence, get ready to send it, and then accidentally hit the wrong key, erasing the message so I had to start again.

Or I would be thinking of how to respond to something andrewm said, and long before I finished constructing the sentence, he would have sent two, three, four lines of text . . . which changed the conversation and the currently appropriate response. I would have to start over.

Many users will tell you that quick wit makes a person more attractive online. Needless to say, I felt completely outranked in this conversation, barely able to keep up with the dazzling wit on the other end of the ether.

andrewm: "Would you like to meet again"

andrewm: "You know for coffee"

Annette: "Only if you want to be interviewed over a cup o java"

andrewm: "conversation in the virtual café"

Annette: "what better place to talk about virtual lives"

andrewm: "Hey lets do it"

Annette: "when?"

andrewm: "how old are you"

Annette: "hey. stop stealing my interview questions!"

andrewm: "ooops"

Annette: "LOL [laughing out loud]"

andrewm: "right we don't want to confuse you"

andrewm: "seriously I want to know more about you"

Annette: "Yeah. I definitely don't want to confuse the interviewer from the interviewee . . . let's see . . .I am."

andrewm: "just the basic nominal data, Annette"

Annette: "Oh, I am the interviewer."

andrewm: "teacher student studetn teacher whats the diff. don't you learn at purdue"

Annette: "so, interested in an inteview in the next couple of days?"

andrewm: "so you have done an excellent job of avoiding any answers to my questions. I hope you have better luck with me"

Annette: "I am thinking Saturday noonish, my time."

That was my first conversation online. It is nothing like face-to-face conversation, at least not at first glance. Later, as it becomes more natural, it feels more like speaking (*to me. Others say it feels like a direct connection between your thoughts and your hands. One person online told me it was like bypassing your voice. I don't perceive it this way; but then again, I tend to say the words aloud in my head as I type them*).

Although my first experience was profound and meaningful (as well as disconcerting), I realized it was probably less meaningful for andrewm. I showed up at the agreed-upon time for my interview with andrewm and was surprised that he didn't show up. I had spent ninety minutes with him online, just trying to get him to agree to an interview. I finally got him to commit, and he didn't show up! I waited for a couple of hours and came to another realization: Because people are anonymous, they can be as flaky as they want. If others don't like it, they can go somewhere else.

Although exact figures vary and shift constantly, we know there are more than seventy million people using the Internet these days. One of Intel's ten-year goals, according to an employee I talked with, is to have as many computers in the home as televisions. If a number like seventy million is meaningless to you, like it is to me, just go to any one of the hundreds of interactive chat networks (Internet

Relay Chat—IRC—is one type; NetMeeting is another) and look at how many thousands of people are logged on. Or visit some online communities. LambdaMOO, the most popular Multi-User Dimension to date, has over three thousand members; more than triple the size of my hometown. These numbers stagger me, but they tell me one significant thing: If you go online, you can and will find someone to talk with. You will find someone who will listen. So why, with all that choice, would a random guy like andrewm (assuming he is a guy) get out of bed early on a Saturday morning to do a two-hour interview (or even a thirty-minute interview) with some random gal (assuming she is a gal) he is never likely to meet? Altruism is not a widespread characteristic of late-twentieth-century humanity; I'm afraid commitment is falling into that same category.

March 21, 1997; 4:19 a.m.: Sheol (a pseudonym), one of the people I interviewed, said that your name defines who you are. Sheol told me that if you don't have a name that captures others' interest, no one will talk to you and you would not be real to them. I agree. When I first logged in, I used my last name. The first question I was asked was "m or f?" Was I male or female? People want a name or a description that will help them fill in some of the blanks created by disembodied presence.

Changing my name online has provided an interesting twist to my experiences. I feel a sense of freedom in a dislocated place where one can be anyone or anything simply by describing oneself through words and names. I also feel a sense of angst in a context of disembodied personae with shifting identities that are largely defined by names.

Once I engaged in conversations online, I realized I could act out a number of personalities. I didn't have to show my face or body or age and be judged by those markers. I didn't have to enact my education or reflect my mode of dress. Every time I described myself differently, others responded to me in particular ways, based on innumerable stereotypes and preconceptions. For instance, if I logged into a chat space as "Annette," I was often called and pestered by self-described male users wanting me to talk dirty with them, or wanting to know what I looked like and if I had the capacity to transmit audio or, preferably, video. When I logged in as Markham, many users mistook me for a male. Once, after working up my nerve for several hours, I logged into an IRC as "Bambi." Within two minutes, I had several requests for private conversations:

```
<aaron69> m or f

<Bambi> f
```

```
<aaron69> wanna cybersex?????

<cowboy> Hello want to chat

<Bambi> hi

<cowboy> Do you want to chat?

<Joe> hello bambi

<Joe> are you there bambi?

<Bambi> yeah, just talking on the phone at the moment; back in
a sec

<Joe> ok

<Joe> in the mean time, i'll talk to you when you're done.


<Justin> hello

<Justin> are you busy?

<Justin> age?

<Justin> sex?!
```

My mixed feelings about the power of naming represent only one of the dilemmas I face as I continue to engage these new contexts. All of my experiences online are displacing my understanding of my own identity, to the point where I can't even say for sure how old I am because I'm not sure what the real self is supposed to be, and therefore, what "age" really means . . . or whether it matters.

In an interview with Beth (who said she was twenty years old), I said I was twenty-five years old. In an interview with BobZ (who said he was forty years old), I said I was thirty-two. I thought a lot about this both as and after I did this, and wondered at the ethics of "lying" about my age.

Now, I don't really know that I lied at all. If I were conducting face-to-face interviews, most people would assume I am in my late twenties because I *look* that way, and people don't typically ask the age of the person interviewing them. But what is my *real* age? I'm not sure I can even answer this question, or understand to what end I (or others) ask it. Is age determined by how one looks? Or how one acts? I know that age is determined by counting the number of years one has been alive, but our everyday understanding of age is something calculated with a much more complex social formula of mental acuity/maturity, job title, possessions, marriage, children, physical appearance, health, and so forth.

The bottom line of this tangent, however, is not so much that age is a complicated and socially constructed concept, but that online I'm not certain age represents what it does in more physical environments. Moreover, although most people I encounter are interested in finding out the age of their online conversation partners, the truth of the matter, as measured in actual years of life, is irrelevant, or at least less relevant, because it cannot be known. I, for instance, have no way of validating the declared ages of my participants; and in many ways, it does not matter. (*Yet it is strange to me that people are so concerned about age, especially since it can't be verified. As Carolyn, one of my editors, suggests, perhaps they want to know what age I plan to take on as part of my online identity so they can determine if that declared age is compatible with their own declared or presumed age. Perhaps there are things we wouldn't say or do to someone in a particular age range, with a particular presumed set of experiences.*) And, of course, age is only one of many identifying characteristics that must be reconsidered and perhaps reconfigured in cyberspace.

March 3, 1997; 8:00 p.m.: I have just found my way to Diversity University, a Multi-User Dimension (MUD) of the Object-Oriented type (MOO). These are programs that allow people to interact simultaneously with one another, using text, in "places" created through descriptive texts, like in the examples below. Before I could get there, I had to download a software "client" to help me interface with the MOO program. Then I had to learn to use this interface program. When I finally got to Diversity University, which was a process of learning the proper responses to various questions that appeared on the screen, I ended up in a tiny cubicle, big enough for two people. I know this only because I saw the following description:

```
Quiet Cubicle No.3

This is a quiet room flooded with warm light in which you can
prepare yourself for the MOO world waiting outside. Only two
people could conceivably fit in here. If you want to learn
more, explore and meet other people, type OUT.

You are standing here.
```

```
You see a note here.
```

```
(You can take a closer look at the note by typing: LOOK NOTE)
```

Hmmm . . . not much warm light. I guess I'm supposed to imagine it. The light in my office is cold, bright fluorescent. The background of the screen is black and the text is green. I can't see it very well, and it strains my eyes. To write this journal, I am clicking back and forth between windows. And because the light is so raw and I've been sitting here so long, I'm typing with my hands closed—wow, what a slip of the Freudian tongue. I meant to say "with my eyes closed," because they are, but I typed "hands" instead. That may be the oddest event of the evening; to think of this as seeing with my hands. Now that I process it, that's exactly what was/is happening.

March 3 (still); 10:30 p.m.: This was it! I was in a MOO for the first time, and I actually interacted with a stranger here. While I was still in the cubicle, I typed "look," and a description of the cubicle appeared on my screen. Then I typed "out" and I "emerged" in the orientation center, where I saw the following text:

```
Orientation Center

Welcome to Diversity University! Ambient lighting conveys a
calm and friendly atmosphere, and there is always plenty of
space on the red couches here. This center is located in the
Student Union, so when you feel ready to explore, just leave
for the foyer by typing OUT.

Type HELP NEWBIE for a quick summary of commands.

Exits include: [west] to the Quiet Cubicles, [out] to Student
Union Foyer, [tutorial] to Tutorial Center, [north] to Help
Desk (Not just for Newbies), [southeast] to Tour Center

You are standing here.

You see Mr. Besenstiel, a large banner, an application folder,
and a map here.

You listen up to make out the words of an announcement,
"ATTENTION Guests! To find out how you can apply for a regular
character at Diversity University MOO, type HELP @REQUEST."
```

```
You  hear  a  faint  voice  coming  from  the  large  banner, "READ
BANNER..."
```

Funny how it says "you listen up," and then I read it with my eyes. It's going to be a challenge to figure out how to write about this feature of online contexts. When I'm "in there," I feel like I'm moving, but I'm not. Actually, I don't feel like I'm moving as much as I can imagine a body moving; I visualize it as if it were mine and watch it move, sometimes from outside the body, sometimes from the inside out. At some point, I'll probably have to stop putting quotes around every word and phrase that implicates the body or physicality.

I didn't see anything except the text on the screen. The descriptions are vivid, though, and I could imagine a banner, red couches, and ambient lighting. There were several directions possible from this location. So I went north (typed "go n") to the help desk. There I saw a description of what was located around and on the help desk. By reading some information (typed "look LEAFLETS"), I found out that "Cindy T's Emissary" was on duty at the help desk and that if I wanted help I should speak up (funny that I didn't "see" this emissary until I read the leaflet located on the help desk itself!). So I said "hi" (typed "say hi" and hit the return key on my computer keyboard).

```
You say, "Hi."

Cindy T's Emissary says, "hi."

You say, "I wonder if I could ask a question if you're not busy
. . . I'm new here."

Cindy T's Emissary says, "sure."
```

So began a conversation. I sound awkward as I write about the experience because it was a very awkward experience. To say something, I had to type "say" before I typed my comment. If I performed this task incorrectly, the MOO program would react with the message, "I don't understand that." At first, I thought Cindy T's Emissary was saying it didn't understand me. Twice, I said to it, "Oh, I'm sorry. What I meant was . . . ;" to which Cindy T's Emissary would respond, "huh?" I finally figured it out, but only after much embarrassment. Luckily, Cindy T's Emissary made a couple of errors as well, which reassured me that it was human, or at least had human traits. The lag time between Cindy T's Emissary's question and my answer, its comment and my reply, seemed immense, primarily because I was trying to use the proper command, type an appropriate response, and hit the right button to send the message so Cindy T's Emissary would actually see what I said. Thankfully, it was very patient. It told me what one could do here at Diversity University (DU) as a guest, such as play games, meet and talk with people, build rooms, teach classes, or do research.

I then asked Cindy T's Emissary what an emissary was. It told me that it was a program that allowed Cindy T to be in two places at one time; an agent of sorts. Cindy T was actually playing Scrabble with her daughter in another location at DU, so she had her emissary watching the help desk. Cindy T's Emissary was very kind and gave me many good suggestions.

When I left the help desk, I had learned much about how to say things in this context. I couldn't emote yet (this required different commands I had not learned), but I could at least express myself through words. I browsed through the help files and found many additional commands that would help me move and communicate. Cindy T's Emissary told me that I could conduct interviews for my research here, but I would have to build a room to do them in. It suggested I read the Builders' Guides before asking more questions; but to even have access to the guides, I had to have an established character in the MOO. In other words, I couldn't be a part of the community unless I had a name and a persona—talk about the power of naming. So as of today, I have applied to become "Markham," a member of the DU community. I'll find out tomorrow whether I am official or not.

March 4, 1997; late evening: I can't believe my evening! I am exhausted! I just got back from a long evening of learning, talking, and traveling online. *(Interesting that I use such spatial metaphors. I can't help but talk about **going** to various **locations** or **places** where I meet and talk with people. I am simultaneously in cyberspace and here in the real world. I went **there** and then said I was **here**. Spatial metaphors are certainly ingrained in our language; we hardly notice how much we use them. It isn't until I am **in a place** (ha!) that defies spatiality that I notice how un-useful these terms are if I want to be accurate in my descriptions . . . or how much I rely on them to have a sense of being.)*

I'm exhausted. My back hurts. My hands hurt. I'm very thirsty. I don't know how people can sit in front of their computers for so many hours at a stretch, but I am beginning to see why they do.

Earlier tonight, after last night's successful online interaction with Cindy T, I decided to traverse a different sort of place, Internet Relay Chat (IRC). Before I could go there, though, I had to have a program (called a "client") on my computer that would allow me to interface with this part of the Internet. I downloaded an IRC client called mIRC and, after figuring out how it worked and learning some basic commands, I logged onto several IRC channels, also known as chatrooms, on a server called the Undernet located in or near Chicago, apparently.

First, though, I went to the Worldwide Web (WWW), searched for help with IRC, and read through a massive document by some IRC guru that talked about how to customize this mIRC interface software program. His website was definitely weird (that really is the most appropriate phrase), and his suggestions were so advanced I couldn't understand them at all. It was as if this person who lived next door to me all his life were speaking in another language. I just wanted to know if it was possible to create a private chatroom and archive conversations. He never got to that. I know how to have unlimited chatrooms going at the same time, how to "kick ban" someone off the channel if they are irritating, and how to chat while at work with something called a "boss key," which apparently allows a person to hide the windows they're chatting in when the boss comes in.

I have been in various online contexts for about seven hours straight. After all that trouble finding a program, learning how to maneuver there, and logging into IRC, I logged off; it was insane. I'm not sure what the point of chatting there is, except to show how adroit you are with your keyboard. To have a normal conversation is impossible because the texts roll by so quickly. It is difficult even to keep up, much less to add to the conversation, if I can even call it "conversation." The norm in most chatrooms is to create short, snappy sound bytes that will draw attention to yourself. As more people participate in the conversation, the texts on the screen scroll up and out of sight faster and faster. Timing, combined with catchy responses, is everything. In mIRC, as with many interface programs, you can assign shortcuts for phrases to save time. Many users thus respond to each other using predetermined sets of phrases, rather than typing out unique responses. For example, if someone says something funny and I want to acknowledge their comment, I can preprogram a shortcut phrase such a "crk" that would appear on the screen as "You crack me up . . . but don't give up your day job!"

I was in nine chatrooms at once; they were all there on my screen, each room a different pane. Odd chatter scrolled by in each chat window. Pointless banter, conversations that had begun long before I ever knew about this place. And my computer beeped incessantly. I found the entire process difficult to comprehend or appreciate. They say that, if you stick with it, everything starts to make sense, somewhat like MTV does if you watch it long enough.

I went back to the MOO and logged in as my new character, "Markham." I was wandering around when I got a message that said, "You sense that someone is trying to talk to you." I knew, from reading the help files, that this message meant someone was yelling at me from some distant location in DU. Then another message notified me that, "Beth_ANN in Hut X (Room 1703) is paging you." Almost immediately I got another message, "Hi, I'm Ellen, do you want to talk? use @go." Then another message, "type '@join Beth_ANN' if you want to talk, i'm in my bungalow." (*If you are confused reading this, think of how confused I was experiencing it in real time, wondering, "Who is Beth_ANN? What now? Who is Ellen? What do I do? What comes next?!" I didn't know who was who, or why two strangers wanted to talk to me all of a sudden, both at the same time.*)

I didn't know how to answer Beth_ANN or Ellen because they weren't in the same room as I was, but I knew the command to tell me who was logged on and where they were. So I saw that Beth_ANN was in Hut X. I couldn't tell where Ellen was—I couldn't even find her name. I was very confused. So I went to the tutorial room, determined to get straightened out in this nonexistent, mapless, nongeographically dislocated space. All of a sudden, I realized I was being paged again by Beth_ANN. By this time, I had figured out how to page back, so I typed "Page Beth_ANN with 'Hi there!'" A moment later, a message appeared on my screen, "Your message has been sent." I soon received another message asking if I would like to join Beth_ANN in Hut X.

I typed "help movement" and got the following message:

```
To go in a particular direction, simply type the name of that
direction (e.g, 'north', 'up'). The name of the direction can
usually be abbreviated to one or two characters (e.g., 'n',
'sw'). You can also type 'go <direction>' to move; this is
particularly useful if you know you're going to type several
movement commands in a row (see 'help go').

In addition to such vanilla movement, some areas may contain
objects allowing teleportation and almost all areas permit
the use of the 'home' command to teleport you to your desig-
nated home (see 'help home' for more details).

Two additional ways to teleport are the "@go" and "@join"
commands. Use "@join <person>" to teleport to the room where
the person is. It's often considered polite to page the person
("page <person> <message>") or use "@knock <person>" first to
see if they're busy. You can use "@go <room>" to move directly
to the specified room. Use "@rooms" to see what places you can
specify by name.
```

```
Related topics
exits — a more detailed primer on MOO exits
ways — tells you a room's obvious exits
go — move through an exit or several exits in succession
@go — teleport to some distant location in the MOO
home — return to your MOO character's home
@rooms — report the list of rooms you can @go to by name
@join — teleport to someone else's location
@knock — a polite way to ask if you may join someone
@move — teleports objects around the MOO
```

Using the proper command, I teleported to Hut X. The screen told me I had just "appeared out of nowhere" in the room. A description of the room told me that:

```
Hut X looks a lot like RedWriter's room on Lambda, bokhara
rug, plants, lots of light from a big window. It's on a
nonspecific studio lot just north of Burbank, and outside
studio lackeys scuttle back and forth on desperate errands.
The room has leather chairs, green plants, not much else. Only
imaginary work gets done here. Davy and Ellen are cuddling on
the couch. Beth_ANN is here.
```

Beth_ANN and I struck up a conversation, but Davy and Ellen, who were cuddling on the couch, never spoke. After awhile, I found out that Ellen and Beth_ANN were the same person. (*Actually, Beth_ANN told me later that her real name was Ellen. . . . and it isn't really Ellen, I just made that up to protect her anonymity. Strange, the names I use in this book are many times removed from the authentic, as well as the declared names of the participants.*)

I was there just a few moments when Beth_ANN said "Are you male or female? You're supposed to declare a gender." I guess I had assumed a gender came with my character or that people would either know or not care. Frankly, I hadn't even thought about it. But then I hesitated; should I be male or female? She said she was "20 from arizona." I told her I was "25, in Indiana." (*I don't know why I said I was twenty-five versus thirty, my real age. (Ha! There's another odd slip. I am thirty-two, not thirty. Wonder what that means.) I guess I figured she would be more comfortable talking with someone in their twenties, or maybe I have some hang-ups about my age. But that's a topic for another time and place.*) She asked again, "Are you a male or a female?" When I figured out how to declare my gender (I could choose from Spivak, Splat, male, female, object, and a host of other possibilities), I chose female.

A couple of other people joined us, and we had a marvelous conversation, which I archived. Now I am absolutely exhausted. To give you a sense of what a conversation in this context looks like and how it flows, I've included some slightly edited excerpts below:

Diamond_Guest arrives from nowhere.

Beth_ANN says, "hi"

Markham says, "hi"

Diamond_Guest exclaims, "Hiya!"

BobZ arrives from nowhere.

Diamond_Guest settles into one of the leather chairs

Beth_ANN says, "hi what's your name Diamond"

Diamond_Guest says, "Cheryl"

BobZ smiles at akk

Markham asks, "Beth, did I ask you before if this was your room?"

BobZ winces at his own spelling

Diamond_Guest smiles at BobZ & understands spelling frustration

Beth_ANN says, "good because I have a lot of spelling frustrations e"

BobZ nods to Diamond/Cheryl

. . .

Markham asks, "Beth, was it hard to build your room?"

Markham says, "I'm asking because I need to build one and interview people for a research project."

Beth_ANN says, "no this room was already here I haven't started building my room yet becaus I haven't gootten upgraded to builder yet but I don't think it will be that hard"

Beth_ANN says, "what research project"

BobZ gapes, having finally noticed that he overlooked Markham's clear declaration of gender.

Markham laughing

BobZ . o O (Is that bcz Markham abbreviates to Mark?)

Markham says, "what, BobZ? "

Markham asks, "Is markham abbreviated to mark?"

Diamond_Guest blushes realizing she make the same mistake as BobZ

Beth_ANN says, "what's your research project about you can interview me if you want"

Markham asks, "it's alright. Hmmm....would you have said things differently if you thought I was female?"

BobZ [to Markham]: in the MOO it definitely works (unless there is another Mark.... person or object in sight).

Markham asks, "I'm not sure what you mean, BobZ. What "it" works?"

Diamond_Guest says, "absolutely not"

Diamond_Guest gigles

Beth_ANN says, "what's your research project on Markham"

BobZ [to Markham]: Not that i am aware of, but everyone i meet in cyberspace has a little mirror or sword-and-shield next to their name anyway ... I like to think it doesn't matter to me, but there is clearly a part of my brain where it does!

Diamond_Guest apologizes to Markham for confusion

Markham says, "Diamond It's okay! I'm so new, I'm very wet around the ears."

Beth_ANN says, "that's ok you have the right to be confused is there anything I can do to releave the confusion"

.   .   .

Markham asks, "So can we interview around then?"

Beth_ANN smiles at you

Beth_ANN says, "that works 7ish my time"

Markham asks, "Beth, is it 10 something your time?"

Markham asks, "i mean now?"

Beth_ANN says, "yes 10:15"

Markham says, "oh, it's 11:15 here. "
Beth_ANN says, "I can be on anytime if this is better for you that's cool"

Markham asks, "so I'll see you at 7 YOUR time, eh?"

Beth_ANN says, "that works 's "

Markham says, "that time is cool"

Markham says, "sigh. this was very fun. "

Beth_ANN says, "cool I'll see you here you have my e-mail address right"

Markham says, "I gotta get to bed too. You're the last at the party."

Beth_ANN says, "yes it was I'm glad you enjoyed it"

Markham asks, "hmmm...had it earlier. can you give it to me again?"

Beth_ANN says, "that's the truth I always am awwal"

Beth_ANN says, "it's K_smak@mars.edu"

Markham asks, "what? what's awwal? "

Beth_ANN says, "and yours is "

Markham says, "markhama@mgmt.purdue.edu"

Markham says, "and by the way, my name's Annette"

Beth_ANN says, "yes that's all"

Beth_ANN says, "cool and mines Ellen"

Markham asks, "how do I get home? just say out?"

Beth_ANN says, "your welcome anytime"

Beth_ANN says, "type 'home'"

Markham exclaims, "I'll see you tomorrow!!"

                          .   .   .

home

You click your heels three times.

Quiet Cubicle No.3

This is a quiet room flooded with warm light in which you can
prepare yourself for the MOO world waiting outside. Only two
people could conceivably fit in here. If you want to learn
more, explore and meet other people, type OUT.

You are standing here.

You see a note here.

(You can take a closer look at the note by typing: LOOK NOTE)

March 4, 1997 (still); 1:35 a.m.: Night. Falling. It began to feel as though I were really there. I was more free with my thoughts. I quipped more than I otherwise might. It was more like a conversation with people in an elevator when it gets stuck . . . without the terror. Maybe more like airplane or bus conversation. No, more like a conversation in a pub with a group of people you know only vaguely, but they are all talkative and friendly. The conversation went very smoothly, as if I knew them. We joked and laughed at and with each other.

Funny how the computer tells me how I move or speak based on the commands I type in or the punctuation I use, respectively. When I type "sit," the computer tells me and everyone else that "Markham settles into one of the leather chairs," or whatever object happens to be "sittable" in the room—it could be a couch or a bed or a bench depending on what the owner of the room has designed. When I type a question mark at the end of my message, it automatically indicates I'm asking a question. When I type an exclamation point, I apparently "exclaim." But if I type a question followed by a statement, it indicates only that I'm saying something—it only notices the punctuation at the end of the line.

In addition to the computer inserting some of the paralinguistics, people seemed much more emotionally expressive than in face-to-face conversations, perhaps because they/we expressed their emotions. I wonder if this is because people are forced to use the emote command to create and show facial expressions or emotional actions such as laughing, crying, sighing, gesturing, and so forth. Using a computer command (typing "emote" or ":") and then writing out the desired emotion ("laughs," "Sighs deeply") may make participants more aware of emotional expression as part of every conversation and as part of the presentation of self. Certainly, I was more aware that emotional and nonverbal communication was happening. If I wanted to indicate that I was smiling, for example, I would type "emote smiles understandingly," and the words "Markham smiles understandingly" would show up on my and their screens.

This experience of being a body in and through text is unusual and unique. I had to think about what I was feeling in order to write it down and show the other participants. Unless I was able to preprogram a keyboard shortcut, I can't imagine how I could ignore my nonverbals (you could, for example, create a shortcut to express vigorous laughter and name it "s-gut," so that whenever you typed "s-gut" the message "Markham splits a gut laughing and then gasps for air" would show up on the screen). Sighs, frowns in frustration, face-splitting grins, you name it; emotional outpouring became something to think about. If someone made a mistake or misspelled something and "blushed in embarrassment," I found myself thinking of ways I could emote in turn to make them feel better. Yet as intriguing as this capacity to express emotions literally is, I feel somewhat constrained. My nonverbal expressiveness tonight was limited to what I could describe in words.

Very interesting; would be the subject of a great study. Does the expression of emotion influence the level of intimacy between conversationalists in online contexts? Could this element of online conversation enable people to be more emotionally expressive in offline contexts? At the moment, however, I am far too drained to think about it.

March 10, 1997; midnight: I did my first interview tonight, online. It was very strange in some ways and at the same time very comfortable, probably because it was with Beth, with whom I'd already had a long conversation. I first logged into DU and entered my comfortable (by this point in time) little cubicle, where "Markham is resting" (that's what the help file told me). I feel like this is a place where I can collect myself before going out into the rest of DU. (I probably feel this way because that's what the description of this cubicle tells me its purpose is.) When I went out, I found I couldn't navigate very well. Of course, I knew where the help desk was, and I learned what was in the orientation room (I came out into it from my cubicle) by typing "look."

But I'd seen all that. I realized I missed the visual image that a gaze, or even a map, provides. I just couldn't get my bearings. You can get into DU in various ways, using different clients. I had heard that if I went to DU through the Worldwide Web, rather than the zMUD interface I was using, I could see things more graphically because the Web is much more graphic, and because it offers more detailed maps. So I switched windows and opened a connection to DU through the Web. It was more visual and offered an overview map, but it still did not allow me to see ahead of myself as I was moving, or to look back as I went through various doorways. The map seemed incomplete, as well, so I couldn't locate the room where Beth/Ellen lived, or the rain forest where Beth mentioned she had gone on a virtual date recently.

Using the Web to navigate through the MOO was much slower; I had to wait much longer for my actions to materialize. So I went back to the text-based DU and stumbled around, encountering many messages such as, "you can't go that way." I found the TV room, though, and remembered that if I wanted to build my own interview space, I would have to watch certain "videos" on what was called the "Big Screen." I figured out how to watch (read, actually) a video (a series of typed comments). But instead of watching the required "Builders From A-Z" video, I watched the "Features and Objects" video, which sounded more interesting and was supposed to tell me where (or how?) to get features added to my character, like the emissary feature, an auto smile, or a picnic basket full of treats I could carry around like BobZ had when we were all in Beth's room. Intrigued by the possibilities as I learned about these options, I decided to go to the actual Features and Objects room to see if I could add some. First, though, I had to figure out the command to turn the TV off so that I wouldn't just leave it running. I didn't know what would happen if I left the video running, but thought it safer and more polite to turn it off.

I dashed off (actually I think it said I teleported) to the Features and Objects room. Acquiring character accessories is more difficult to accomplish than I thought, however, and requires more know-how than I currently possess, so I didn't get any. Oh well. Then I realized it was almost 8:00 P.M. and Beth would be waiting for me. I found out where she was (typed "@who" to see a list of who was where in DU) and joined her (typed "@join Beth_ANN").

Now it is midnight. I have been interviewing Beth for almost four hours. The interview is winding down, which allows me to write this journal at the same time she is thinking about answers. I just click back and forth between windows, which allows me to "multi-task," as they say.

The most amazing thing happened just now! Beth_ANN and I were ending the interview, and I was asking her how to type a command that would allow me into her room when she wasn't there. (It turns out I don't need any special permission. Most places are just open . . . I guess there's no real need for locks here <grin>.) Earlier, Beth_ANN had offered to let me use her room to conduct interviews, which was a kind and generous offer.

```
Markham asks, "say, when you log on, what do you do to get to
this room? Is this Hut X or Room 1703?"

Beth_ANN says, "either will work"

Beth_ANN says, "just a second Ill try to get this to be a home
for you"

Markham asks, "Beth, you are kidding! really?"

Beth_ANN says, "sure"

Beth_ANN says, "I'm going to have to log off soon I was
invited to coffee in a friends room but Ill be back soon"

Markham says, "I think I'm going to go home.....sleepy. Been
at work since 8 a.m."
```

Markham says, "so I'll let you go now. Have good coffee."

Markham smiles

Markham exclaims, "thanks again for everything....letting me use the room tomorrow and spending so much time thinking about and answering questions. I really appreciate it!"

Beth_ANN says, "just a second I'm trying to @set your home"

Beth_ANN says, "just type'@sethome' now"

Room 1703 (Hut X) is your new home.

Beth_ANN says, "are you there"

Markham exclaims, "yeah! it worked!!!!!!"

Markham exclaims, "wow!"

Markham grins ear to ear

Markham hugs Beth in her enthusiasm

Beth_ANN says, "good now you have a home with me and you can do your interviewing here from now on"

Markham says, "wow, I feel like I've just been welcomed into your home."

Beth_ANN says, "your wellcome."

Markham says, "thanks, again"

Markham waves bye

Markham exclaims, "bye Beth!"

Beth_ANN says, "you have learned all I know at this point"

Beth_ANN says, "see you later"

Markham exclaims, "I seriously doubt that. Bye!"

```
Beth_ANN says, "I've passed all my knowledge on to you"

Beth_ANN says, "bye"

Beth_ANN says, "see you soon"

Markham exclaims, "yeah. see you!"

Beth_ANN says, "I'm leaving for coffee now bye"
```

Without any solicitation from me, Beth effectively opened her home to me and is letting me stay there for as long as I like. I feel so welcomed. I also feel like I've "exclaimed" a lot tonight. I am thirsty and my wrists hurt, but I'm very happy.

March 16, 1997; 9:40 p.m.: I read scholarly books during the day and cyberpunk novels at night to get my mind off theory so I can sleep. I have started doing research and writing from afternoon to after midnight, not just because there is more activity online at night, but because there seems to be more action in my brain as well. I get distracted by the sunlight, or the sounds of other people. I write best in my office, ten feet by ten feet of white concrete with two doors; one leads out to the physical world, and one leads into the cyber world.

*(I realized just as I was writing that sentence that I automatically began to write "one that leads **out to the real world**," as if the real world were the physical world outside both my office and my computer, and it was the real place to be, as opposed to the artificial(?) world of my office or the computer. I also didn't think about my words, "into the cyber world," until after I had written them. After I wrote the sentence, I looked back at it and deliberated over the use of "out," "in," "real," and "cyber," putting various other words in place of these, rearranging them, and so forth.*

Let me analyze my own words for a minute, if I might. What did my words imply by saying that the real world was out there [not in here, my office] and that another world [not real, but not artificial or virtual either] could be reached through a doorway that looked very much like my computer? All this editing over one sentence has left me bemused enough to write this brief analysis of my own actions, because it reflects precisely the questions about space and place that I am pursuing in this study.

Interestingly, I seem to believe that my office is the center of the universe at the moment. I also have separated my physical office from both the world that is implied by the hallway, building, campus, and university beyond, and the world that is embodied by my computer, which sits on its own little stand and acts as a portal to a different world of experiences.)

Described in another way, my office seems to embody the tiny waist of an hourglass placed exactly on the fulcrum of a teeter-totter, and I sit at that exact point in the center with complete agency. I can tip the entire mechanism one way or the other, making life alternately real or virtual. (*Believe me, I winced as I wrote those two words—**real** and **virtual**—and have just spent fifteen minutes deliberating over them again. I decided to leave them there only because they point to the difficulty and irony of the entire project of describing sand on one side of the hourglass—or my experience of it—as "real," and that same sand on the other side of the hourglass—or my experience of it—as something else, not real.*) In short, though it seems a simple conclusion to the confusion, my own struggles to name and frame my experiences both influence and are a part of this study, and they are not likely to get easier.

When I am in my office, I can't see whether it is day or night. The walls always look the same. The computer's clock tells me what time it is, though the numbers seem quite arbitrary in a space that is neither day nor night and where I spend much time traversing information territory that is neither here nor there. My world is becoming less guided by the clock and my biorhythms. It is always the same temperature in this office. The computer is always on. I work until I'm tired and then go home to sleep, regardless of whether it is really night; and at the moment, the reality of it matters little. I eat when I can or when I'm hungry, not when traditions dictate I should.

Not only is my body readjusting to this new time I spend in front of the computer screen, but we (me and my body) are thinking differently about what it means to be somewhere. I am learning that I can be in several places at once. This is not so different from daydreaming, but the experience is more tangible.

I can be linked to many different online experiences at the same time. Each program is tiled on my screen, and each pane is a window into a separate space/place. In the IRC pane, conversations flow quickly, and the lines scroll steadily up and out of sight. In the MOO pane, I wait for Beth_ANN to respond to the last question I asked. She types very slowly but is very thoughtful, and if I give her enough time, she will continue to think of things to say in response to the question.

The waiting was difficult for me at first; when she would stop responding, I would charge on with another question, only to see that her next words were in response to the previous question. I learned to slow down, and having several window panes open helps me do this. Meanwhile, I am writing these words in a third pane, and if I feel compelled to comment on the interview I am conducting, I have another pane open to my research journal.

Below these panes, at the bottom of my computer screen, I have a series of buttons that, if clicked on, will reveal yet other windows that are available, but not visible. For instance, I have Netscape running, which allows me to surf the Web for research, shopping, or entertainment. I am also working on my web page, so I have a Netscape editing window open. Finally, I have a program called Microsoft Exchange running, so if I receive email, a message box will automatically appear over the top of everything else, asking me if I want to read my new mail. I must respond "yes" or "no" before I can continue with whatever else I was doing. These various windows allow me to work on several projects at once and talk with many people at the same time. I have access to a multilayered desktop that never gets as cluttered as my physical desk would. Of course, this capacity also brings with it a dizzying array of potentially superfluous information to manage.

This setup allows me to do several things at once, but it also keeps me focused on the computer as opposed to other elements in my office. For the time being, the computer is both my world and my portal to that world. It is many things at once. As Steven Jones says, online communication "not only structures relations, it is the structure within which the relations occur and the tool that individuals use to enter that space" (1995, p. 16).

In this place, time and space are meaningful in different ways. I am in an office with no windows, no day, no night; yet in cyberspace I am talking with Beth_ANN and other people. I am looking at three-dimensional representations of some trousers I have been thinking about buying from Eddie Bauer. I am putting gourmet Italian groceries in my "shopping cart." I am writing the results of an ethnography. I am doing all these things simultaneously, or close enough. Worlds get carried on through my fingertips and my ability to interface with these vast, invisible webs of connection.

Yesterday, as I was trying to figure out how to connect with an interviewee in an IRC ("Gargoyle" was meeting me in a place called irc.warnerbros.com in a private room called #interview), my sister Louise called me on the phone. She was logged into Microsoft Network and wanted to know how to get to this MOO (Diversity University) where I've been doing interviews. As I talked with her on the phone, I guided her to my home page on the Web; and by logging in through that portal, she could link to Diversity University. Then, as I talked her through the process of getting into the MOO as a guest, I simultaneously opened my connection to DU and logged in as Markham, so I could be there to greet her when she got in. I connected and found myself in Beth's room, which is now considered my home. Beth was there and began talking to me, asking me how the interviews were going, how I liked my research, and so forth.

Let me summarize the chaos that ensued: I have a phone pressed between my ear and shoulder and I am talking to my sister Louise, telling her what to do to get online. As she carries out a command, she passes the phone to her son, Vincent, so he can talk to his Aunt Annette. Meanwhile, I am typing in a command to talk with

Beth. All of a sudden, a page from Susan_M (whoever that is) just appears on my screen; she wants to say hello. I quickly send the message I've been writing to Beth, which seems odd because she is "standing" right next to me in our room, and then compose a responding command to page Susan_M. And now, within seconds, Louise tells me eagerly (over the phone) that she is "in a small cubicle . . ." (she continues reading to me the description she sees on her computer screen). I quickly type in a command that effectively pages "Moonstone_Guest" with the message "Hi Louise! You made it! Now type '@join Markham' and you will teleport to my room." She excitedly repeats (in my ear) the words I have just typed because they have just appeared on her screen, and at that same moment, Beth's question "So who are you interviewing tonight?" appears on my screen. Seconds later, as I am composing a response to Beth and listening to Louise talk to herself about what she is typing on her keyboard (she is reading everything on the screen aloud, as well as repeating everything she types into the computer), Moonstone_Guest "arrives from nowhere" in the room with Beth and me. So now, as I congratulate Louise (on the phone), I compose and send a message to Beth, saying, "Beth, Moonstone_Guest is my sister Louise, who has just come into DU for the first time." Immediately after I punch the send button, I compose another message to Moonstone_Guest that reads, "Louise, this is Beth and this is her room, which she is letting me use for interviews." Thankfully, Beth asks Louise a question, which gives me a split second to breathe. As I take in a deep breath, I remember that I forgot to answer a second page from Susan_M, asking me what I was up to. I type a command to page Susan_M with the message, "Sorry for ignoring you, Susan, I'm swamped at the moment in an interview but maybe we can talk later." I slowly let my breath out, wonder why I am here, and think briefly of disconnecting everything. But the sound of my sister's voice grows more persistent in my ear. . . .

The amazing thing during this entire experience is that I was able to do it all, though I felt quite out of breath the entire time. Depending on what I typed into my computer, different things would show up on different people's screens, despite the fact that we were logged into the same computer program/network/server. I could "whisper" to Louise and only she would see the message. I could page Susan and no one in the same room (or anywhere else) would see me "yelling" at her across the virtual university. I could say something and both Louise and Beth would see the message.

I could type "@who" and get a list of everyone who was currently logged into DU, how long they had been connected, how long they had been inactive, and at what location within DU they currently were. Louise and Beth would not see that I had done this, and they also would not see that I had, with another command, looked at their personal information (real name—if offered—email address, physical location, etc.). And, of course, Beth didn't realize that Louise and I were talking on the phone.

When I think back on the experience, I am amazed that it all transpired within two minutes, because so much took place in so many places and with four people. Time seemed to slow down, and I accomplished many things in a very short period of actual time. Even though I could do all these things at once, however, I found it draining. I told Beth I was late for my interview and had to leave. Louise said she had to go as well and disconnected, and then Louise and I said good-bye again on the phone.

I clicked on another pane of my screen and connected to the IRC, where I was meeting Gargoyle for the interview. He was waiting for me in the room, and I realized that the instant switch of venue had thrown me off. The commands here were slightly different than those in the MOO, and I felt a bit like a United Nations translator stuck in the middle of a heated negotiation.

March 17, 1997; 2:00 a.m.: Going online has been a unique, fantastic, and troublesome enterprise. In many ways, I am still being transformed by my experiences of the past few months. Two years ago, my first timid forays into the realm of cyberspace began as many online experiences do, with email, a useful way of communicating with people inexpensively, especially if you are at a university. Although it took some getting used to, I quickly learned how to use my program and started communicating in bits and pieces with friends and colleagues. I was intrigued by the idea that I could write to people I didn't know, but I never actually did—I was too shy.

Over time, I learned about various group communication possibilities online. I could subscribe to a group of tens or hundreds of people joined together by common interests. I joined a group called Comgrads (communication graduate students) and learned that I could send an email message to this group and everyone would see it, perhaps even respond to it. (This type of interaction is asynchronous. The common name for these groups is "listerv.") Of course I never sent any messages—I was too apprehensive about saying something stupid and getting flamed. When I think back, I also felt like my presence was somehow concretized by the text in which it was embedded. In a face-to-face conversation, my statements were not written in stone. In cyberspace, they were not written in stone either, of course, but I was daunted by the thought that my sentences would land on hundreds of personal computer screens to be scrutinized, saved, and held against me at some future unknown date. Paranoid delusions of a "newbie," I suppose.

That seems a long time ago.

In the past few months, I have completely shifted my stance toward communicating with strangers online. I have posted replies to several comments in public forums among other communications scholars. I probably would not do this at a face-to-face meeting of these people at a national conference, but I am beginning to think that people who are communicating with each other online care less about formalities or titles. First of all, people do not necessarily know the real names of other interlocutors, and most of the time the content of the message gets more attention than the person attached to the message. In certain small online groups that are preoccupied with their real-life titles and positions, this may not be the case, but in most online settings I feel free to comment. As I conceptualize it now, a person has made a public statement in a public forum; if I think it warrants a response, I am just as capable of making one up as someone else.

Of course, even as I say this I must disagree with myself. I recently spent forty-five minutes composing a six-sentence message to a well-known author and five times longer deliberating over whether to send it. I sent an email message to a prominent scholar in my field of study the other day, but only after serious arguments with myself. I sent an email message to the editor of an electronic journal today, to ask her if she would like to be interviewed. All of these personal communications were troubling and painstaking because they made me feel exposed and vulnerable.

Yet I have to smile to myself as I realize it gets easier with each passing day. For instance, I sent a message to the dean of the business school today and didn't deliberate over its phrasing at all. I just wrote it and hit the send button. I suspect I am experiencing a pendulum effect rather than a learning curve, and after I commit some grave error and get flamed, I'm sure I'll calm down. In the meantime, I continue to feel a growing sense of freedom in this space. For example, physical disembodiment allows me to experiment with imaginary bodies (which I describe and try to perform) so I can experience how others respond to me; disengaging from my actual name and physical location allows me to escape for a few moments from the categories that hang like placards around my neck in everyday life. I realize that I cannot completely transform myself into something other than my embodied self, even through my words; but I am beginning to experience things that I couldn't in a physical setting.

March 21, 1997; 3:00 a.m.: However it happened, and as long as it took, I think I'm almost there. I feel strange as I write this, knowing that the *there* is both here in front of my computer, where I have been spending an inordinate amount of time, and in many other strange places . . . also here, but not, really. It makes me a little nervous. It is currently 3:00 A.M. Tonight, as I worked on this chapter, I simultaneously interviewed a user online and helped a student—who happened to catch me with my door open—with an assignment.

Another student dropped by and told me I was "quite the geek," and I realize that it might appear so. I am camped out in my office with wrist guards, take-out Chinese food, and coffee. I seem to live most of my hours through this computer screen. I am actually beginning to understand the language I hear in the chatrooms and MOOs I visit. Last night I spent more than four hours talking with a hacker whose goal in life is to build a virtual fortress of information that no one can penetrate. I just finished a two-hour conversation with a person who said she would rather live life through language because she could be herself through words better than she could be herself through her body.

At the same time, I realize that we all struggle with issues of self, identity, and embodiment, whether we are online or not. Each of us enacts multiple, often conflicting roles, some of which would surprise those closest to us. I am learning and knowing as I write, and what I write is a representation of who I am, so perhaps I, too, am living life through language. Perhaps these contexts I have encountered are not so alien to those I enact at other times; simply less familiar.

Ambivalence and the Body

When I spend a lot of time in disembodied spaces, I forget my body. Often, I don't remember it until the physical pain is extreme, and then I resent my body's intrusion on my life online, and my online life's impact on my body.

Sometimes I will take a deep breath and realize I haven't been breathing. Then I'll feel giddy with the rushing intake of air. Sometimes I blink and realize I must not have blinked in a long time because it feels so good. I'll close my eyes for awhile, enjoying the sensation of not staring bug-eyed at the glare of the computer screen. After a few hours of work, my body is screaming with pain. My back constantly aches, no matter how I adjust my chair. If I don't chew gum, I clench my teeth; if I don't talk, my throat gets raw and sore. My hands take the most punishment. They ache and throb because I forget to stop typing.

I'm dehydrating into a shell of myself, a dry husk filled with salt and caffeine. So why can't I stop? I lose track of time, and three, four, five hours will pass before I realize I haven't stood up, stretched, or even taken a sip of water. I haven't had hot coffee in months; it always gets cold before I remember to drink it.

My body hurts, yet I'm actively participating in life online. I talk with people; I walk here and there. I feel the breeze as I walk down the avenue at DU and pick up a Frisbee to throw to Beth. At the same time that I'm engaging in these "embodied" activities, my eyeballs are drying out, I don't speak a word, and no part of my body is moving at all except my hands.

In a way, I resent the encroachment of my body into my life here. This frightens me. I'm afraid this project will go on too long. I'm afraid I'm getting accustomed to it, learning to live with certain aches and pains. I'm afraid I'll get so used to this position that I won't notice my back hunching over and my hips spreading over the edges of the chair. I'm afraid I'll just increase the size of the letters on the screen if they begin to blur before my tortured eyes. Maybe I'll need the humming sound of the computer to wake up in the morning . . . maybe I'll need it to help me sleep at night.

Somehow, the more I try to ignore my physical body to create a textual one, the more my physical one reminds me it is here and needs attending to. I wonder if this is just a stage I need to work through.

Perhaps my body just needs to get used to being avoided.

Chapter 2

The Shifting Project, The Shifting Self

The Internet changes so rapidly that few aspects of it now resemble the online world I first knew, the online world I studied, or the online world you may be familiar with. Odd to think I'll never be in the same place I was when I first got connected. The fact that things change over time applies to any place one encounters and connects with, but it is perhaps more noticeable online because the foundations of these contexts are unique and easily transformed. Of course, newly developed technologies will alter the media through which communication takes place. Even so, the social dimensions of online contexts are constructed primarily through the texts of participants. As participants come and go, the context also shifts, sometimes radically.

In this chapter, I address some methodological issues related to studying this shifting ethnographic site. After describing the logistical nightmares of collecting data in online contexts, I share my thoughts as I progressed through the initial stages of interpretation and tried to make sense of the relations among the users, the project, the context, and me. You'll discover, as I did, that this ethnography seems to have a life of its own—a life that is intimately connected with mine, yet inseparable from the dialogues that constitute the study. It continues to change, even as I write these words.

Deciding how to frame and present this ethnography was a process of attempting to maneuver it into a traditional report and then accepting it for what it wanted to be—a study that honestly came into being through me. I have spent several years learning about and interrogating the practices and processes of ethnographic inquiry. I am informed and intrigued by the contemporary debates among ethnographers regarding the practices of coming to know and write about others. And I have spent time exploring alternative modes of ethnography. It should not be surprising, then, that as I discuss how the study progressed I raise several concerns:

the elusive goal of trying to validate and legitimate my project using traditional social scientific norms; the ongoing dilemma of trying and failing to separate artificially the "official" interview texts from myriad other texts influencing my interpretation; the quandary of trying to represent adequately and honestly the voices of the participants; and the paradox of conducting a nontraditional ethnography in a nontraditional nonspace with traditional sensibilities. These issues are important in any interpretive ethnographic study, and they certainly plagued me here.

Perhaps the most difficult issue I faced throughout this project, however, was that my original assumptions about online experiences significantly influenced the way I framed and asked questions in interviews, as well as the way I tried to interpret those interviews. Although my goal was to learn about the ways people experience cyberspace, I tried to fit their experiences into my own conceptual and grounded understandings of social life, even before I met them. I believe all qualitative researchers must at some point face this struggle between wanting to be open and flexible, yet needing to design and justify a study; so I talk about it here.

SETTING UP THE INTERVIEWS

Over the course of this study, I experienced a shift of perspective that significantly altered the trajectory and design of the project. I realized as I moved closer to the project that I could not work with abstracted texts to address meaningfully the questions I had set before me. I wanted to know how users were making sense of the concepts of identity and reality in computer-mediated contexts, but I realized I was not talking with users and asking them this question. Instead, I had sought to study them from afar. In other words, I was trying to *get at* the question without *directly asking* the question. Only after the study began did I realize I needed to participate online to truly get at their understandings of their experiences.

After consulting with several colleagues about how to generate texts for analysis, I decided to conduct what I call "User on the Net" interviews, following the general concept used by Studs Terkel, whom I admire for his rich and nuanced interviews of everyday people. Rather than selecting participants and bringing them to his office for interviews, Terkel simply carries a tape recorder with him wherever he goes and lets "improvisation and chance" help him find people to talk with (1974, xxi). Terkel's books—such as *Working* (1974), *"The Good War"* (1984), and *Race* (1992)—address current issues from the perspectives of the people experiencing those issues in their everyday lives. My goal was similar. The scope of my research question, "How do users make sense of reality in online contexts?" allowed me to choose participants from many randomly encountered online contexts. I did not want to confine the participants to one group or community online; instead, I wanted to head out into the Net and, with keyboard in hand, so to speak, talk with people and get them to tell me stories about their experiences. The great advantage of doing the study online was that my range was not limited by physical space. I could contact people in any geographic location, interview them online, and use the interviews, which became "transcribed" in the process of doing the interviews, as the basis of my analysis.

It seemed so straightforward. I contacted colleagues and asked them if they knew people who would consider themselves "heavy users." Although many people gave me the names and email addresses of users who might be interested, I found it immensely difficult both to contact and correspond with potential participants and to set up and accomplish the actual interviews. I realize now that I was fairly naive to expect to complete the interview portion of the ethnography within a few weeks. (*No doubt many of you are saying to yourselves, "Wow, what a naive expectation for the interview portion of any study!"*) I asked myself, "How hard could it be to do ten interviews online?" Just go there, chat with people, and get them to interview with me, right? Even with complications, I figured the entire process would take no more than three weeks. I even developed a series of logical steps to follow:

- Create or find a way to conduct interviews.
    Must be accessible to both interviewer and interviewee.
    Must allow real-time (synchronous) interaction.
    Must allow interviewer to log and archive the transcript.
- Establish contact with participant.
- Negotiate date, time, location of each interview.
- Go to agreed-upon location, meet participant, conduct interview.

These steps *seemed* straightforward, until I moved from thought to action. The first one caused me many nightmares, some of which you heard about in the last chapter. Before I could tell people where to go for an interview, I had to figure out where to go myself, how to manage the setting once I got there, and how to communicate in this setting. For example, I didn't know how to get to an IRC or a MOO; and once I figured out how to get there, I didn't have the right software to interact easily in these environments. So I had to go online (mostly to the Web), learn about what software people used, and find out where they got the software.

But this was only the beginning. Most people who have the nerve to say they study computer-mediated communication know how to "download" software. I did not. I had to learn how to get the software from the Internet to the computer in my office. Once on my machine, I had to figure out how to "unzip," or "decompress," the software so it would run on my PC (which required that I download yet another software program called WinZip... I had to get help on that one). Finally, when I got the interface or "client" programs running on my computer, I had to learn how to use them. I had to make sure I could get to a MOO through the client (zMUD is the name of the client I chose), learn how to work the zMUD commands, and learn the basic commands common to most MOO environments. I also had to be able to teach all of this, if necessary, to a potential participant so they could participate in the interview. All in all, this involved slightly more work than setting up another chair in my office next to a microphone.

As I set my mind to these challenges, I began contacting possible participants and setting up interviews, a process that is still giving me headaches. When we plan meetings with someone over the phone or face-to-face, we take for granted the ease and speed with which details and logistics can be negotiated in a simultaneous communication environment, but this is not so with email, which was my method of contacting and communicating with participants.

At this point, I began to realize how unrealistic a three-week projection for interviewing was. I can attribute part of my vast underestimation to my overly optimistic nature, but the medium itself and the way we deal with online information (and overload) contributed significantly to my misunderstanding.

We frequently and commonly make the error of conflating *information transmission* with *communication*, and believe that because information gets transferred instantaneously between people, or their computers, communication speeds up as well (or that communication *happens*, at least). This is not always the case.

I thought that the entire data-collection process would be expedited through online communication. Besides the great benefit of not having to transcribe the interviews after conducting them, I could do several things at once. As I was contacting one potential participant, I could simultaneously be in contact with another participant, setting up an interview. It was feasible that these two tasks could be taking place as I was interviewing yet another participant.

I also thought that contacting people would be a simple matter of sending one email message, getting a response, and nailing down details in a third or fourth message. This would surely be faster than using the telephone. I could send a message at any time of day and it would be waiting for the other person as soon as they logged on. I could also do the interviews at any time of day the participants were available. Finally, because we wouldn't be meeting physically, getting to the interview was a simple matter of running the correct software.

I suspect my reasoning is not so different than that of many who mistakenly equate information transfer with communication. Intellectually, I know they are not equal, but the medium—the promise of instantaneous communication with others—is very deceptive, as I came to find out the hard way. I envisioned my packets of information zipping around the globe at unimaginable speeds, making connections with others as easy as the press of the enter/send button on my keyboard. Instead, I should have envisioned piles and piles of post-it notes—some personal, some official, some important, most unimportant—growing higher and higher on everyone's desks.

People who are really on the ball go through each message as it arrives, decide whether to read it or not, and then if and how to respond. Others, like me, read through all the messages, think about responding to them, and put off the entire project until later . . . and later. Still others accidentally delete messages, or don't respond because they don't know the sender personally.

By this point, you probably understand what was really happening and why three weeks was a naïve timetable for this stage of the ethnography. Online, negotiating a simple detail like "What time will we meet?" takes multiple messages at best, sometimes days or weeks, depending on how often people check their email or how complicated the two schedules are. In general, the people I contacted were willing to be interviewed, but establishing a date, time, and place for the interviews was more complicated than I ever suspected, as the following two examples illustrate:

February 13, Annette writes:

Hi Sherie,

I'm Annette Markham. I've been working on an ethnography about cyberspace and my colleague told me you were in her class. I know your name from an online list, where I have occasionally lurked about. I would love to talk with you sometime about your experiences.

Anyway, the purpose of this message is to ask if you would be interested in being interviewed online for a study I'm doing. I am using a "user on the street" approach, sort of in the Studs Turkel fashion, and interviewing people that tend to use the Internet a lot. I thought you would have some interesting perspectives.

What are your thoughts? I can give you more info if you are interested. Let me know.

February 15, Sherie writes:

I'd be glad to. How do you want to set this up?

February 15, Annette writes:

Great! Thanks!

I'm trying to get my office computer set up for interactive sessions that will also log the interviews, and the tech people here are working on it at this very moment. For our interview, since you are on a linked system, we could try the talk function, although I have never been able to get my talk function to work. Anyway, when they get my computer's capabilities figured out, I'll let you know.

If you have any suggestions, let me know.

February 25, Annette writes:

Sherie,

Sorry to delay getting back to you...was out of town for a few days. I have a PC platform, on which I have set up netmeeting, which allows real-time talk. Do you have a PC or Mac? If you have a PC and netmeeting, we're set. If you don't have netmeeting, I can tell you where to download the shareware (it's very easy...if I can do it, anyone can).

Let me know what your preferences are. I have a very flexible schedule and could meet almost any time.

February 26, Sherie writes:

i have a pc but don't have netmeeting, so you'll need to tell me how to download it. in terms of scheduling, weekends are generally best. also, i'll want to ask you some technical questions because i have a similar idea in mind for a project. but i don't have time to go into it right now.

February 26, Annette writes:

on netscape, go to http://www.microsoft.com and under free
stuff or products, find netmeeting. pretty user friendly from
there. If you have trouble, let me know. weekends are good for
me too. And ask away on the technical stuff. Not sure if I can
answer it or not, but I'll try.

just tell me a date, and I'll work things out.

March 9, Annette writes:

Hi Sherie!

Just wanted to let you know that I can do the interview any
time you like. Also, I now have another alternate location for
us to do our interview. I have a room in a MOO (Diversity
University) that we can use for real-time interviewing. If you
have a MOO or MUD client, it will be easy for you to use. You
can also log in as a guest through the web.

If you go to my home page, I have a direct link to Diversity
University). If you log into DU from the web, you can simply
Telnet in...not as user friendly, but workable. Also, you
could easily download a mud client (I did it, so I know most
other people could).

I downloaded zMUD and really like it.

Anyway, I'm here all of spring break if you are around. If
not, maybe when you get back, eh?

Let me know how it's going.

March 15, Annette writes:

Hi Sherie,

Hope you had a restful spring break! Thought I would let you
know that I now have three options for interviewing. IRC, MOO
(Diversity University), or NetMeeting. Just let me know what
medium works best for you and I'll work out the details.

I'm free all week and weekend for interviews, except St Patrick's day. Let me know what works for you or if you're too busy we can do it next week.

March 19, Sherie writes:

The moo might work best for me. As for the best time, Thursday evening might be best.

March 19, Annette writes:

Hi Sherie!

How about 8:00 p.m. Thursday?

March 19, Sherie writes:

that sounds good.

*

February 27, Annette writes:

Hi! My friend Kelly told me you might be interested in participating in an online interview for a study I'm doing.

If you are, let me know and I'll set something up!

I am free almost all the time during the next week or so. I could easily work around your schedule, day or night.

The interview would take about an hour, depending on how much you want to talk. And it would be strictly confidential.

Let me know if you're interested, or if you need more information.

Thanks very much,

March 8, Annette writes:

Hi!

I wonder if you are still interested in interviewing with me about your online experiences. Please let me know either way. If you're not interested, I'll definitely stop bugging you :)

March 12, Gargoyle writes:

Sorry it took me so long to get back to you.
I would be more than interested, but could I find out a little bit more info like what I would be questioned about???

March 12, Annette writes:

Hi! Thanks for getting back with me.

In the interview, I would be asking questions about what you do, where you go, who you meet. Questions about what it's like for you to be online. I would also be asking you to compare your online experiences with your off-line experiences. AT ANY TIME during the interview, if you decide you don't want to participate, you can disconnect and I will never bother you again...but really, it won't be that kind of interview.

Basically, I am collecting stories and experiences from all kinds of different users.

If you are worried about anonymity, I guarantee I won't refer to you by any of your real or online names. Also, I will never reveal where you live or work or any of that. Nobody would ever be able to trace what I write about back to you.

Hmmm...anything else you would like to know?
Let me know what works for you. The only times I am not available are Thursday (March 13) afternoon through Saturday late afternoon (out of town for spring break). Oh, and I can't do it St. Patrick's day....going to a concert.

March 14, Gargoyle writes:

How about tonight??? Could it be in a chat room or something, as I am at work right now, but if you would like we could do it tonight???

March 14, Annette writes:

```
That's cool :)
```

```
You will have to walk me through the chat room thing......I
have mIRC so I think I'll be able to get there, but as far as
going to a private location, you'll have to be the guide,
okay?
```

```
Where should we meet? When?
```

March 14, Gargoyle writes:

```
I will be on at the server irc.warnerbros.com as the user
Gargoyle I plan on being there in about 1/2 hour - an hour.
just look for me and I will be there.
```

March 14, Annette writes:

```
Where will you be? What channel? I'll look for you....hopefully
I'll get there :)
```

March 14, Gargoyle writes:

```
I'll set one up called #interview
```

Setting up the interviews was, needless to say, a complicated matter of accom-
modating the participants and getting them to commit to a date and time. I became
very frustrated with the process before I ever conducted a single interview.

CONDUCTING THE INTERVIEWS

The actual interviews ranged from less than one hour to more than four hours.
During the first interview, I followed the interview protocol fairly closely, modify-
ing various questions and probes as I went along. My mentor and colleague, Bill, sat
in on the first interview to help me formulate follow-up questions and for general
moral support. He had not conducted interviews online either, but he had spent
many hours interviewing people from all walks of life. About halfway through the
interview, we both realized that online interviewing is a singular, frustrating, and
exciting experience. Two specific issues are worth commenting on in further detail:
First, online I only see the text—not the nonverbals, the paralanguage, the general
mannerisms or demeanor of the participant. Second, because writing takes much
longer than talking, being a good interviewer means being patient.

Online, you can't see their faces

Online, I can't see the other person's face, hear their tone of voice, or get any sense of who they are beyond the words I see scrolling up my own screen. This does not mean the interview is less interesting. Through their words and through my interaction with them, I could sense joy, anger, passion, bitterness, happiness. In fact, I was surprised and impressed by the intensity of the conversations.

However, I found it difficult to manage the basic elements of conversation, such as taking turns at the appropriate time, nodding, or mm-hmm-ing to imply, "Go on, I'm listening." I couldn't give a questioning glance or wrinkle my forehead or frown slightly to let the other person know I didn't understand what they were getting at. I couldn't smile, chuckle, or laugh spontaneously. Indeed, if I wanted to react to something I found amusing, funny, striking, or in some other way noteworthy without interrupting the flow of the story, I had to type something such as "emote smiles" or "emote grimaces understandingly." Then a message would appear on the interviewee's screen that read "markham smiles" or "markham grimaces understandingly."

Each time I felt compelled to react nonverbally to something the other person said, I had to decide whether or not to risk disrupting their thoughts to let them know I was listening and was engaged in the conversation. This issue became less troublesome as the interviews progressed, but not less salient. How much of good conversation is based on reading the other person's face? How much of good storytelling relies on the listener's nodding head, chuckles, gasps, or raised eyebrows?

During one interview, the participant answered many of my questions with very few words: "Yes." "No." "It was nice." "It was different." "Not much time." "OK." I thought she was shy. For almost two hours, I tried every technique I could think of to get her to talk more. I was struck by the disjuncture between her obvious reluctance to open up, and her statement that, "my net sense of self is myself in language. I get to express myself as a writer, in writing, more than in any other aspect of my life. I'm a good writer." I asked for specific instances, descriptions of events, examples of what it felt like. I finally gave up. Toward the end of the interview, she told me I would never understand what she was talking about unless I read the things she had already written (and published).

I'll never know if she was shy, bored, or put out by the interview, but at that moment, I decided I had just wasted two hours with a rude, pretentious, self-absorbed, cerebral person who felt she was too far beyond and above me to engage my questions with more than monosyllabic responses. I felt as if she were telling me that if I wanted to know what she felt about being online, I should read her publications rather than pester her with questions that are so simplistic they could be answered with mere yes/no responses.

My reading may be harsh, but I only have her short phrases, a painstaking dialogue, and my interpretation of the text. Perhaps she spoke more in those few words than she ever had in a face-to-face conversation. My point here is that I might learn other things, or reach other conclusions in a face-to-face interview, but here I was working from my own experiences of conversation and thus drew conclusions from that reference point. I'm convinced that the absence of body language, tone of voice, and other quintessential elements of conversation make a difference. (*This is clearly a judgment on my part—many users of this technology would disagree.*) Whether this difference is relevant or not is a good question for future study. Regardless, in this study, I was frustrated by the lack of face-to-face cues.

Writing takes longer than talking

```
Beth_ANN smiles

Markham nods understandingly
```

Beth said, "I think I like it this way because I can just type what comes to mind and not have to think about it as much; thinks seem to be communicated better through my fingers than my voice."

I tried my best not to type something back immediately, because I had been running over Beth's sentences constantly since we started the interview. I just couldn't stop myself; I tend to jump into the middle of face-to-face conversations too, so I guess I shouldn't be surprised.

Sure enough, Beth eventually continued, "that's why I like being on here so much."

I asked, "do you think that talking with your fingers better than your voice is the major difference between RL and online communication?" And then, as an afterthought, I added, "for you, I mean?" (RL is a common online acronym for "real life.")

I had been talking with Beth for almost an hour when Bill knocked on my office door. "Come on in," I yelled through the door. I distractedly pointed to an empty chair and Bill sat down.

"Hang on, Bill. I'm talking with Beth. . . . Hang on."

"Hey, no problemo. Take your time. I'm just here to help."

I was glad that Bill, my advisor, had agreed to sit through my first interview because I was nervous about how to ask questions in this context and wanted his expertise to guide me.

Beth wrote, "I use the internet for a lot of things even now to find information, chat, look for things just use it for everything but I haven't brought anything off the Internet yet."

"Is this your interview protocol?" Bill asked, gesturing toward the sheets of paper hanging from a clip attached to the side of the computer.

"Mmhmm . . . Just a sec. Yeah, yeah," I mumbled, distracted. I was typing a message to Beth, and was having trouble concentrating. I wondered if Beth meant to type bought instead of brought. I typed, "What do you mean by brought off . . ." I considered this for a moment, then erased the message. Better to buy myself some time, I thought, and wrote a different message. "Beth, can you hang on a minute while I use the restroom?"

Beth said, "yes it is because I can type what i'm feeling better then I can voice my . . ." A few seconds passed, then Beth continued, "feelings it just comes a little easier seeing things to answer then hearing and having to answer I like to worrk with my hands a lot."

I looked at the screen, trying to decipher her response to my question. After a moment, I realized she was answering my previous question about the relative advantage of using one's fingers versus voice to communicate online. Good thing I didn't press on with the question I had just erased. As usual, I was racing ahead of Beth and she was plodding along, answering questions in the order I asked them.

"Yes I can!"

Ah-ha. She means yes, she'll wait while I'm in the restroom.

I quickly typed, "thanks! back in a flash!"

"ok that's cool"

I sighed with relief, leaned back in my chair, and looked over at the person physically present beside me. "Hi! Hey, I'm glad you're here! Okay, we have a few minutes to talk while I'm in the 'restroom.' You won't believe this. Very cool! I had to start without you, because Beth was waiting for me. But it seems to be going okay." I started scrolling back through the logged transcript, pointing out to Bill some of Beth's more interesting comments.

"She takes forever to answer questions, Bill." I said excitedly. "And sometimes she repeats herself. I think when I send a message to her, it just appears on her screen and it interrupts her own writing of her message. She doesn't have the same interface program as I do. I think she's using Telnet . . ."

"Wait, wait!" Bill interrupted me, laughing. "Slow down! I have no idea what you're talking about."

I laughed. "Okay, okay. How are you?" Without waiting for an answer, I went on. "Let's just get to the interviewing part. I'm only on the second page, and I'm having trouble sticking to the questions. Look here . . ." I showed Bill places in the transcripts where I had strayed significantly from the protocol.

"Well," he said, "I can't stay for very long. Let me watch for awhile. I'll see if we can't stay more on track."

I noticed a message had come on to the screen from Beth,

```
You sense that Beth_ANN is looking for you in Hut X

Beth pages, "is a girl who's at Purdue and it's on here that
she's interviewing"
```

I quickly sent the message, "hi again."
Beth replied "hi. your back. that's cool."

```
Beth_ANN smiles

Markham smiles back
```

From my side, Bill asked, "How long has it taken for you to get through each page so far?"

As I typed, I replied, "I don't know. Maybe thirty minutes? I'm not sure."

I wrote to Beth, "What do you do mostly when you are online? Where do you go?"

"I'm usually on the MOO when I'm in my room. But I go all over the place I have lots of bookmarks on my computer. I just love to look around at everything and anything. Plus my teacher my English professor likes us to search for things in class for projects and stuff she's an Internet junky too."

"Mostly the moo? Or do you IRC too?"

Bill flipped through the interview protocol silently for a few moments, then pronounced, "At that rate, the interview will take over four hours."

"Well," I replied worriedly, "I'm not sure if I can go any faster. Do you think there are any questions I can cut out?"

Beth continued her response, "I love the internet and my professor likes it that I like the internet because she says it's the wave of the future and there are not enough women on the Internet. The Internet is a place we can make the most impact."

I gave Beth time to catch up with my questions, which gave Bill and me time to discuss various questions we could collapse or delete.

"I only moo you can't IRC very well from my room and I'm too busy in the computer lab to do it so I'm just here and it keeps me busy."

Thinking Beth had finished her response, I asked another question, "How do you think women can make the most impact online?"

Noticing the question I had just asked, Bill commented, "Annette, maybe you should get to the next question on the protocol." Then he added, "I can't stay that long, you know."

I shot him a sidelong glance. "Yeah, I know. You told me that when you came in." I turned away from the computer, frustrated, and looked my mentor straight in the eye. "Bill, I can't just do the questions as I planned. I know I keep getting off track, and I'm not going very fast. But I don't know how to go faster. I think it just takes longer to interview this way."

He nodded, "Maybe so, maybe so. But these interviews could take a long time, given where you're at now. Do you think the participants will agree to such long interviews?"

"Well, look," I said, trying to explain. "It's like small talk. I can't just ignore the small talk to jump into the interview. And every time I smile, I have to type it. Every time I say "mmhmm" I have to type it. Every time I say something or nod or do anything, I have to type and send a message." I sighed, feeling exasperated, "You see? It takes forever to do the things that you just need a few seconds to do in a face-to-face interview."

Bill had been nodding throughout my outburst, and I knew he was trying to understand. "You're right," he said thoughtfully. "That never occurred to me. I guess I do the same thing in my interviews, but I don't have to think so much about it." He smiled and started to chuckle as the implications struck him. "It's a good thing I don't have to type everything that I do and say in an interview! It would never get done!" Bill exclaimed, and suddenly burst into laughter.

Beth asked, "is that clear enough?"

I realized I had taken too long to send a message, and now Beth was reminding me that I was supposed to be focused on a different conversation.

I quickly typed and sent another message, "very clear," and then asked another question.

Bill and I realized that when I strayed from the questions, I still was accomplishing a vital part of any interview by allowing the participant to relax, encouraging a conversational mode, and letting the conversation guide the questions rather than the other way around. Whether it was small talk, comic relief, or a new conversational direction, we came to realize all interviews have these elements; they are just less noticeable in face-to-face contexts—and less time-consuming. Here, even clarifying a participant's response took time to write and several messages back and forth to complete. In short, the basic elements of good conversation seem to steal precious time from what I had been taught was the heart of the interview, the set of protocol questions. The solution was fairly simple—accept this fact and make sure everyone involved knew that the interview could take much longer than expected.

I also had to learn to slow down to give participants enough time to respond fully to the questions. When I was interviewing Beth, I would ask a question and wait for what seemed like a long time for her to respond. Sometimes, if I didn't see writing on the screen shortly (don't ask me how I define "shortly"; I'm sure the actual passage of time was much shorter than the multiple minutes I imagined), I would wonder if she had received the message. Then I would wonder if she was still there. Then, to make sure she was there, I would send the same message again, or another message asking if she got the first one. I'm sure it drove Beth crazy. At other times, after Beth would send a message, I would ask the next question (a logical enough conversational move, I thought), and Beth's response would be a continuation of her previous message.

In effect, I interrupted almost every story she tried to tell. She would be warming up to the question, getting started on an in-depth answer, and I would abruptly ask a different question. I couldn't help myself. I felt compelled to fill the blank, black void with more green writing. I couldn't stand what I thought to be silence. Meanwhile, Beth was chatting away. I just couldn't hear it yet.

To solve this problem, I forced myself to focus on other things. I started writing a research journal at the same time so that she had time to respond in peace. Learning to be patient was crucial for another reason as well. If I asked a question, got a complete response, and still remained silent, the participants would often fill the empty space with more stuff—more detail regarding their previous answer or another related story that occurred to them during the silent period. Most interviewers learn to wait patiently in face-to-face contexts, but here it took concentrated effort to not type. Sometimes I resorted to sitting on my hands.

In general, interviewing online took more planning and time than I thought it would. One significant advantage of online interviewing is worth mentioning, however: I had time to think of good follow-up questions. I could see the story unfolding, or the response developing, as the participant sent segments of text. This meant I could attend to the message more than once. I could reread what the participant had just sent, and while he or she was composing the next message, I could think of possible follow-up questions.

Not only did I have more time to consider the direction of the discussion, or scroll back to previous comments, I could revise the form of the question to make it more precise, open, and evocative. For instance, I could ask Sheol a closed-ended follow-up question, "Are you an addict?" or, after typing that and thinking more carefully about what I wanted, I could ask a more open-ended question instead, "What would define 'addict'?" In another instance, I started to ask (write), "Why did you start using the Internet?" and changed my question to, "What drew you to the Net?" because I thought Sheol would be more enticed by the second question. These questions vary only slightly, but as any interviewer knows, the form of the questions is vital for facilitating the participant's response.

Having more time was good for another reason as well: If I was having trouble formulating a question or deciding what direction to go next, I could pretend I had been interrupted by the phone or something else (which I learned by actually being interrupted by people who didn't realize I was conducting an interview while sitting at my keyboard). These contrived interruptions gave me time to think without looking like an inept, amateur researcher.

EVERYTHING CHANGES, BUT SHOULD THE RESEARCHER ADMIT THIS?

May 1997: Reading through the interviews, I am realizing a number of things about my project and my preconceptions about cyberspace. First, I changed my interviewing style significantly over the course of the interviews; not only did my questions shift but the responses also changed, perhaps because the questions were asked differently. Second, the interviews do not say what I thought they would. Third, I am beginning to question my own methods as well as traditional methods of collecting and analyzing discourse and reporting research findings. Having noted these realizations, let me explain their significance to the course and shape of the study and my understanding of the research process.

If my thoughts throughout this discussion seem nonlinear, it is because they are. I cannot in good faith write a completely orderly narrative of precisely how I collected, encountered, and made sense of (am still making sense of) these texts. The ethnography is taking me in particular directions—directions I did not predict or expect. Even as I write, I continue to make sense of the entire project, process, and product in shifting ways.

The interview protocol changed significantly as the interviews progressed. Because I concentrated more on the conversation with the participants and less on the protocol, I ended up with richer discourse. (*Of course, the protocol didn't like this. I could sense it glaring admonishingly at me from the side of the computer, waiting impatiently for me to get back to the proper questions.*)

For awhile, I worried about the potential problems associated with straying from the interview protocol; many methods teachers had warned me against such deviations. One suspicion and two realizations have eased my mind considerably. I suspect all researchers stray from their interview protocols to a certain degree, and I realized that recognizing when one crosses the invisible threshold that indicates one has strayed "too far" is a matter of interpretation. Indeed, many researchers don't even begin with a standard protocol, so the thought that they have strayed too far might never even enter their minds as they engage in richly generative conversations with others. I also realized that although I set up a research question to guide my investigation, I am not really trying to get a set of answers to a standardized set of questions. I just want to get people to talk about their experiences, to tell me stories. Adhering strictly to a standardized protocol actually impeded my progress toward this goal. The users I interviewed are very different; different ages, different stages of life, different reasons for going online, different ways of talking. We all are prompted to tell our stories at different moments, depending on numberless contextual factors. I would be presumptuous to expect these users to respond exactly the same way (or even necessarily comparatively) to the same set of questions.

In fact, as I continue to struggle to make sense of this project (to make sense both of the context I am studying and the process of studying it), I am beginning to question at least two underlying assumptions of traditional research reporting—that the researcher can and should separate the planning from the doing from the presenting of research; and that the researcher should present research projects as if they were a sensible linear process, when in fact the linearity is made sense of retrospectively.

March 30, 1997: I have gathered all my interviews and have been reading and rereading them, looking for themes, patterns, or whatever seems salient. This is a difficult process, as any qualitative researcher knows. Interpretive research is generally thought to be inductive and emergent. In theory, I look through the data until something comes to me. But as many scholars have noted (Ashmore, 1989; Grumet, 1991; Van Maanen, 1988; Wolf, 1992), the process is not so neat and linear in practice. Certainly, I look for themes and patterns to emerge from the texts, but I also follow hunches (some of which came out of my research questions long before I actually went online, some of which came out of my interactions online) with my nose to the ground.

For example, in my research proposal I asked, "How do online users make sense of the concepts of reality, identity, and community?" As I began researching literature for this project two years ago, I became intrigued by the issues of reality, virtuality, and hyperreality. I found that many scholars theorizing about cyberspace and computer-mediated communication focus on the difficulty of determining what is real and what is virtual, or on the blurring of the two in or through various technologies (e.g., Baudrillard, 1988; Benedikt, 1991; Gibson, 1986; Jameson, 1991; Rheingold, 1991, 1993; Slouka, 1995; Woolley, 1992). Still other scholars focus on the identities of users, as these identities are fragmented, multiplied, disembodied, or decentered through their interaction with various technologies (e.g., those listed above, as well as Stone, 1991; Turkle, 1984, 1995).

As I continued to engage the project, I realized I really wanted to listen to people's stories. I knew what the theories suggested they would say, but I wanted to hear about lived experiences. I wanted to know how they would answer the question, "What is Real?" To get at these questions, I developed an open-ended interview protocol that would get participants to talk about what it was like to meet others and be with them online. I wanted to ask them questions that would get them talking about their perception and presentation of self, both online and offline.

Many of my questions were crafted so that participants would compare their online and offline experiences, identities, and relationships. I asked, "How would you compare your sense of self as a person online with your sense of self offline?" If they indicated they felt differently, I asked the follow-up question, "What about your online experiences makes you feel as though you are a different person from when you are offline?" I also asked, "How real are your experiences online?" and "How would you compare communicating online with communicating in RL?"

Now as I look through the transcripts, I don't quite know if I am more interested in what they say about these issues of reality and identity, or what they do while they're online and what they think about their online experiences. I'm not sure, but it seems I am not getting what I thought I wanted out of the interviews.

WHAT AM I LOOKING FOR? AND IS THIS THE SAME QUESTION AS "WHAT AM I FINDING?"

Frankly, most of the participants do not think about being online in the ways I assumed they would before I talked to them. Some users perceive computer-mediated communication as a means of keeping in touch with friends and relatives inexpensively. Others talk about the Internet as a vital connection to the rest of the world, a place where they can be more like themselves because they can backspace and edit their words prior to uttering them. Cyberspace allows them to interact as and with words rather than bodies. Some users seem to separate their real-life selves from their online selves. Of course, some of the people I interviewed would not have distinguished between the two if I had not pressed them to think in those categories.

March 31, 1997: I keep reading the transcripts, wondering vaguely what I am looking for now that I have determined they don't say what I thought they would. I see many possible themes:

- CMC is a tool for virtually all the participants.
- The Internet is a window to the world—a way to get connected to more things and people.
- Online communication is real, friendships and relationships are real, but "being" is for the most part located in the physical body.
- Across the board, the online self is more outgoing, more eloquent, more confident.
- Each user is different and unique.

This last item is most bothersome at the moment. If they are all different, how can I say they have similarities? Why don't they all talk about the same issues? I am attempting to say something meaningful about online users of online communication, but I'm not sure what I can legitimately begin to say about them as a group, based on these interviews. Let me back up, recap my goals. By conducting "User in The Net" interviews, I am addressing the question "How do users make sense of identity and reality?" If I am pressed, I say I'm looking for themes or patterns in their discourse; otherwise, what's the point?

Basically, this goal seems incommensurate with the type of interviews I conducted. This project is somewhat analogous to trying to say something about Americans by talking on the phone with a dozen people who claim to be American. I am interviewing self-described "heavy users" who spend a lot of time online, who perhaps even live much of their lives through computer-mediated communication. I have found, though, that heavy use is individually determined, and "a lot" can range from two to eighteen hours per day.

*

This entire discussion, of course, emerged just as the official interviews were ending. I was trying to make sense of the interviews prior to interpreting them. The process of interpretation is a never-ending cycle of reading, thinking, interpreting, writing, questioning, and rereading, reinterpreting, thinking, finding patterns, rejecting patterns . . . and so on. Clearly, this process evolves as the project does. Do we include all the stages in the final presentation of research? Not usually; we present findings as if they came through a logical process of making sense of the data. But I want to share my interpretive dilemmas, those crucial moments in the research process where I questioned the research process itself. Besides, discussing these moments allows me to explore a methodological issue very relevant to conducting interpretive research, namely: "How do you justify the choices you've made?"

If my goal is to find themes and patterns, and I don't seem to be finding any in the discourses I have collected, can I really say anything meaningful with these texts? Do I just present eight stories, eight sets of sense-making practices? I asked a colleague this question recently, and he suggested I collect more interviews. This sparked a long conversation about the number of interviews required to justify interpretations.

My colleague believes I should keep interviewing to reach "critical mass"— that I should interview until I see patterns repeating, which is fairly standard practice in qualitative research. In other words, more interviews might yield critical insights that tie the rest of the interviews together. He also suggested that doing more interviews would be a strategy to gain some credibility for what I did eventually decide to say. (This was my term—he wouldn't call it a strategy.)

I was and still am confused by this discussion. More importantly, I am confused by my own (and many of my professional colleagues') conviction that enough discourse is something we can somehow quantify, even as we spend seemingly endless amounts of time trying to convince our social constructionist, interpretive, anti–hypothetico-deductive selves otherwise. What is enough? How much is critical mass? How many interviews equals saturation? How many does it take to validate the results of a qualitative study?

These are not trivial questions. Indeed, they invoke heated discussion even among the most agreeable of colleagues. I have asked these questions for several years and have yet to receive adequate answers, not because those whom I ask give unsatisfactory answers but because they, too, struggle with these issues and do not profess to have the definitive answers themselves. The most common answers seem to be: "You will know when you have enough," and "Ten."

In the final analysis, the questions still remain: How do we know we are saying something meaningful? How do we represent and speak for others adequately and honorably? I think it is important to confront these questions throughout the research process, not because I can find definitive answers, but because the honest pursuit of these questions leads me to a fairly honest conclusion—we can never get to the bottom of it, we can never have enough, we can never know it all. Even if I am saying something meaningful about a particular context, I am not saying an infinite number of other things. I can never exhaust all possibilities. Yet, as Geertz says, "it is not necessary to know everything in order to understand something" (1973, p. 20). In other words, all social inquiry focuses on particular aspects of social life at the expense of other, potentially interesting features. This is a good thing.

SO WHAT AM I REALLY STUDYING?

June 1997: At the moment, I consider myself a newcomer to the Internet. My view of this world is as an outsider. I see cyberspace in particular ways. You, the reader, undoubtedly see it in other, singular ways. My research is centered in cyberspace, but it is also centered in me. Considering all the things in my life that influence my research and writing, my research becomes a polyvocal, dialogic process of retrospective sense-making and storytelling.

I created research questions that I was interested in exploring. I created an interview protocol that led interviewees in particular directions that I chose. Yet as I engage this context to study it, the very context changes. Each interview changes slightly, because I get to a different place in my own understanding of the context and, consequently, I ask different questions. I am changing as a result of my inter-action with this context. In turn, this changes the way I see the participants, changes the way I seek out and obtain participants, changes the way I interview the par-ticipants, and most importantly, changes the way I interpret the transcripts of the interviews. (I should add that writing for different audiences also has altered my interpretation of the interviews, and the version you will read is another rendition of this ongoing process of making sense of Other.)

I'm trying to comprehend the connections among texts—texts I have writ-ten, texts I've encountered, texts I've generated with others online. Layer upon layer of dialogue; within me, the texts I bump up against, the Others I meet, the various selves I perform and embody.

Frankly, it's a complicated but challenging mess. I am studying other peoples' dialogues with each other. Simultaneously, I am influencing and altering their conception of themselves and others as I converse with them. I also am contribut-ing to the shape of cyberspace through my presence and interactions. Meanwhile, I am reconsidering my own understandings of identity and reality as I encounter and engage this world. And my transformation of self influences every aspect of the project. What is part of the research and what is not? What do I consider part of the ethnographic experience and what do I edit out as irrelevant?

My understanding of cyberspace comes in moments, fragments, glimpses, and dreams. I might perceive and experience it one way and completely revise my understanding of it based on any number of things that happen—conversations I have that spark new ideas, scents on the wind that provoke particular memories, cyberpunk novels I read, a student's speech about nanotechnology, the titles of books that glare at me when I'm trying to think. (*What do I do with this dream I had after a particularly long night online, in which I was asking someone a question and I could see the words coming out of my mouth, letter by letter, to form themselves in sentences superimposed over my vision?*) We might come to understand our experiences as a coherent narrative, but the process we go through to get to that semblance of organization is not as linear as we might like to think, and the experiences we remember and retell are not the same as the experiences themselves.

May 10, 1997: I should have expected that the reporting part of this project would get complicated. This is not a linear process, and the more I find out, the more I realize how little I know. Some colleagues tell me I just need to stick with it, stay there until I have discovered and recorded enough facts, and then stick to those facts. But for me, embedded as I am in this study at this moment, this traditional stance to ethnographic inquiry (voiced to me in many books, personal conversations, and a decade of social scientific education) is limiting. I cannot quell the voices of innumerable texts, each influencing and being influenced by the project. The other day, my colleague Bill urged me to stop trying to figure out the ending. He said, "just follow your lights." He said I should stop trying to encapsulate the project based on traditional ethnographic research. This is good advice. (*But order, tradition, and narrow conceptions of validity keep peering over my shoulder as I write....*)

Even as I do this ethnography, I am not separate from it. The more I become a part of the ethnography, the more it becomes a part of me. In the end, I am not sure if I will have learned more about cyberspace, the participants, or me.

January 1998: How do we study and come to know the "Other?" And how— when we think we know something—do we write what we think we know? Throughout this project, I have grappled with questions like these, sometimes because I wanted to, but mostly, because I couldn't help it. During the early stages when I was preparing for the study, these questions did not seem so important. When I wrote the first version of this manuscript and I was writing the Other into my text, however, the questions were crucial. Now, many months later, as I reflect back on my experiences and retell the stories of the participants for the book you now hold in your hands, I believe the questions of how we represent others in our research are paramount. In the end, though, it is not so important to find the answers; I gain insight and humility just by considering the questions.

Sheol says it beautifully: "What I know is like filling a thimble full of water, and saying I hold the ocean in my hands." These words give me strength.

Chapter 3

Themes Of Life in Cyberspace

Internet users do not comprise a single culture, but enact innumerable cultural forms. Through the course of this study, I encountered only a tiny fragment of those users, and for only a moment in time. When I think about this—frequently, these days—I begin to ask questions such as, "What can I say about the experiences of those I study that will both honor their individuality and help scholars understand the Internet as an emerging cultural force? How can I contain the multiplicity, or thematize the idiosyncratic?"

Each of the users I talked with engages Internet technologies for different reasons, with different degrees of attachment and commitment. Throughout the interviews, if I didn't know better (I knew better because I was asking the questions), I would have thought we were talking about completely different modes of experience. And perhaps we were. As I pored over the transcripts of these conversations, I knew intellectually that we were all talking about similar tangible technologies; but the *meanings* of online technologies derive from the users' interactions with, in, and through them, and those meanings offer much more complex stories.

Even though these participants related distinctive accounts of their experiences, over time and through many rereadings, their reports coalesced into patterns that I could render in a larger narrative sense. (*Or, I eventually fit their experiences into a pattern, because I needed to grasp some sense of connection among their descriptions.*)

Three themes guided and emerged from my interpretation. First, in terms of how users frame computer-mediated communication, their definitions fall along a continuum from *tool* to *place* to *way of being*. Second, in terms of how they experience computer-mediated communication, they experience it as *real*, but they use this term in intriguing and nuanced ways. Third, in terms of why they use, go to, or exist through and with computer-mediated communication, they appear to gain a certain measure of *control* from the technology.

Before you read about these themes and my depictions of the interviews, let me offer two specific caveats: First, these three themes can be separated heuristically, but they also are inseparably woven into lived experiences. Each theme is nested within and encompasses the others. I could not prioritize these themes into levels of relevance or importance for the users, or into any causal sequence (e.g., if one thinks of the Internet as a place, it becomes more real and affords a greater degree of control over the self). They are simply different moments of lived experiences.

Second, I have separated these themes artificially for purposes of presenting a somewhat coherent narrative, but not all of the participants' discourse falls neatly into the themes I created. They don't always address these themes directly in their conversations with me. I have gleaned from their texts an understanding of how they experience and define Internet technology, as well as what keeps them there, or compels them to return.

ONLINE TECHNOLOGY AS A TOOL . . . OR A PLACE . . . OR A WAY OF BEING

Online communication engages most users at a number of conceptual levels. The extent to which we mix metaphors when speaking of this technology (highway, frontier, community, web) hints at our complex understanding of it. Certain users describe this technology as a communication medium, a conduit that transmits information from one place to another, a means of keeping in touch with friends in faraway places—or of avoiding face-to-face contact with the people just upstairs. For these users, the Internet is primarily a *tool* they utilize to facilitate research or communicate with others.

Other users talk about cyberspace as a *place* they can go to meet and talk with others. Although such online worlds may not have physical substance, they are thought of as meaningful places where things happen that have genuine consequences. Some users talk about these online spaces as virtual communities. Others call cyberspace "home."

Some users do not focus on the technology they use or occupy; rather, they focus on the expression of self and other through the text. These users, most of whom have integrated online technologies into their lives to a high degree, talk about their experiences *in* or *as* the text. For these users, online technology is a *way of being*. Some consider themselves cyborgs—a state in which mind and body merge with the computer, or the mind separates from the body to be inside the machine, creating and expressing the soul in abstraction through language.

The participants shifted their terminology frequently. You will no doubt notice some of this slippage as people talk about going there, using it, living there, editing the self, doing research on the net, being with others in cyberspace, and so on. Everyone framed cyberspace as a *tool*, whether they called it a tool directly or not. Everyone also talked about it as a *place*, but this is where the terms began to lose their coherence. For example, some speak of *going* online, but they don't conceptualize themselves any*where*, any more than they do when they are on the phone. Everyone also talked about *being* online, but most of them do not seem to mean this literally.

For several of the participants, while discussing technology in inconsistent ways probably indicates they are familiar with current jargon, it does not necessarily indicate they experience the Internet in those various ways. However, for a few participants, particularly those whose lives are intertwined with online technologies, mixing frames is just part of using, going to, or being in cyberspace. These users have integrated online technology into their lives to the point where they conceptualize it as they go along, and use whatever terminology makes sense at the time.

People's perceptions of computer-mediated communication shift and change depending on what they're doing or why they are online at any given time. This makes intuitive sense; people experience cyberspace as they experience life—it is not that profoundly different. All life experiences can be more meaningful at certain times than at other times. Some days, I walk across the campus where I work and feel intensely connected to something important. Other days, I don't even pay attention to where I am; I'm just trying to get from point A to point B in the most expeditious way possible.

I present the interview participants along a continuum of ever-increasing connection of self to the Internet. Three of them, Matthew, Jennifer, and Mist, talk of the Internet as a place to go, but their discourse indicates they think of it as primarily a tool. For another participant, Michael, the Net is very definitely a place, a world even, where people go to live with others in meaningful ways. The authentic self remains stable and rooted in corporeality, however, even though it might play behind masks. Beth and Sheol seem to take this one step further. They live much of their lives online, and their senses of self are integrally connected to their online experiences. Terri not only lives much of her life online, she has integrated her online and offline lives. She speaks so casually of both realms of existence it is often difficult to separate them, and her discussion of experience, self, and other incorporates technology to a high degree. Like Terri, Sherie perceives the interplay of online texts as a way of being, but Sherie actually enacts this way of being. For

Beth and Sheol, and even for Terri, the Internet may offer an ideal way of being, but Sherie lives through and in the text, even as she participated in the interview.

I developed a version of this experiential continuum before this project began as a way of understanding the literature related to online technologies. Early organizational communication scholars, for instance, have viewed and defined computer-mediated communication as a tool (see Sproull & Kiesler, 1991, for a good overview of this perspective) that can both enable and constrain communication practices and processes in the workplace. Once the Internet became popular in the early 1990s and users began to develop online enclaves, scholars began to explore how individual identities, collectives, and cultures are created and maintained through technology (e.g., Baym, 1995; Benedikt, 1991; Bromberg, 1996; Jones, 1995; Ludlow, 1995; Reid, 1995; Rheingold, 1993; Shields, 1996; Turkle, 1995). Cyberspace is conceptualized by these scholars as a place where meaningful human activities take place. At the same time, the written text is where cyberbodies get inscribed and live, so theorists have also focused on technology as a mode of being (e.g., Baudrillard, 1988; Cherny & Weise, 1996; Clark, 1995; Robins, 1995; Senft, 1997; Stone, 1991).

Although I did not consciously think about this continuum as I conducted or initially analyzed the interviews, I found myself categorizing the research participants in groups when curious family members and colleagues asked me, "So, what do they say?" Around this same time, as I looked through my research journals, I realized my own frames had been shifting along a continuum of sorts throughout the project. The starting point for this shift was when I met Beth.

Before I interviewed Beth, I had many preconceived notions of what I would find through these interviews, of what cyberspace would be like. As I interviewed Beth, I initially thought of cyberspace as a tool to facilitate my research. The interviews were a way to get at certain sense-making practices, and conducting these interviews online was necessary to preserve anonymity and to increase my geographical range. Using this medium also facilitated the transcription of several hours of interview data.

One of the first questions I asked the first being I encountered on my screen once I found Diversity University was: "Would it be possible to conduct interviews for research here?" I needed to know whether I could use this elaborate software program to accommodate several interactive, private interviews. Later, when Beth—who calls this domain home—said "hello," it seemed an interruption of my research, or perhaps of my time. After all, I was faced with the daunting task of building a room (writing a subprogram) in which to conduct interviews. For me, this was not yet a meaningful place; it was simply a tool.

A few days and two online conversations later, I interviewed Beth. As this interview progressed, I found myself struggling to force our interaction to fit into my made-for-face-to-face interview protocol template. In retrospect, it seems I wanted simply to add online interaction to my research procedures; but the more I talked with Beth, the more I realized that merely incorporating online interaction into my research efforts as a tool to collect texts wasn't working very smoothly. More importantly, this wasn't just a tool to study the context, it *was* the context of the study.

As time and conversations with Beth went by, I came to think of online as a place, although I was still caught up in learning the commands that would allow me to communicate and move more easily. It still seemed more like a mechanism with complicated working parts. I would go to the MOO and join her in her room, and we would chat with others who came there. But when she offered to let me conduct interviews in her home, I honestly felt like I had a place to go.

One day I was chatting with Beth in her room and asked her if she wanted to go for a walk through the MOO. Our experiences during our exploration of this interactive space were telling.

✳

You say, "hey Beth, what's up? I was just hanging out in an IRC...looking around."

Beth_ANN says, "taht's coo, Annette"

Beth_ANN says, "that's cool which one"

Beth_ANN asks, "is it cool?"

You say, "hmmm...Hades/Dalnet. and I was just in a basic room, like cyberchat or something."

You say, "it's okay."

Beth_ANN says, "that's cool"

You ask, "what are you supposed to be studying?"

Beth_ANN says, "government and english"

Beth_ANN says, "lots of reading to do"

You say, "sounds boring........snore, snore. No wonder you're here :)"

Beth_ANN says, "yes I know"

Beth_ANN says, "I have been on Spring Break for the past week and just got home I'm going back to school tonight or in the morning"

You ask, "so Beth, how have you been!? Haven't talked to you in awhile. Was spring break relaxing?"

Beth_ANN says, "yes it was very relaxing but I was away from my computer and taht was hard"

You ask, "why so hard?"

Beth_ANN says, "I don't know I like my computer and do so much on it that it's hard to be away from it I don't know why though but Florida was cool anyway"

You exclaim, "wow. I didn't know you were in Florida! Cool!"

Beth_ANN says, "so when was your Spring Break or have you had it yet"

You say, "oh. we had it two weeks ago. I didn't go anywhere. Too busy here...sigh."

Beth_ANN says, "that's cool you don't live in the dorms or do you"

You say, "no, I have an apartment across town."

Beth_ANN says, "that's cool"

You ask, "hmmm...I'm thinking of exploring this place. Wanna go?"

Beth_ANN says, "sure that would be cool"

You say, "hmmm....never walked around with another virtual persona before..."

You ask, "I guess if we get separated we can page each other, huh?"

Beth_ANN says, "that's cool a new experience doesn't hurt"

Markham laughs

Beth_ANN says, "that's cool"

Beth_ANN smiles

You ask, "so where should we start? in the hallway?"

Beth_ANN laughs

Beth_ANN says, "that's cool"

Beth_ANN goes out.

You go Hallway.

2nd Floor Hallway

You have entered the second floor of the Grand University Hotel. Please type 'exits' to see the list of rooms on this floor. To go to these rooms one needs only to type the room number in. Thank you.

Exits include: [E] to Grand Hotel Elevator, [201A] to Room 201A (Grand Hotel), [201B] to Room 201B (A Single Adjoining Room), [202] to Room 202 (A Large Suite), [203] to Room 1703 (Hut X), [204] to Room 204 (A Large Suite), [205A] to Room 205A (A Single Adjoining Room), [205B] to Room 205B (A Single Adjoining Room), [206] to Room 206 (A Large Suite), [207] to Room 207 (A Single Room), [208] to Room 208 (A Large Suite)

Beth_ANN is standing here.

You ask, "do you know people in these rooms?"

Beth_ANN says, "yes in 204 I think I do"

You ask, "is it considered impolite to just barge into a room?"

Beth_ANN says, "I don't think so"

You say, "then let's go! I'm going to try some doors..."

Markham giggles

You ask, "how bout 206?"

Beth_ANN says, "okthat's cool"

You go 206.

room 206 (A Large Suite)

A very large sectioned off room. When you first enter the room you notice a spectacular view out the window. As you move further in the room you see a hot tub, a small bar, a huge bed, and a table that seats 6.

Exits include: [Hallway] to 2nd Floor Hallway

P+T_Johnson-Lenz (asleep) is standing here.

You go Hallway.

2nd Floor Hallway

You have entered the second floor of the Grand University Hotel. Please type 'exits' to see the list of rooms on this floor. To go to these rooms one needs only to type the room number in. Thank you.

Beth_ANN is standing here.

You say, "not much there."

Beth_ANN says, "that's cool"

You go 208.

Room 208 (A Large Suite)

This room is a fantasy room. On the ceiling above the bed are mirrors (for your enjoyment of course), you will find a comple-

mentary bar (both alcoholic and non-alcoholic drinks), a hot
tub, and a bathroom you could probably open up a roller
skating rink in.

Exits include: [Hallway] to 2nd Floor Hallway

Tyisha (lays like sleeping beauty waiting for her prince to
come. You have the sudden urge to join her: she appears soooo
relaxed and comfortable.) is laying on the huge bed.

Beth_ANN has arrived.

You say, "wow, Beth. Look."

Beth_ANN says, "I like the hot tub idea"

You say, "yeah. I could use one about now."

Beth_ANN says, "me too"

You ask, "how do you look around or go somewhere?"

You ask, "I mean in this room?"

Beth_ANN says, "type look"

You ask, "yeah. I did that. Can you get more specific descriptions of objects in the room?"

Beth_ANN says, "I don't think there's anywhere to go"

You exclaim, "ah. well, then, I'm outta here!"

You go Hallway.

2nd Floor Hallway

Beth_ANN has arrived.

You exclaim, "lets go to 207!"

You go 207.

Room 207 (A Single Room)

This is a private, single room. It contains a bed, a bathroom, and many conveniences for just one person.

Exits include: [Hallway] to 2nd Floor Hallway

Beth_ANN has arrived.

You say, "boring."

You go Hallway.

2nd Floor Hallway

Beth_ANN has arrived.

Markham laughs

You say, "this is sort of fun."

You exclaim, "let's get in the elevator!"

You go E.

Grand Hotel Elevator

A bird-cage elevator that links the lobby with the second and third floor. Bird-cage elevators were quite the rage when the century was new.

Exits include: [Main] to Grand Hotel Main Entry, [B] to Basement, [Fl2] to 2nd Floor Hallway, [Fl3] to Third Floor Hall

Beth_ANN has arrived.

You ask, "hi! where to, madam?"

Beth_ANN says, "I don't know you choose"

You say, "basement. could be spooky......"

Markham grins and pushes the button

You go B.

Basement

This is the place where the laundry is done and the water is
heated. The pumps for the pool whirl in a corner. John has his
office east of where you are now and you can reach Strathmore
schoolyard to see Weaver by going down into the manhole.

Exits include: [east] to John's Office, [Elv] to Grand Hotel
Elevator, [down] to Stratmhore schoolyard

Beth_ANN has arrived.

You ask, "sigh. not too spooky. Who is or what is 'weaver?'"

Beth_ANN says, "boring"

Beth_ANN says, "where is that"

You say, "let's go down into the manhole. I think it is down."

Beth_ANN climbs down the ladder into the hole and disappears
with a whoosh.

You start to climb down the ladder but lose your grip and fall
weightless right through the planet ... finally decelerating
in time to grab hold of a rope and haul yourself up and out
through a drainpipe.

Strathmore schoolyard

You would think you were in a transportation school rather
than an above average K-12. Trains run past, planes land up
the hill, a freeway connects to two arterial roads just outside the yard. A thick rope hangs down a stormwater drain.

Exits include: [down] to Basement

Weaver (off enjoying other times and other seasons) and Beth_ANN
are here.

You say, "hmmm. can't go anywhere except back to the basement"

Beth_ANN says, "are you here"

You say, "yes"

You ask, "back to the basement?"

Beth_ANN lowers herself down the rope into the drainpipe and disappears with a whoosh.

You start to lower yourself down the rope but lose your grip and fall weightless right through the planet ... finally decelerating in time to grab the bottom rung of a ladder which you climb up and out of the hole.

Basement

Beth_ANN is standing here.

You say, "okay, elevator."

You go Elv.

Grand Hotel Elevator

A bird-cage elevator that links the lobby with the second and third floor. Bird-cage elevators were quite the rage when the century was new.

Exits include: [Main] to Grand Hotel Main Entry, [B] to Basement, [Fl2] to 2nd Floor Hallway, [Fl3] to Third Floor Hall

Beth_ANN has arrived.

You ask, "main entry?"

Beth_ANN says, "go"

You go Main.

Grand Hotel Main Entry

THIS IS A HUGE LOBBY reminiscent of the majestic hotels from long ago. There is a split staircase that curves up from the back of the lobby. At the end of the desk a wrought iron elevator was installed to provide service for those staying at the hotel. The hotel contains a restaurant and conference center as well as a swimming pool and gift shop. Lining one wall is an elegant *sofa with several *chair(s) facing it in a semi-circle. In the center of the room you see a large poster on an easel saying:

<====== West to the DU Conference Center

Exits include: [south] to LSU Street (100 block), [EV] to Grand Hotel

Elevator, [north] to Pool Entryway, [east] to Windsor Hallway, [west] to DU

Conference Center Foyer

You are standing here.

Beth_ANN has arrived.

You say, "hi. This is cool"

Beth_ANN says, "yes it is very cool"

You say, "okay, your turn. Lead on, I'll follow :)"

Markham smiles

Beth_ANN goes south.

You go south.

LSU Street (100 block)

This part of LSU Street is newer than the rest and paved with concrete. The School of Hotel Management is on the north side and includes an actual hotel where visiting potential students, families and friends may stay. You may find an adjunct faculty member or guest speaker staying there as well.

———————————

Exits include: [east] to Intersection of LSU and Houston streets, [west] to Intersection of Mogue's Run and LSU Street, [north] to Grand Hotel Main Entry, [south] to Business and Accounting

Building

Beth_ANN is here.

Beth_ANN goes east.

You go east to the intersection with Houston Street.

Intersection of LSU and Houston streets

_____

Giant pine trees tower over your head, swaying their fluid limbs and dropping pine needles onto the intersection. Every once and a while you hear a pine cone drop, plop, to the ground. And when you do, you duck, out of habit.

There are large signs on each corner of the intersection pointing to the School of Hotel Management, which also houses a real hotel. Parents and significant others of dorm-residents often stay there while visiting. It is to the west, down LSU Street. LSU Street continues to east, as well, past the Student Union and Free Speech Alley.

Houston street runs north and south. The Communication Building entrance is to the southwest, off this intersection, while the Center for the Development of Human Potential and the Technical Complex are to the north and south, respectively, on the west side of Houston Street.

_____

Exits include: [east] to LSU Street (200 block), [west] to LSU Street (100 block), [north] to Houston Street (400 block), [south] to Houston Street (300 block), [southwest] to Communication Building Foyer

Beth_ANN is standing here.

You ask, "hi. Are we on a street?"

Beth_ANN says, "yes I think we are"

Beth_ANN says, "at an intersect I think"

You ask, "what is the center for the development of human potential? Sounds official, eh?"

You ask, "where do most of the people hang out?"

Beth_ANN says, "I don't really know"

Beth_ANN goes southwest.

You go southwest.

Communication Building Foyer

You have entered the Communication Building of Diversity University, here you will find the communication department, Journalism and Media departments. There is a fully functional tv studio and a moderated debate room.

Exits include: [northeast] to Intersection of LSU and Houston streets, [south] to Communication Building Lobby, [west] to IRC Uplink Forum

Beth_ANN is standing here.

Beth_ANN goes west.

You go west.

IRC Uplink Forum

You are in a large meeting room, with several long tables arranged in a U-shape. Speakers are mounted at one end of the room, and microphones are on the table before each chair.

A sign says: Welcome to the IRC Uplink forum. This room is able to connect to the Internet Relay Chat system, linking MOO users and IRC users into a common discussion medium. Please contact one of the DU administrators if you wish to use this room for purposes in line with DU's theme.

Exits include: [east] to Communication Building Foyer

Beth_ANN and you are standing here.

You see a quick intro to IRC here.

You ask, "wow, what do you do here?"

The IRC Uplink Forum room can be connected to the IRC network by any MOO wizard. Once connected, it can be made to join an IRCchannel, so that whatever is said on that channel is repeated to everyone in the room, AND anything people in the room say or emote is broadcast to the IRC channel. If you want to communicate ONLY to people in the room use "think <message>" and the message won't be seen by outside IRC listeners. Use "look here" to find out if the room is linked to the IRC network and which channels it is listening to.

Beth_ANN says, "that's what I'm trying to figure out"

You say, "oh. looks like we need a wizard to turn it on."

Beth_ANN says, "yes it does"

You say, "hmmm.....we should do it sometime."

Obvious exits:

east (east, e, out): Communication Building Foyer

Beth_ANN says, "that would be cool"

You go east.

Communication Building Foyer

Beth_ANN has arrived.

You ask, "hmmm, now where?"

Beth_ANN goes northeast.

You go northeast.

Beth_ANN walks east on LSU Street, towards the Student Union.

You continue walking east on LSU Street and begin to hear laughter. At that point you realize you are not approaching a building where classes take place.

LSU Street (200 block)

This street was named after Louisiana State University, the alma mater for one of the campus administrators. To the North is the Student Union, while to the South is the northern part of the Southern Quadrangle. LSU street runs East/West.

Free Speech Alley lies between the Student Union and the Administration Building and provides a setting for impromptu political rabble rousing. Sometimes you can even hear the pontificator all the way out here!

Exits include: [south] to The Southern Quadrangle (north end), [east] to Intersection of LSU and Sandoz streets, [northeast] to Free-Speech Alley, [west] to Intersection of LSU and Houston streets, [north] to Student Union Front Lawn

Beth_ANN is standing here.

You see Pretzel Wagon here.

You check your watch to see if you have enough time to run into the Student Union for something to drink before class.

You say, "wow."

A food vending machine for hungry people.

(Best viewed with @playeroptions -no_drawing)

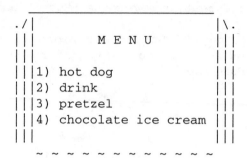

type 'order <number> from wagon' to get that item.

Markham orders pretzel from the Pretzel Wagon.

```
              //~~~~~~~\\
           //||          || \\
         //  \\        //    \\
        ||    \\    //        ||
        ||     \\//           ||
         \\    // \\        //
          \\__//    \\__//
```

Hope that you enjoyed the pretzel from Pretzel Wagon.

You exclaim, "Beth, get some ice cream from the pretzel wagon!"

A food vending machine for hungry people.

(Best viewed with @playeroptions -no_drawing)

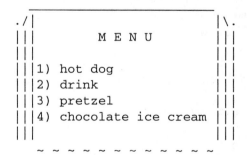

type 'order <number> from wagon' to get that item.

Markham orders chocolate ice cream from the Pretzel Wagon.

Hope that you enjoyed the chocolate ice cream from Pretzel Wagon.

Beth_ANN orders drink from the Pretzel Wagon.

Beth_ANN orders chocolate ice cream from the Pretzel Wagon.

Markham grins, wishing this food was real.

Beth_ANN says, "that's cool"

You exclaim, "yeah!"

You ask, "okay now whereZ?"

Beth_ANN says, "mee too"

Beth_ANN goes north.

You go north.

Student Union Front Lawn

You see a large grassy expanse that has numerous *benches (bench) to relax on or you can just relax on the cool green *grass. There is a winding *walk that goes through the various well kept flower *gardens (garden). It seems like a great place to relax between classes or chat with friends. Or, you can play frisbee.

Exits include: [south] to LSU Street (200 block), [north] to Student Union Foyer

Beth_ANN and you are standing here.

You see frisbee here.

You take frisbee.

You throw frisbee.

Frisbee lands.

You exclaim, "Beth! Look!"

Beth_ANN catches the frisbee

You ask, "oh! well done! How did you do that?"

Beth_ANN says, "I did : catches the frisbee"

You say, "cool."

Beth_ANN throws the frisbee to you

You take frisbee.

You already have that!

Beth_ANN throws the frisbee to you

You already have that!

Markham catches the frisbee

Beth_ANN says, "see you did it"

Beth_ANN says, "that's cool"

You say, "yeah."

You ask, "I think I am holding the frisbee. How do I put it
down?"

You drop frisbee.

You say, "oh. I got it. I dropped it"

Student Union Front Lawn

You see various garden plots of flowers in full bloom. Some
are all in one color. (The purple orchids are beautiful!) Some
are mixtures of plants with colors in pleasant harmony.

You see a well worn wooden bench that looks extremely comfortable to sit on or even take a nap between classes.

Beth_ANN says, "that's cool I think"

You decide to take a break and sit on the bench.

Beth_ANN says, "do you know Ben would you like to @ join him
next"

You ask, "huh?"

Beth_ANN says, "Ben one of the people I know here invited us
to see his place"

You ask, "oh. let's go! Should I type @join ben?"

Beth_ANN says, "would you like to do that next"

Beth_ANN suddenly disappears.

You exclaim, "yes. Let's go!"

You reluctantly stand up from the bench.

Mr. Cruz's Flat (Dial M for Murder)

Welcome to the Flat.

Fenster, the caretaker, greets you.

You immediately sense that all is not right in this place.
What's that sound? Do you smell smoke?

"There ain't nothin to worry 'bout now," says the caretaker.

The Flat is lit like an old Fritz Lang movie. You realize that
you're only seeing black and white. There are no colours here.

Someone is whistling Beethoven's Ode to Joy. There's also a faint heartbeat coming from underneath the floorboards. The uneasy feeling passes.

Ben (L'Enfant Terrible..), Beth_ANN, and you are standing here. Jury (asleep) is sleeping. Please do not attempt to waken the sleeper as you will suffer the wrath of Fenster.

You see Fenster, trapdoor, Miki, A note to the ECIAD scholarship jury, your guide (listening), Resident_Alien, and Crush here.

Ben says, "hey you"

Beth_ANN says, "Hi Ben"

Miki [to Beth_ANN]: Hey... how's it going.

Ben hushes Miki.

Beth_ANN [to Miki]: ok

Ben says, "your talking to a robot, Beth..."

You say, "Hi! Great place"

Ben hushes Resident_Alien.

Beth_ANN says, "did you see the robots"

Ben says, "i turned em all off"

Crush sits down and starts scratching her shoulder.

Beth_ANN [to Markham]: I like Crush

You ask, "who is Crush?"

Ben says, "hello markham"

Ben says, "thats my dog"

Beth_ANN says, "it's a dog"

You say, "hi Ben, nice to meet you."

You exclaim, "Hi crush!"

You ask, "what kind of dog is Crush?"

Beth_ANN [to Ben]: so how's Canada

Ben [to Markham]: are you new here?

You say, "yes. Beth and I were exploring. I am very wet behind the ears."

You say, "good thing for Beth, or I'd be lost."

Ben cheers for Beth_ANN.

Crush sits down and starts scratching her shoulder.

Beth_ANN smiles thanks

Markham smiles

Crush sits down and starts scratching her shoulder.

Ben says, "well.. im here too to help anyone"

Ben says, "cept when im not here"

Beth_ANN [to Ben]: "that's good"

You say, "pardon my asking, but does Crush have fleas? She keeps scratching."

Ben says, "ill fix that"

Ben picks up Crush.

Markham laughs

Ben says, "she just wants attention"

You say, "sounds like a lot of humans I know."

Beth_ANN says, "yes it does"

You say, "(me included)"

Ben says, "me too"

Beth_ANN says, "a lot of people I talk to like to help"

Ben asks, "if they can, right?"

Beth_ANN says, "right"

You say, "well, at my level, anybody is helpful. :)"

Ben [to Beth_ANN]: how was spring break

Beth_ANN [to Markham]: I'm glad to be of help

Markham smiles

Beth_ANN [to Ben]: it was great

You exclaim, "thanks, Beth, you are very helpful!"

Ben tackles Miki to the ground.

You ask, "Ben, Who is L'Enfant Terrible?"

Ben says, "thats what my french tutor used to call me"

Markham laughs

Markham scratches her chin thoughtfully, pondering....

Ben . o O (terrible infant)

You say, "oh, oui, oui."

You ask, "Ben, where are you from?"

Ben says, "oh i thought you were a guy"

Ben hmms.

Markham smiles

Ben . o O (mark ham)

You ask, "it's funny how a name can lead us to different places, eh?"

Ben says, "markham, ontario"

You say, "when I logged onto an IRC as 'Bambi' the other day, it was a completely different experience."

You ask, "are you really from Markham, Ontario?"

Ben says, "no, Toronto"

You say, "ah Toronto. Nice place"

Ben says, "but i know people in markham"

You say, "I used to live in Seattle. I miss the Northwest"

Ben says, "kewl"

Ben asks, "where now?"

You say, "Oh. Indiana for the moment."

You say, "soon to be in Blacksburg, VA"

Beth_ANN says, "ben you don't"

Beth_ANN says, "here"

Beth_ANN says, "where"

Ben [to Beth_ANN]: what???

Beth_ANN says, "that's cool"

Beth_ANN says, "I like the panda"

Ben GOT LOST IN THE SPAM

Beth_ANN [to Ben]: never mind

You ask, "Ben, can you breath?"

Ben says, "very well...yes"

Beth_ANN [to Markham]: what did you mean by that?

You ask, "are you still in the Spam? Do you need any help?"

Ben laughs.

You say, "Ben said he got lost in the Spam. I thought he might be covered with it, and might not be able to breathe."

Markham sends the panda over to eat some of the spam.

Ben . o O (SPAM-verb-to overload with text)

Ben says, "wow you ARE new"

You ask, "yes, but it's much more fun to turn that useless overload of information into something else, eh?"

Ben hmms.

Markham . o O (not *that* new, but close enough)

Ben says, "oh"

You ask, "Beth, do you come here often?"

Beth_ANN says, "yes I do come here"

You ask, "Ben, what is 'personal white pages?'"

You say, "sorry. Didn't mean to be gender-ist."

Markham looks abashed.

Ben says, "address, phone and e mail book"

Ben says, "like a litl blak book"

Beth_ANN [to Ben]: do you give your number out on here

Ben [to Beth_ANN]: not usualy

Beth_ANN [to Ben]: just wondering

Ben says, "if people ask maybe"

Beth_ANN says, "that's cool"

You say, "Sigh.....I think I'm going to have to go soon. Procrastinating too much."

Ben says, "me too"

Beth_ANN says, "me too"

You ask, "I might be interviewing someone in your room tomorrow afternoon Beth, that ok?"

Beth_ANN [to Markham]: that's cool

You say, "Hey, Ben, if you ever feel like telling stories, or are bored and want to talk about your experiences in the net, just let me know....I'm doing some interviews for a project."

You say, "That's how I met Beth, sort of."

Ben says, "sure"

Ben smiles.

Ben says, "i gotta hit the darkroom soon"

Ben pokes at Beth_ANN.

You say, "yeah....I gotta go do some work too. See you two later.'

Ben says, "bye"

You exclaim, "Thanks for letting me hang out!"

You say, "Bye Beth. Bye Ben."

Ben says, "no prob panda markham"

Ben cheers you up with a *live* panda!

```
                              ,;;;;;;;,/;;;;
                 .,aa###########@a;;;;;/;;;,//;;;
          ..,,..,aa###############@a;//;;;,//;;;
       ,;;;;;;;;O#####OO##############OOO###a,/;;;;'
    .;;//,;;;O####OOO##########OOO###OOO####a'
   .;;/,;;/;OO##OO##########################OOO####.
   ;;;/,;;//OO#######OOO###############OOO###########.
   ';;//,;,OOO#########OO############OO#############.
  ;.  """OOO#####;;;;;;OO#####OO;;;;;;#####O####.
  .;;,       OOO###O;;'  ~';##OOOOO##;'  ~';;O#####OO###
  ;;;;      ,  OOO##O;;;;,.,;O#########O;,..,;;O####OO###,
  ';;'     ,;; OOO##OO;;;;OOO(??????)OOO;;;;OO###OO###%,
   '\    ;;; 'OOO####OOOO##\?????/##OOOO#######O####%O@a
    \,';'  'OOO####OOO#####;#####OOO###########%O##a,
    .,\      'OO####OO"#####;#####"OO##########%oO###O#;
  ,;;;; \   .::::OO##OOOaaa###aaaOOO#######',,OO##OOO##;,
  .;;''    \:::.OOaa'##OO#######OO###':;aOO.;;OO##OO;::.
  '       .::\.OO####O#::;;;;;;;;;;;;;:O#O@OO.:::::::://::
          .::::.O\########O#O:;;;;;:O#OO#O###@OO.;;;;;;;;;//:,
         .:/;;.OO#\##########OO#OO#OO########@OO.;;;;;;;;;;//:
         .://;;.OO###\##########O############@OO.;;;;;;;;;//:.
       .;,,,.OOOOO###########\#######@OOO.;;;//;;;;;;;;;;;//;.OO,
       //;;.oO################@\OOO.;;;;;;;;;;;;;;;;;;;;//;.oO#O,
       //;;;;O#############@OOO=;;;;//;;;;;;;;;;;;;;;;;;;;//;.oO##Oo
       //:;;O#########@OOOOO=;;;;;;;//;;;;;;;;;;;;;;;////;.oO###OO
  .n.n.n'n';O########@OOOOO=;;;;;;;;//;;;//////';oO########OO
  .%%%%%%%%%,;;########@=;;;;=;;;;//////////////'::::::::a######@
  /%%%%%%%%%.;;;;""""=::://:::::::::::::::\:::::::::://:.####@'
  /%%%%%%%%%//.;'   =::://:::::::::::::::::\:::::::::://:.###@
  /%%%%%%%%//'      =::://:::::::::;::::::::::\:::::::://:.##@'
   /%%%%%/          =::://:::;;::::::::::::::\:::::::
    %%%%%            ://::::::::::::::::::::\:::
```

Markham laughs

You exclaim, "wow! great big bear!!!!!!"

Ben says, "you get the hang of things soon enough"

You exclaim, "bye, all!"

Ben smiles.

Beth_ANN says, "who's got a real bea"

Ben asks, "bea?"

Beth_ANN says, "bear"

Beth_ANN says, "bye Harkham"

∗

Late night, March 23, 1997; just after my trip through the MOO: I don't seem to think about the issues of space and time much when I'm online. Time passes much more quickly than I am accustomed to. But, now that I think about it, I felt a definite sense of movement as Beth and I went exploring through DU. I could sense spatiality, perhaps because it was written into the scene around us. When we went "outside," I felt like I was outside . . . more than when I read a novel, more than when I'm watching a movie.

Cyberspace is definitely taking on dimension.

Maybe I feel an increased sense of "being there" because the context is interactive and I have agency. I moved through the space and my movements caused certain things to happen (caused certain descriptions to pop up on the screen). I walked down the street to the front of the student union, where I saw a pretzel stand, a bench, and a Frisbee lying on the ground. I wondered why someone had provided that description, out of all the things they could have mentioned. I wondered if I could pick up the Frisbee. Sure enough, when I typed "get Frisbee," a responding message appeared, "you pick up Frisbee."

All of a sudden, I felt as though I had really picked it up. And when I threw it, it disappeared. I felt as if my arm were going through that familiar throwing motion. And then I saw it land, because the computer told me "Frisbee lands."

"Look!" I shouted to Beth. Then I saw the message "Beth catches Frisbee," and—the spell was broken just as quickly as it began. The scene was out of sequence. Beth couldn't have caught the Frisbee, I thought to myself, because I just saw it land on the grass. Suddenly I wasn't in the scene anymore, but just observing it; and the action wasn't real at all. After that, it became a game to see how to make the text work in sequence. I picked up the Frisbee. Then Beth threw it to me. I tried to catch the one she threw at me, but the program said I already had it in my hands. I quickly tired of trying to make the computer simulate what I wanted to be real. Of course, it was real in the sense that it was actually happening, but not real in an embodied kind of way.

But then, moments later, I could visualize the ice cream I got from the pretzel stand. And when I sat on the bench, I actually thought to myself, "how nice it feels to rest a bit after all this adventuring." But then Beth got paged by her friend Ben, and she said "Let's Go!" So I got up ("reluctantly," the computer told me) and teleported over to Ben's room.

*

I realized my vocabulary was changing. When I revisited the journal entry above, I was surprised that I wrote "I shouted," as if I were really doing something that constituted shouting. Then I realized that I was doing something that constituted shouting, at that moment. And I felt like I was shouting when I did it. So my own way of talking about doing things in cyberspace was shifting toward a more embodied sense of self or presence in this place. I also noticed (first in this entry, then throughout my journals and field notes and in the text you are now reading, in fact) that my vocabulary slips from describing it as a place back to describing cyberspace as a simulation via a machine, depending on how I am experiencing what is happening.

I find myself thinking of my online character, and the people I've met and hung out with in these online places, at odd times of the day and night. When this first happened—one Friday night I was lying in bed wishing I had a computer at home so I could be out, so to speak, with my new friends—I worried about my own sanity, wondered if I wasn't a little too involved in this project. But now I realize I was experiencing a significant shift in my level of connection to online communication. I was beginning to perceive cyberspace not only as a place, but as a potential way of being. (*If I weren't so busy writing this book, I am certain I would be learning who I am and who I want to be online.*)

The continuum of *tool . . . place . . . way of being* does not begin to capture the nuances of how people understand their experiences online, but it provides a starting place for us to see how diversely people experience similar technologies. It also helps us understand why users and nonusers refer to the phenomenon with such variety, using terms like *information superhighway, electronic frontier, digital revolution*, or *cyberspace*. These labels reflect the numerous frames we are using as we try to make sense of communication technologies. Over time and continued use, these metaphors become templates we apply to our experiences of these technologies—or as Lakoff and Johnson write, they become "Metaphors we live by" (1981).

ONLINE EXPERIENCES ARE REAL . . . HOW COULD
EXPERIENCE BE OTHERWISE?

Annette: "How real are your experiences in the internet?"

Sherie: "How real are experiences off the internet?"

The second theme that guided and emerged from my interpretation of the online interviews addresses how the subjects perceive the reality of their experiences. I began my study with the question, "How do users make sense of the concept of reality?" About halfway through the study, though, I realized that although it *seemed* I was asking that question, I was actually asking—or at least trying to get at—a significantly different question, namely: "How do users make sense of virtuality, as compared to reality?" It might seem obvious to say, but the frames offered by these two questions make a lot of difference, and this is something I didn't notice as I forged into the new cultural context of cyberspace. Framing *real* as something different than *virtual* is my conceptual move, not theirs. Fortunately, my participants encouraged me to value and give voice to the concept of reality as they experience it themselves. I've had to learn not only about how they experience their lives both on and offline, but about how much I was limiting my understanding of them through my presumptions about the term *real*. I suppose, at some level, I am still stuck on what the term really means to them (or me), which might help explain why I focused on it throughout the project.

As the participants talked about their experiences both online and offline, I realized they were using the terms *real*, *RL* (real life), and *IRL* (in real life), as if these terms distinguished their "not real," or virtual online identities and lives from their real offline identities and lives. However, as I continued to read closely and interact with the transcripts, I realized this was not the case. The participants were not using these terms the same way I was (or as I was wanting them to). You will see what I mean when I present their texts in chapters 4 and 5. I realized that, for almost all of these users, *real* does not so much indicate a state of authenticity or genuineness as it indicates both "that which is experienced" and demarcates "those experiences that occur offline." When they do use the term *real* as a marker of authenticity, they seem to be trying to make sense of other people online. In these cases, real means that which is known (as in "I know myself, therefore I am real," or "I have more information about Other, therefore Other is more real").

As I analyzed what they said, I began to understand that *real* and its opposite, *not real*, are becoming less valid frames, not because we are not having real experiences, but because online our experiences cannot be classified into binary states. Even the term *virtual,* if defined as *nearly real,* doesn't encapsulate online experience. For these participants, every experience is as real as another. This makes sense intuitively. For most of us, every experience is an experience, to the extent that it is lived. If it makes sense to us and feels like it is happening, how could it not be real?

What is real? Does it really matter?

As I began this study, I was influenced by recent works that characterized our late-twentieth-century lives and social structures as *hyperreal,* or moving closer to the virtual (e.g., Baudrillard, 1988; Benedikt, 1991; Rheingold, 1991, 1993).

When it comes to making sense of what is meant by the terms *hyperreal* and/or *virtual,* we necessarily depart from a previously determined and understood starting place, which in this case is the word *real.* In other words, we mostly talk about how things are hyperreal or virtual *in comparison to* other things that are real. While this might be a useful move, it presupposes, and therefore does not contest, our knowledge of what is real.

What does the term *real* do for us when we think about online experiences? Perhaps it makes more sense to begin by talking about what the term means offline, in a colloquial sense. In Webster's *Third New International Dictionary,* for example, real includes:

> real, actual, of or relating to things, 1 a : of or relating to things themselves : existing, . . . 2 a : that is precisely what its name implies : not merely so called : truly possessing the essence of what it is called: as (1) : AUTHENTIC, GENUINE (2) : not merely apparent : ACTUAL, TRUE (3) : not artificial or counterfeit : NATURAL (4) : not illusory : INDUBITABLE, UNQUESTIONABLE (5) : free from affectation or pretense b : actually existing, occurring, or present in fact : corresponding to actuality c (1) having an objective independent existence . . . [and so on]. (1993, p. 1890)

Fully sixty-two lines in this dictionary are devoted to defining this elusive word, and at least three times the term *real* is used to define the word *real.* Needless to say, *real* is a complex term that chases itself in search of a definition.

The term begs the question in more ways than one. Not only does it use itself as a premise for describing itself, it doesn't ever land anywhere except back where we began. Real is real. Or sometimes, as Beth would say, things are *really* real—as opposed to *just* real, I suppose.

The process of coming to know what something is also is a process of trying to know what it is *not*—what is "not real." As I mentioned above, most authors presuppose a particular understanding of the term real (similar to the definitions above), and often contrast real—when talking about computer technologies—to the term *virtual*. According to Richard MacKinnon (1998), for instance,

> The primary difference then between the real and the virtually real
> is the interposition of some mediating and transforming agent or
> interface between the senses and the shared perception" (p. 4).

MacKinnon seems to define real as that which is experienced by the senses and virtually real as that experience which encounters something between its existence and our senses. Presumably he means a computer, but he could also mean spectacles, or a mirror. More importantly, there is a baseline reality out there, and something is happening to it.

In another essay, Keeps (1994) wonders about the epistemological status of the real, asking,

> If the virtual can offer the complete range of sensory experiences
> available . . . and even optimize those experiences such that the real
> comes to seem a pale shadow of the virtual, how will one still
> differentiate between the sign and the referent?" (p. 2).

Here, real is equated with "sensory experience," and the virtual is that which reproduces or optimizes sensory experience. The idea that we will no longer be able to differentiate between the two implies that we once could, and that these two states (virtual and real) were once apparent and distinct.

Howard Rheingold (1991) writes that computers

> are only beginning to approach the point where people might
> confuse simulations with reality. Computation and display
> technology are converging on hyperreal simulation capability.
> [Through this capability, we] will be able to put on a headset, or
> walk into a media room, and surround ourselves in a responsive
> simulation of startling verisimilitude. . . . That point of

convergence is important enough to contemplate in advance of its arrival. The day computer simulations become so realistic that people cannot distinguish them from not simulated reality we are in for major changes. (p. 388)

Rheingold, who seems to understand that we will need to redefine our basic conceptualizations of reality, still clings tenaciously to an objective, grounded sense of reality. Real describes a specific set of experiences; namely, those that are lived through the body, without the intervention of computer technology. Simulating these embodied experiences comprises virtual reality, and these simulations are hyperreal. As such, these experiences may be realistic, a state that is like real, but not really real.

(The bottom line is that I don't get much help from these authors, who seem to talk about issues of reality but presuppose the term even as they try to reconceptualize it; the loop around the word grows tighter, even as it does not hold anything steady.)

Baudrillard's various discussions of hyperreality serve as a starting point for many writers who conceptualize cyberspace. Reading his and others' works, I struggled with the concept of the hyperreal, the idea that, in the postmodern world, the image becomes the reality so that the real is evermore lost in the infinite regression of mirrors, forever reflecting only the reflection from other mirrors. This image is compelling. It might seem that in technologically-mediated contexts, everything that exists is all and nothing but a reproduction of something else, a collapse of sign and referent. And if everything is a representation of something else, everything, yet nothing, is real.

(We can take this image further, bring it offline, if you will. Baudrillard argues that when the image and the real become less distinguishable from one another, our world becomes hyperreal. For me, the perfect world of Disney exemplifies hyperreality. The newly established township of Celebration City, owned and incorporated by Disney, seems to be hyperreality gone mad. People actually live in the community envisioned by Walt himself and created by the Disney Corporation. Of course, the houses all look similar, and the people in them must abide by certain codes of community living, dictated by the town leadership. And, as you might guess, the law, the city government, the shops, and the maintenance services are owned and controlled by Disney. And the rules for living in a town that represents "The Happiest Place On Earth" are fairly comprehensive.)

As compelling as the image of the hyperreal is, as much as Baudrillard and other postmodern theorists might long to let this concept explain our lives at the end of the twentieth century, it leaves me feeling empty and dissatisfied as a researcher. How do we begin to talk about what is real when we are all focusing on what is not real? More importantly, though, the never-ending recursivity of the hyperreal does not adequately speak to or begin to explain the experiences of humans dwelling in cyber/cyborg spaces.

Real as a Double Negative

At some point in my research and thinking, I began to realize the slippage—the dilemma of where I was going, what I was seeking, and what I was (and was not) finding. I wanted to understand what people really thought of their online (or virtual) experiences, but by asking them about their virtual experiences, and asking them to compare their online experiences with their offline experiences, I was ultimately asking them to make a distinction between real and virtual experiences.

As I said above, I commenced this study by presuming the existence of the hyperreal. My reasoning went something like this: We live in an increasingly hyperreal world of images without referents. Virtual realities such as the Internet encourage people to see the virtual as real and vice versa, or to accept the virtual as an adequate way to experience various places and others. (Online, I can seem to walk through a rainforest without actually going there—or perhaps needing it to be there at all. I can walk around the pyramids in cyberspace, and as long as the program that created the representation is preserved, I might not be so concerned that pollution is eating away these wonders of the world. I can share meaningful discussions with people who care about me online, so I might not feel compelled to acknowledge or get along with the people who live next door. The examples go on and on.) As I reasoned, this ungrounded foundation of living does not bode well for the preservation of the planet because we are progressively distancing ourselves from it, disappearing into the idealized, usually more interesting, pleasant, or less stressful hyperreal world of virtual realities such as cyberspace. Hence, I wanted to see just how people are experiencing the (hyper)reality of cyberspace.

I've reached a point in the project where I am reasoning differently. I realize now that when many writers (myself included) describe cyberspace, they use the terms *reality* and *virtuality* in traditional ways. We presuppose a binary composition and opposition between real and virtual. This helps us integrate various communication technologies into current vocabularies and ways of thinking. We use real (and whatever we term its opposite; virtual being the trendy choice at the moment) to juxtapose nature versus technology, referent versus sign, science versus fraud, genuine versus reproduction, authentic versus fake, human versus machine, and so forth. While I might know theoretically that these distinctions are faulty, I (and I suspect many of us) still split my understanding of the world into these categories.

How useful are these distinctions for describing one's experiences online? The users I talked with indicate that the term *real*, as traditionally defined, is not very useful to them at all. Whether online or offline, everything that is experienced is real, and everything that is not experienced is not experienced. Real becomes a double negative; simply put, when experiences are experienced, they cannot be "not real." In a broader sense, terms such as *real, hyperreal, not real,* or *virtual* are no longer valid or meaningful as definitions of our experiences because our experiences are not easily separated into these binary oppositions.

CONTROL OF THE TEXT EQUALS CONTROL OF SELF, OTHER, AND SOCIAL STRUCTURE

Consider this version of Annette Markham: I am sitting here by myself in front of the screen, with almost-empty containers of Chinese take-out, several cups of coffee at varying stages of decay, and a package of M&Ms littering the surface of my desk. If you were looking out into my office from the other side of the screen, you would see various books on the shelves behind my head: Critical organization studies, feminist theories, virtual reality, ethnography, a smattering of science fiction, a collection of management-communication handbooks. You might also see, if you could peer around the corner—photographs of me in the mountains, me sailing, my sisters, places I've visited or lived, my friends—and a poster of Audrey Hepburn. If you saw me, you would notice I'm not in such great shape—hair unkempt; chapped, water-deprived lips; a face that hasn't seen much sunlight. I haven't been to the gym in ages, and I'm slouched in my chair, my posture perfect for a backache later. My eyes are glazed from a combination of computer screen glare, too much caffeine, and not enough sleep.

Or this version:

```
<pejay> heya

<pejay> do i know you?

<Bambi> i don't think so, do i know you?

<pejay> hmmmm, where ya from?

<Bambi> Seattle, but I live in indiana now
```

<pejay> nope, I don't think I know ya, but I'd like to get to know you

<Bambi> where are you from?

<pejay> Texas, where the big boys live, yup

<Bambi> hmmm...well, I wouldn't know much about that. Do you come here often?

<pejay> a lot. I'm a founder. Do u?

<Bambi> no, never been here before. But I've seen some pretty great conversations so far. That story you told about the girl who sent you those naked sex pics was really funny.

<pejay> Thanks. Age?

<Bambi> ancient. 24

<Bambi> age?

<pejay> man was it a straaannnnggeeee night! Sorta fun, tho! <evil grin>

<pejay> im 23

<pejay> what do you do? do you have a pic?

<pejay> ...not necesarily a nude one though...unless...

<pejay> hehehe

<Bambi> lol

<Bambi> hmmm, I'm sorta new at this, no pic.

<pejay> ohhhh, well, too bad.

<pejay> well, wlecome anyway!

<Bambi> thanks

<pejay> need any help? I'd be more than happy to help out!

<Bambi> do? oh, I'm a stripper paying my way through school. The story about the girl sending you pictures cracked me up. What do you do?

<pejay> Hmmm, glad to meet you, very glad indeed. I'm a student, too, tho I don't strip...for a living

<Bambi> hmmm.....I may need help, after all. Right now I'm just looking around, going to various channels, learning how to talk, basically

<Bambi> what are you studying?

<pejay> criminal justice

<Bambi> what you wanna be when you grow up?

<pejay> a police officer

<pejay> u?

<Bambi> big bad cop with billy club, eh?

<pejay> yup...and you should see it, bambi!!!

<Bambi> Ha! got a pic? huh? huh?

<pejay> ohhhhh, well....

<Bambi> I can see you now, swinging your billy club, looking for crime to stop :-)

<Bambi> Actually, I think some of the coolest cops live in Seattle.

<pejay> well im cool too

<Bambi> I used to try to get them to do things they weren't supposed to while on duty.

<pejay> so what do ya look like?

<Bambi> I'm sure you are cool!

```
<pejay> lol
```

```
<Bambi> takes her hands off the keyboard and leans back in her
chair to stretch her long, sometimes dancer's legs, her back
arched like a cat. She runs her hands through her black hair,
ruffling her long curls and scratches her head, idly. Her
almost black Spanish eyes gaze out through narrow slits,
watching the screen for some action.
```

```
<pejay> w00 w00
```

```
<pejay> wow, I'd really like to get to know you better
<grins and winks>
```

```
<Bambi> and you??
```

```
<pejay> 5'11'' brown hair green eyes tight wrangler jeans and
spurs…
```

```
<Bambi> I once tried to get two cops to have champagne with me
in a limo my friends and I rented.
```

```
<pejay> and?
```

```
<Bambi> they declined, but gave me a complimentary set of
handcuffs
```

```
<pejay> no way, really?
```

```
<Bambi> I'm not kidding!
```

```
<pejay> w00w00!
```

```
<pejay> lol
```

When you are what you say, and you can say anything, the possibilities are as endless as your imagination. In an online context, if I control the text, I have control over the presentation of self, provided we have never had face-to-face contact. I have the capacity to control what you see and know of me.

Of course, this is possible only to a certain extent. It would be more accurate to say I have a choice about what to present deliberately. After all, I might present a version of my self, but whether that self is interpreted by you to be the same (as the) self I presented is unclear, and unlikely. For general purposes, however, my conviction is adequate; I *believe* that I control what others see, read, and therefore know about me, and the channels available to them to think otherwise are limited or nonexistent.

The capacity for control through online communication is undeniably tantalizing. Everyone I interviewed expressed this, and I experienced it myself. Control is an issue that is woven into all the participants' discussions about why and how they engage online technologies. Furthermore, control is perceived as a benefit of the technology or a power the self possesses, not a threat from outside the self or some power possessed by the Other. Perhaps physical isolation or separation from the context enables a perception of limitless agency.

For many users, examining and editing their words before they "utter" them gives them the feeling that they have control over their presentation of self as well as control over the other's perceptions of the self. Jennifer, one of the participants, says she can control the tenor and movement of a conversation by attending carefully to what the other person is saying and how they seem to be saying it, and then carefully crafting her own responses. In addition, electronic text-based media lend themselves to manipulation of conversational content and style through various conventions—or lack thereof—if i do not capitalize first person pronouns, for instance, or refer to "ourself" as "We." Other conventions, such as adding <grin> or "LOL" or graphic accents—such as smiley faces :) —to an utterance allow the user to exhibit certain nonverbal behaviors. Of course, because the user chooses the type of nonverbal expression he or she wishes the other to see, a powerful measure of control is granted to the sender of the message.

A crucial feature of online communication media for some is that users can limit the extent to which others can view or touch them, physically and, presumably, psychologically. Shutting off the computer, altering one's description of oneself, and not describing in text or graphics accents what could easily be seen on one's face are just three ways that distance can be achieved. Hence, control can be directed inward (that is, one can control what is presented to others, or be "in control"), or control can extend outward from the self to put restraints on the Other.

All the participants see control as a considerable benefit of, if not the very reason for, being online. Ironically, each of them talks about the benefits of controlling the self and others, but none of them seem worried that, online, others might be exerting similar control over them. As you will see in our conversations, their perceptions and knowledge of their experiences are centered in the self. It doesn't seem to occur to the participants, as they reflect on their online experiences, that the Other might play an important role in the construction of their own subjectivity.

Most people I met online perceive self to be a performance controlled by the sender of the message. This perception is no doubt strengthened by the fact that, for many users, viewing and revising their utterances and choosing facial expressions or degree of spontaneous responses—chuckle, gasp, roll on the floor laughing (ROFL)—is a newly discovered and seemingly limitless ability. These users seem to believe that the text transmits meaning to the other person, and the meaning derived from the interaction is determined by the correct interpretation of the message. Thus, if a person can edit and refine his or her description of self to others, and clarify misunderstandings with more precise messages, shared understanding should be possible. Of course, it's never that easy because communication is not a simple linear process of sending and receiving carefully constructed messages; it is an ever-evolving web of relationships. (*The term* **they** *might be more accurately expressed as* **we** *in this case, because I fell into this one-way pattern of thinking as well. I did not question my ability to control others' perceptions of me, as long as I could find the right way to express myself. I did not consider the other person's role in the construction of my persona. In fact, it never even occurred to me to wonder what they thought of me, or how they pictured me visually when I was using my real name, because at those points I was just being "myself." How and why would anyone doubt that? Ha. Pretty naive, if you ask me.*)

✳

All of the people I talked with engage online technologies in meaningful and distinctive ways. Yet even as they talked about their unique experiences (and talked uniquely about them), the three themes I discovered in their conversations created a way for me to make sense of their stories. Like me, they seemed to experience the Internet along a continuum from *tool* to *place* to a *way of being*. Moreover, their descriptions bespoke an expanded definition of reality, and they each expressed satisfaction with an increased capacity for control in their online environments.

Of course, what you see in my interpretation is largely the product of my deciding that, in order to say something meaningful, I had to make choices that necessarily limited the full expression of their voices. Perhaps my uneasiness about this stems from my own fears of having others speak for me, trapping me in definitions and categories without my consent. I had to remind myself constantly that interpreting and editing was not just my right, but my responsibility as a researcher. What you see when you read my interpretation in the next two chapters, then, is what I think these people mean by what they say.

I feel limited by the fact that I have not asked their opinions about what I've decided they think. I consider this an ethical dilemma that was probably intensified by the online structure of our dialogue. I could not see their faces or hear the meaningful sounds that accompany words in other settings. I could not judge their words on anything but their words, and because of this I feel frustrated and cut off from them somehow.

Yet this points to an important characteristic of doing research online. I have only the text, and I consider this a limitation. Yet they, too, have only the text—to create identities, to perceive and know others, and to carry on their lives. Some of the participants are more comfortable with this feature than others; all of them seem more comfortable than I am.

I talked with dozens of users whose words helped me make sense of this emerging and evolving cultural form. I joined several online discussion groups and visited many of the prominent communities online. I created an online persona at Diversity University, and I actually feel like a member of one online community. As I became more connected to the online world, the study changed considerably. That I became increasingly connected to my experiences online is not surprising, of course; but the extent to which my conversations and my experiences with others changed how I understood and interpreted the experiences of being online was something I hadn't anticipated.

In other words, not only do the results of the ethnography merge with my experiences of communication technology, the very objects of analysis for the ethnography are derived from my engagement with them. I helped create—through my dialogues with others in various online contexts—the context I am writing about. As I now endeavor to complete this inquiry through the writing process, I am creating a text that talks about creating worlds through texts. And in creating that text, I am continuing the process of structuring this social world in specific (*that is, Annette-centered*) ways.

What I produce in writing, then, is my shifting understandings of my experiences of the participants and these new contexts, inasmuch as these can be written (*not to mention understood by the reader, which is another question altogether*). As John Van Maanen reminds us, "social reality is presented, not known. Culture . . . is created, as is the reader's view of it, by the active construction of a text" (1988, p. 7). The text I present to you interacts with the participants' texts and the other texts you read about cyberspace, thus providing a working frame for online technologies that is actively constituted, one that will continue to grow and change as we continue the dialogue.

Chapter 4

Stories of Tools and Places

January 5, 1998: I am revising the appearance of the conversations I had with the participants. I originally intended to provide an analytical interpretation of the interviews in a traditional format—I presented large excerpts of the participants' words, but wrote my thoughts as a researcher interpreting texts after the fact. The result was a lot of me and not much of them. Art, the coeditor of this ethnography series, told me that I could have more narrative license. He suggested I rewrite the interpretations so the readers would be more involved in the story. He told me to be true to the experience but also to show the experience, not just talk about it from a removed position. So now I'm moving statements around and presenting these conversations with a cleaner linearity, which didn't exist before.

This version is richer and more nuanced than earlier versions. The dialogue format allows you to be a part of the interviews and to know more about the participants (and me) as you watch the conversations evolve.

For each of the participants, you will read a combination of interview excerpts and my analysis of the interviews. To present the conversations as dialogues, I sometimes made minor changes in the transcripts: First, I frequently altered the font and form of our dialogues so conversation appears as it would in a novel. At other times, I leave the font and form unaltered so the conversation appears as it does online—like the dialogue in a play. I leave some descriptions in their original font and form to maintain some of the place-ness of the interviews and to remind you where and how they occurred. Also, because I interviewed certain people using different interface clients or software programs, you'll notice some variation in the appearance of the dialogue.

Second, I retained each participant's exact phrasing and words, regardless of the font or form alterations with which they are presented here, unless the spelling or grammar was so atrocious that a reader could not possibly decipher a word or phrase. I also significantly condensed and sometimes rearranged the conversations.

To present a narrative that the reader could step easily into, I was compelled to smooth out some of the awkwardness present in most online conversations. I don't intend to illustrate that we accomplished a great deal in a short amount of time and in smooth writing turns, but I also could not present the interviews in their entirety.

Third, I added my embodied presence to the interviews so you could follow my thoughts between questions and my immediate interpretation of what was happening. Some of these additions I've gleaned from my research journals. In other places and paragraphs, I've tried to go back to those moments to recall what I was feeling and thinking. I did this to bring my lived experience to the interviews rather than to present the conversations as if they occurred merely in the text.

(As I rewrite my conversations with these participants, I realize I am rewriting my past as if it is the present, which is somewhat disconcerting at the moment. We do this all the time, of course, whenever we tell stories; I just never experienced it so viscerally before. Maybe I feel more responsible for my words because they will be printed and distributed. I feel as if the voice that appears in these printed conversations is not the same as the voice of the person who did the study. Of course, the thoughts in this version that I claim to be mine are mine—but they are the thoughts of an Annette Markham located in a different time and space than the Annette who did the study.

When I was having these conversations and writing about them, I spent almost all my waking hours in my sterile and windowless office staring at a computer monitor. This was my window to a world of relationships and visions and emotions I had never experienced before. To accomplish the study, I immersed myself in this online world. Now, a year later, I'm not emotionally or physically as close to the conversations as I was when I first wrote about them.

My new office has a tall, paned window that frames the western sky. I'm looking at gray clouds today. Yesterday I gazed at a bright blue winter sky and saw day turn to night in my peripheral vision as I looked at the computer. I shut my eyes, trying to remember what it felt like to be in an office without a window. I pull the blinds down to attempt to re-create the moments in time and space when and where I had these conversations, but the changing sky seeps around the corners of the shade, reminding me that I'm not then and there anymore.

*Perhaps I'm struggling with the issue of presentation because I was trained early in my education to think about the **process** of research as distinct from the **product**. Now, with each new version of this ethnography, I am experiencing—with all my senses—the extent to which each rendering represents me and the participants differently. And, as the product continues to shift, my lived comprehension of research reporting shifts also.)*

MATTHEW
I'M JUST ME, REALLY OR VIRTUALLY

I fell behind several slow cars pulling into the parking lot, unhappily realizing I would be late for the interview. I nervously scanned the next row over, hoping for a lucky break. How could I be so out of touch that I didn't remember the concert was tonight? Damn, I hope Matthew waits for me. I finally found a spot, grabbed my bookbag, and ran across the street to the building.

After writing several messages back and forth for two weeks, Matthew and I had found a mutual gap in our busy schedules. Starting ten minutes ago. When I reached the fourth floor, I was gasping for air. Fumbling for the right key, I opened the office door, threw my briefcase on an extra chair, and practically dove for the computer.

"C'mon, c'mon," I muttered impatiently as the MOO interface program slowly opened. As soon as the right screen appeared, I quickly typed my user name and password.

```
***connected***
```

```
Hut X looks a lot like RedWriter's room on Lambda, bokhara
rug, plants, lots of light from a big window. It's on a
nonspecific studio lot just north of Burbank, and outside
studio lackeys scuttle back and forth on desperate errands.
The room has leather chairs, green plants, not much else. Only
imaginary work gets done here. Davy and Ellen are cuddling on
the couch. Beth_ANN is here. Obsidian_Guest is here.
```

```
Beth_ANN says "that's cool that your from the west. I'm origi-
nally from Wisconsin, Whitewater but now in arizona I'm 20 and
a college student."
```

```
Obsidian_Guest says "Now Whitewater, that's a nice town."
```

```
Beth_ANN exclaims "yes it is I would have liked to go to UW-
Whitewater but I still may I love it there. Hi Annette!"
```

I sighed in relief. I should have known Beth would be in her room—she was online practically half her waking hours. It was only coincidence that she had not been present at any of the other interviews. I presumed she was talking with Matthew, but I couldn't tell, because the other person was only identified as Obsidian_Guest. It made sense, though; Matthew would have logged in as a guest because he's not a member of this community, and guests were always assigned gemstone names randomly. I quickly began typing.

```
Markham asks, "Hey, Beth. How are you?"

Obsidian_Guest says, "Hi Annette! Beth and I were just talking
about where we were from."

Markham asks, "Hi Obsidian, are you Matthew?"

Beth_ANN exclaims, "I'm fine!"

Obsidian_Guest says, "Yeah, it's me, at least the virtual me."

Markham says, "Sorry I'm late!!!! got stuck in concert traf-
fic."

Obsidian_Guest says, "no problem. I found the room okay, and
found Beth here. We've been chatting."

Markham asks, "Good! Sorry to do this, but can you wait
another second while I get set up here?"
```

Not waiting for an answer, I quickly reshuffled my interview questions and pinned them back up on the clipboard hanging from the left side of my computer monitor. I glanced back at the screen. They were still chatting. Beth_ANN, my savior again. Not only did she make this my default home in the MOO, but she was now entertaining my study participants so I could waltz into interviews at any time. I was very lucky to meet her, I thought, and grinned. She was still plying Matthew with questions, so I took an extra moment to shrug off my coat before I began typing again.

```
Markham smiles and wipes sweat from her brow.
```

Beth asked, "What happened?"
"Oh, I just ran up four flights of stairs, so now I'm sweating," I said.
"ok that's cool. Are you two going to interview now?" she asked.
"Yeah," I replied. I didn't know whether to ask Beth to leave or not. After all, this was her home. But if she stayed, I couldn't interview Matthew. His anonymity would be compromised, and he probably wouldn't be as candid.

Beth solved the problem for me. "ok, I'll talk to you guys later then."

I quickly typed, "Oh! Well, maybe I'll talk with you later, Beth! Sorry to push you out like this."

Beth added, "have fun and Matthew have good answers to Annette's questions!"

"Okay, let me give you some official information before we begin," I said.

Matthew said, "bye Beth!"

```
Obsidian_Guest salutes and says "Yes'm."

Markham laughs.

Beth_ANN suddenly disappears.
```

"Okay, Annette," Matthew said, "ask away. Let's start with the tough questions. Let's see, I should give you RL answers since this is RL research."

"Hey Matthew, feel free to give whatever types of answers you like!" I said, and added, "I can't start typing yet anyway, on account of I'm laughing at the fact that I got saluted."

Matthew answered, "Hate to break your heart, but I was saluting Beth_ANN for commanding me to answer you."

```
Markham sighs in very apparent disappointment, which she is
trying to hide.

Obsidian_Guest doesn't answer the sign because he just spilled
popcorncrumbs into his keyboard :-(

Markham laughs—I mean looks concerned...bummer about that

Obsidian_Guest laughs
```

"So don't get concerned if you see me going away for awhile—you know I went to make more popcorn ;-) "

"Okay. And just to let you know, I have a tendency to ask questions too quickly," I said, trying to get serious. "If you want me to be quiet because you are thinking, give me ellipses at the end of your message . . ."

I typed another message, "so I will know you want to say more. . . . and I won't be tempted to break in with a barrage of questions."

Matthew replied, "Probably a good idea with the ellipses."

"Well," I said, "they help to slow me down. If I see them, I'll watch the clock and give you two minutes of silence before I interrupt you."

"Wow, it sounds like you really have that planned out!" Matthew exclaimed.

I suppose it did seem strange that I would watch seconds ticking by in a conversation, but online interaction was so difficult to facilitate or control. This wasn't my first interview, and I'd learned the hard way how to interview in this strange context. Every time I assumed I had waited long enough for someone to type a reply, I ended up interrupting a thought or question. To prevent myself from sending a message too soon, I pretended I had to answer my own question; but I talk to myself pretty quickly, whereas the actual response was composed with the hands and sent to me through several electronic networks. So I had begun to use the clock to compensate for the nonverbal signals that would otherwise let me know the other person in the conversation was thinking or talking or finished with his or her conversational turn.

I replied, "Yeah, well you'll be glad. You might be the first interviewee who gets to finish a sentence before I ask the next question."

```
Obsidian_Guest laughs, but can't respond at the moment be-
cause he's busy opening a bag of rice cakes.
```

"Ha! Okay. So how much time per day do you spend online?"

Matthew said, "Really, what happened? Did you get any answers at all?"

I laughed out loud. "See what I mean?!" I had asked my first question too quickly, probably at the same time Matthew was writing his response to my previous statement.

Matthew politely ignored my outburst, and simply dealt with the next question in line, saying, "Please define online."

I said, "I mean connected to a network. You might call it cyberspace, the internet, the web, etc."

"Complicated answer..." he began. "I'm probably logged on about 50 hours a week and perhaps 75% of that time I'm connected to Netscape, e-mail, etc. ... Now, some of that time I'm writing documents or code locally or I'm searching for something, but when new mail pops up I answer it. I also test programs online."

"Do you consider yourself 'connected' much of the time?" I asked.

```
You sense that Beth_ANN is looking for you in the Student
Union.
```

```
She pages, "Is the interview going ok?"
```

Wow, I thought. Talk about interruptions. I definitely deserve this for interrupting others all the time. I quickly typed a message to her.

```
Page Beth_ANN with "yeah! thanks for asking. And thank you so
much for letting me use your room.....I hope I didn't put you
out!"
```

Meanwhile, Matthew replied, "Usually. If I'm at home, programming locally, I will still log on once every half hour or so to see what's happening."

I asked, "In your opinion, is 50 hours a lot of time?"

```
Your message has been sent.
```

"I'd say so," Matthew replied, "I mean you hear stories about these people, especially kids, who are logged on almost all their waking hours, but I think that they are far out on the extreme end. . . . far beyond a mere 'lot of time.'"

"Yeah," I agreed, 50 hours was a lot of time. "Would you spend more time online if you could?"

```
You sense that Beth_ANN is looking for you in the Student
Union.
```

```
She pages, "sure! your welcome anytime you need it it's cool
I like to see things going on in there."
```

Matthew replied, "Yes, but real life interferes."

Wow, this could get complicated if Beth keeps paging me, I thought. I was having trouble concentrating, so I didn't respond to her page and hoped she got the message that I was busy.

I asked Matthew, "What do you do mostly when you're online? Where do you go?"

He replied, "Mostly, I'm doing one of two things. Firstly, if I'm doing research much of what I need is there, so I fire off a web search. I also build Web tools, so I use it for testing things a lot." A moment later, he said, "A lot of tools to play with are there, too. Also, I use it for news and information, the way I used to use the radio. (I'm an unrepentent real-lifer). For instance, if I'm going to go run (or bike or something else outside) I check the weather on the web when in years past I would turn on the radio. Ditto for news. And I'm a newsgroup reader, of course. And lots of email. Finally enough nontechie people are getting email to make it a useful communications medium."

I was intrigued by Matthew's use of the term *real life*. I scrolled back to scan the interview log, and then asked, "What's an unrepentant real-lifer?" In a very short span of interview time (relatively speaking), Matthew had contrasted RL interview responses from other types of questions and responses—real life as something he wasn't repentant about, and real life as something that interferes with being online.

Matthew's answer came after a long pause. "Unrepentant real-lifer. If you read something like Sherry Turkle's book 'Life on the Screen' you'll see the argument that a lot of people are really different people online from what they are in RL, and that this is an important part of the totality of their being."

"On the other hand," he continued after a few moments, "I'm just me, really or virtually."

Hmmm . . . It was difficult to decide where to go next in the interview, which of his statements to follow up on. "So how would you describe yourself?" I asked, and as an afterthought, clarified, "I mean, who is the 'me' you're talking about?"

"Kind of androgeneous. Plenty of women for friends. But I was never good at dating or any of the romantic/sexual stuff. . . . Also somewhat intellectual. And a fitness nut."

```
Obsidian_Guest does pushups.

Markham stares.

Obsidian_Guest leaps up, does ten jumping jacks, and sits back
down.

Markham wonders if she should be doing something...
```

"You should be asking questions, Annette. (the interviewee becomes the interviewer) . . ." Matthew said.

```
Markham sighs and refocuses.
```

"Okay, how would you compare your sense of self as a person online with your sense of self offline?" I asked.

```
Obsidian_Guest has a delayed blushing reaction to the androgeny
comment.
```

Matthew said, "More confident online, because I'm a better editor than writer/speaker. I do well when I can backspace." I laughed aloud at this statement, because I happened to be backspacing as the message appeared. I knew exactly what he meant—I imagine I could find that backspace button on the keyboard in an earthquake, on my deathbed, or with amnesia.

I replied, "I know what you mean. I love that. What a great (and accurate?) thing to focus on when describing the computer-mediated self. Ha! the ability to correct everything you say and therefore are."

```
Obsidian_Guest smiles confidently.
```

Then he added, "But I'm the same me in both places. I guess I've been me too long to be anybody else without a lot more practice than I have time for." He paused a moment (or perhaps he was simply editing his next comment), then went on, "Now 'virtually'—there's a word that's undergoing a metamorphosis of meaning, much like 'gay' did a couple decades ago."

I asked, "How so?"

"Virtually used to mean 'nearly,' but now it means something so very different. If I were to say I'm really a man but virtually a woman, this used to mean that maybe I was getting a sex change. Now it would just mean I had a female online persona."

```
Obsidian_Guest smiles at this somewhat pathological example.

Markham chuckles.
```

"Okay Matthew, tell me about your most memorable experience online."

```
Obsidian_Guest enters state of deep thought.

Obsidian_Guest goes to raid the nearby refrigerator while
composing reply in head.
```

"Now what were you saying? Oh, most memorable experience?"

✳

Matthew and I talked for about an hour and a half, which seemed a short amount of time compared with previous interviews of three, four, and five hours. I was surprised when we had to end the interview; it seemed I had just gotten started. As you might notice, I was distracted by many things during this interview—being late, Beth's curiosity, and Matthew's textual/physical antics. Throughout the interview, Matthew constantly enacted his physicality through the text. I had fun playing along.

When I selected excerpts from this conversation for an earlier draft of this manuscript, I completely ignored—and therefore did not include—Matthew's performances of his embodied status. His words clearly indicated he conceptualized online communication as a convenient and necessary set of tools that helped him do research and keep in touch with family and friends.

When I revisited the original transcripts, however, I was immediately struck by the physicality of this conversation—or more precisely, the physicality of Matthew's presence. Indeed, I was shocked to realize I had ignored and omitted the nonverbal, embodied elements of Matthew's conversational style, and instead had focused on his *explanations* of his experiences on and offline. Ironically, as I was trying to decipher his understanding of real life, I was ignoring his *expressions* of real life in the text of our conversation.

Now, Matthew's constant references to and performance of his embodied status emphasize for me his focus on his real life, offline. In a way, he both upholds and demolishes the distinction between existence online and existence offline. (*It took me months to make sense of his use of the term **real life**, particularly in the context of his very embodied presence online. When I finally stopped focusing on my original research question, I began to perceive Matthew's experiences as he portrayed—and perhaps lived—them, rather than as I theorized and abstracted them.*)

During our conversations, Matthew made a strong distinction between online life and real life (RL), by frequently mentioning real life as something different than our conversational context. Yet, Matthew enacted real life with a vengeance in our conversation. Now, I can see what he meant when he said "I'm the same me, really or virtually." I believe he meant this: I am an embodied being who likes to talk with others. Whether I use my body, my voice, my hands, I'm the same. Whether we talk face-to-face, on the phone, in a MOO, or via email, I'm the same. To illustrate this point, Matthew brings his eating, exercising, blushing, laughing self online along with the text-producing, thinking, backspacing, and talking self. For him, it's all the same, I suspect.

As I read and re-read my conversation with Matthew, I realized that the story he told contained a straightforward understanding of cyberspace: Cyberspace, the

Internet, the Web, whatever you want to call it, is essentially a tool to enhance one's capacity to control both the flow of information and how the self is presented.

While Matthew may consider *place* a useful metaphor for describing the way he interacts with this tool, he more literally equates cyberspace with other "useful communications media," such as radio, telephone, or television. Sure, he says, "Cyberspace is a new dimension." But this dimension is not occupied by people, only information. When he describes being online, he refers to "logging onto" the local network, or "connecting to" various programs and resources to "do one of two things. If I'm looking for something . . . I fire off a Web search. Also I use it for news and information."

I understand Matthew to be saying that we can "go online" to do research, to find and play with various tools, to read newsgroups, to keep in touch with friends, and, most importantly, to retrieve information and news. But going online does not include an embodied sense of being any*where*. For Matthew, going there means getting connected to the network, like when you dial the telephone or turn on the television.

Within the confines of this understanding, then, *real life*, *RL*, or IRL describe those times when you're not connecting to technology through the body (engaging the technology). Real life is when you hang up the telephone. It is when you turn off the television.

For Matthew, this way of defining real life may allow him to separate technology from his everyday life as he simultaneously integrates technology into his everyday activities. When he writes that he is spilling popcorn or opening a bag of rice cakes or doing jumping jacks, he is not so much performing a self that is distinct from his offline self; he is simply illustrating that he is the same physical self in this conversational context as in any other. Significantly, Matthew only enacted a body in online space one time, when he saluted to Beth. I may have responded as if he were really in Beth's room with me when I stared at him doing pushups as if he were doing them in front of me, but he never did anything actively in the MOO, such as looking around, picking up objects, or sitting/standing.

Matthew's understanding of cyberspace is based on a fundamental understanding of computer-mediated communication as information exchange. Cyberspace is a tool that facilitates communication, which is the transfer of information; and if one knows enough about how to wield the tool, one can control the form and flow of information to accomplish certain tasks. For example, Matthew indicated he feels he is a more effective and confident communicator online because he can backspace and edit. He assumes that through careful construction of the message, accurate information can be transmitted to others. Matthew doesn't seem to worry about whether or not his message is received. Effectiveness, or mutual understanding, is assumed.

The extent to which Matthew believes online communication is solely information is illustrated clearly in two instances—when we talked about online sex and when we talked about his daughters using the Internet.

"It's funny, when I briefly explored the Web sex stuff a year or two ago, I remembered why I quit looking at magazines (sex type) 15 years ago."

"How so?" I prompted.

Matthew seemed to think for a few moments before answering. "It is so bloody boring to see or read about sex but not to do it, I think."

"Well, why do you think online sex is so popular, then?"

"I'd say because a lot of people (read mostly younger men) want more information about sex, and if they don't get it then learning about it is better than nothing. It just doesn't hold a candle to the real thing, IMHO [In My Humble Opinion]."

I considered Matthew's response. I suppose I agree, at a certain level, that online sex could be informational, but surely one couldn't dismiss the thousands of sex-based sites as merely a way to get information about sex. Exchanging sex pics (sexual pictures) through the Internet or accessing a pornography site was one thing, engaging in interactive sex either graphically or textually was another. I asked, "Well, that might describe the pornography sites, but what about all those S and M rooms and bondage sites that you can't even get on because they're always full?"

"I suppose it's all a part of learning about different things, exploring the options, if you know what I mean," Matthew said. "It's probably interesting to young people. But as I said, it doesn't hold a candle ..."

"Yeah," I said, "I would tend to agree with you there."

As we continued to talk, his various descriptions of online sex, reality, and virtuality gave a clear conception that being online did not imply "being" as much as it implied "connection to technology." And perhaps because he did not imagine himself having a separate identity and existence online, he was very nonchalant about his two young daughters going online, to do presumably the same things he does ... find and retrieve useful information and communicate with others.

"What do you think of cyberspace?" I asked as I felt the interview draw to a close.

Matthew's answer came immediately, "A new dimension. People have talked for years about the information age, but now it's actually being used, and I think it will have an impact equivalent to the automobile or the telegraph."

I asked, "Do you have anything you would like to add about your experiences with computer-mediated communication?"

Matthew replied, "As a parent of two girls, I am always perking up my ears when I hear about the so-called 'dangers that lurk in cyberspace for our innocent young girls,' or however the media is hyping it today. But I think that's a bunch of paranoia. I'm of the opinion that one need only teach kids not to give out too much RL information on MOOs/MUDs, which is like telling them not to give their names over the telephone or get into cars with strangers. I just hope that we don't lose our liberties as per information access from these kinds of paranoid imaginings of the (often) net-illiterate." A pause, then he concluded, "That's my $0.02."

"Well, I think it was worth at least two bits," I replied. For some reason, though, I was chilled by his words. I shook my head at the screen. As we ended the interview, I thought maybe I'd been spending too much time online, talking with people who said online life was much more interesting than offline life, whose sense of self seemed to revolve around their online personae and the relationships they had with other people through texts. I had just completed a critical analysis of interactive cybersex games, where the user completely controls the behaviors and responses of the woman—and she likes it, of course. Perhaps my research focus had tainted my ability to dismiss so easily the impact online practices could have on young people's attitudes and behaviors.

For Matthew, online interaction is primarily information transfer. Controlling the interaction is a simple matter of controlling the amount and type of information given to others about the self. He thinks that as long as his daughters remain anonymous online, they will not encounter anything dangerous or damaging.

In his last statements, I began to comprehend just how simple and uncomplicated Matthew's conception of cyberspace was. When he mentioned his two daughters spending time in various online spaces, I immediately thought of several things that might never occur to Matthew, such as learning about sex from a dominatrix in a bondage site, putting on the mask of a twenty-one-year-old, getting involved in serious online relationships with much older men without realizing it, or replacing the embodied (and perhaps perceived as less attractive) sense of self with a more attractive or more sexual identity.

None of these is inherently or necessarily damaging or dangerous, but I am still cautious about them. Maybe I see them more complexly because I self-consciously analyze these practices in my research. Maybe it was Sherie's comment that she feels more beautiful online because she can live through language instead of her body. Maybe I can't forget DominO's boastful statement, "I can dominate and control others' minds and actions through my words, which are just as good as my hands." (*When it comes down to it, I really wonder what would have happened if I had spent four to five hours a night interacting with others online when I was in junior high school. It might have been easier than living in my physical body, which was going through changes I did not understand. It might have been nice to experiment with different bodies, prettier faces. I might have avoided processing the angst of adolescence if I leaped over it or ignored it. But would I have learned to accept and live with my physical self with all these other choices?)*

Although Matthew performed an embodied self during our interview, his understanding of computer-mediated communication does not incorporate the body. Matthew is a programmer who spends a lot of time using computer-mediated communication as a tool in his job, to retrieve useful information, and as a way of keeping in touch with others. He might talk about real life as if it were something to be noted separately from online life; but based on the way he talks about it, I believe he experiences computer-mediated communication no differently than he experiences a typewriter, a telephone, or the newspaper. This technology is a tool that connects him to others and to the world.

JENNIFER
THE COMPUTER IS A RATHER HARSH REMINDER
THAT YOU AREN'T THERE

"When you were first online, what did you mostly do?" I began.

"At the beginning, I was primarily following one or 2 Usenet groups. That led to meeting my husband, at which point I was relying heavily on e-mail and then MU* [Multi-User Dimensions of various types] to communicate/talk with him. Since we've been married, my reasons for using online media have changed. More of my friends are online now, as is my immediate family. They're some distance away, so email is great for keeping touch."

Jennifer and I were finally having a "normal" conversation after several starts and stops. We had started talking in her online community, but my computer kept acting up—or shutting down, actually. After a frustrating thirty minutes of creating and losing our connection, we decided to meet a few days later in Beth's room at the MOO. Jennifer had been recommended by one of my colleagues because she had met her husband online, and I was anxious to interview someone who had become so connected and attached to someone online that they got married.

"What do you mean when you say your use of online media has changed?"

After a pause, Jennifer added, "When I say change, I say my usage quantity changed, quite drastically from when I first learned how to maneuver the various on-line environments (email, WWW, Usenet, MU*s).

"How long have you been using internet technologies?" I asked.

```
Jennifer got online in 1993. "Using email and reading Usenet
were my first online activities."
```

Interesting move, I thought. Jennifer had just slipped into third person by using the emote command. In most Multi-User Dimensions, one can perform certain actions by typing different things. To speak, I type "say," followed by whatever I want to say. The words "Markham says . . ." appear on other screens. If I want to indicate I am agreeing, I type "emote nods," and "Markham nods" appears on the screen for others to see. Typically, one uses the emote command to show action or emotion. For instance, I use the emote command principally to laugh or scratch my head. Matthew used it to indicate he was doing pushups, opening bags of food, or meandering to the kitchen (either textually or physically, I was never sure which). But Jennifer was using the emote command to create a metanarrative of sorts, apparently. I had never seen this particular use before, and was intrigued.

Jennifer returned to first person and continued, "To begin with, I didn't quite know what the Internet *was* when I first heard about it—which has likely been the case for a number of persons. A friend I'd met dur"

```
Jennifer made a typo, which kept what she'd just said from
going through.

Jennifer tries again.

Markham grins in understanding.....she does that all the time.
```

"A friend I'd met during a summer job used MU* as a hobby and also read Usenet. When I left the summer job and returned to school, email was a logical way for the 2 of us to stay in touch (cheaper than phone calls, and I had the free university account). So when I got online, I didn't really know what to expect. I wasn't computer literate beyond using MSWord and a Macintosh, so a friend showed me the basics of manipulating the email and Usenet environments. From there I started reading/following a Usenet group—reading for about a month, and then figuring out how to post (contribute to the general conversation of the group). It was on that group that I first started talking (via email) w/ the man who's now my husband."

"How did you start talking?" I asked curiously. I was dying to know how it happened—how two people could start typing to each other and end up married. Just the other day, I had heard another story about a woman who left her husband for another man she had met only through email. A secretary I knew across town met a man online, and he moved from three states away to be with her. At least they met face-to-face once before he made the commitment. Online romance. It apparently happens all the time these days; people meet through the text and love what they see in the other person's words. Actually, the experience is much more complicated than this. In some cases, people develop an intimacy precisely because they are connected only with words. As one of my students recently said, "You talk about each other and express things in words that you might otherwise communicate in just a glance." Intimacy can be expressed in the words themselves or in the act of writing intimate thoughts, which can require a measure of trust and willingness to be vulnerable. It makes sense logically, but for the life of me, I couldn't imagine it.

Jennifer said, "He sent private email in response to something I'd posted to the newsgroup. From there, we struck up a conversation (again, carried on via email), the topic of which began with the focus of the newsgroup itself, and then moved on to other things. . . . Other things being things like school—I was an undergrad and he was getting his master's, both of us close to finishing and working on a thesis (so we commiserated :}) —and then on to other interests we had, what we were studying, what films we'd seen lately, the weather. Often continuing thoughts about the newsgroup topic. And then (I will admit that, at the time, I had no clue about the country abbrevations at the end of e-mail addresses), once I learned he was from a completely different country, we started talking about different cultural experiences, what our home countries were like . . . simple things like 'are you the youngest or oldest in your family?' and 'What's your city/town like?'"

Markham nods

Jennifer continued, "I guess we started the email correspondence in 10/93. During the winter school break, he thought I was blowing him off, b/c he hadn't realized I'd be gone for the school holiday :} But that all got cleared up once I returned :)"

I wondered what Jennifer meant when she made a squiggly smiley face as opposed to the regular smiley face. It seemed deliberate. I made a mental note to ask her about it later, but I didn't want to interrupt her during a good story, so I typed, "Was the conversation and/or relationship romantic at this point?"

Jennifer replied, "It hadn't even occurred to me that a *romantic* relationship was something that could arise from talking to people online."

I exclaimed, "Ha! I *still* can't imagine how it happens!"

"In fact," Jennifer went on, "the romantic interest wasn't reciprocated until nearly a year after we'd first started talking w/ one another. We emailed each other quite a lot throughout those first 10 months—probably about 4msg/day on average"

I interrupted, "(reciprocated . . . by whom?)"

"And too, once I figured out how to use telnet—we found we could talk via a MUD chat system. . . . oh. reciprocated by me—he became interested in me first (which he'd agree with, were you to talk with him :))."

Jennifer continued to talk about her relationship with Brian. During a period without access to email, she began to realize how much she missed their discussions—and how much she missed Brian. "You see, our conversations were pretty lighthearted in tone, but often about topics that we discovered were meaningful to both of us."

"When did you start talking again?" I asked.

"When I got back to school (and the computer), I contacted him immediately, and we resumed the conversation where we'd left off . . ."

```
Jennifer thinks....
```

"Roughly 2 months after that (so 9/94), he asked me to marry him—it was either online or on the phone. Neither of us can remember exactly which—I said yes, and he didn't come in person till 1/95."

"Wow," I typed, shaking my head at the screen in amazement. I was unable to come up with anything better to say, so I added lamely, "Very interesting!" Of course, I'd known that Jennifer met her husband online, but I'd never realized Jennifer had accepted a marriage proposal before meeting him face-to-face!

```
Jennifer grins and adds, "yes, we think so too — we certainly
didn't expect it to happen."
```

"I can imagine!" I exclaimed. I was bursting with curiosity. "What was it like when you first talked on the phone? What was it like when you first met face-to-face?"

```
Jennifer laughs.
```

"Well, I think we were both in slight shock during the first phone conversation we had—he called at 5am. I was barely awake enough to register that the voice on the other end was likely his—there was a little adjustment for accents, too."

I had countless questions burning in my head. I still couldn't get used to the idea that Jennifer—or anyone, for that matter—would agree to marry someone they had never seen. I wondered how their relationship changed when they finally met. Or what it felt like when they saw each other for the first time. "How did your offline relationship compare with your online relationship?"

Jennifer asked, "You mean, were there any surprises when we met face-to-face the first time?"

"Sure," I typed, nodding at the screen, "or in general, what were the differences?"

Jennifer's response came after a brief pause, "There were no differences from one to the other."

No differences? Huh? I couldn't believe that an exclusively online relationship would be no different from the offline relationship. Not satisfied with her answer, I asked the question in a different way, "What was it like when you met him?"

Jennifer replied, "All along, our communication and expressiveness with one another had been very full and very open . . . very descriptive."

Still curious, I pressed, "Were you surprised about anything when you met him?"

"No, there were no differences from one to the other. We hadn't pulled any punches in describing ourselves. I realize that people can easily disguise that sort of thing online . . . but we'd talked a lot about goals and family and experiences in both past and present, more than enough to establish whether the other was being consistent and sincere." I could almost see Jennifer shrug her shoulders nonchalantly.

I couldn't give it up yet, and asked, "So did he look like what you thought he would?"

Jennifer laughs

"Actually, people tell us we look a lot like each other."

Of course, Jennifer emphasized, building and maintaining a relationship took a lot of online time. "After we were engaged I spent a good portion of my weekend on a live chat system talking with him and sending emails a lot during the week, as well as phone calls."

Perhaps being in a MU* together helped create a sense of presence for them. That would help explain why she seemed to treat her first face-to-face meeting with her fiancé so casually. I asked, "Before you met face-to-face, when you were spending all that time in live chat, did you feel like you were with him?"

"The on-line interaction doesn't replace the face-to-face, but supplements it, again b/c of distance factors. That time was very tough on both of us. As a few weeks passed, we realized what a strain being separated was, so we chose to do what we could to get married asap. Yes, it felt like we were together in the sense that we were emotionally connected . . . however, the computer is a rather harsh barrier/reminder that you're not together . . ." She paused, and then concluded, "it's never easy being apart from someone you love."

*

Throughout our conversation, I was intrigued by Jennifer's apparent nonchalance about meeting, getting to know, and agreeing to marry her husband exclusively in cyberspace. Of course, my curiosity stems from never experiencing online romance, and perhaps I overestimate the drama of it all. Even so, as I consider the form and content of Jennifer's statements, I get the sense that Jennifer doesn't really conceptualize cyberspace as some place to be with others. Rather, cyberspace seems to be the space between two people communicating with each other through technology. Being online may have facilitated the connection between Jennifer and Brian, but it is mostly, as Jennifer says, a reminder that you're not with the other person.

Although Jennifer gets a lot out of computer-mediated communication, she uses it primarily as another communication tool or medium. She "maneuvers," "manipulates," and "uses" various CMC environments to conduct research, look for jobs, and keep in touch with friends and family. For Jennifer, being online is comparable to being on the telephone, only less expensive; and computer-mediated communication is like writing letters, only more immediate and interactive.

Throughout our conversation, I was intrigued by Jennifer's facility with this medium and her apparent concern with correct form. Early in the interview I noticed she typed quickly but used correct punctuation, sophisticated sentence structures, and third person to refer to herself in what I felt conveyed a metanarrative. Her skillful use of text made me feel like I was in the middle of a story I was reading. Later, when I asked her about her identity and self-concept in online contexts, Jennifer suggested that measured, thoughtful participation in the interaction and careful control of the form and content of the messages enhanced the effectiveness of her communication via the computer.

Interestingly, Jennifer's use and manipulation of the technology to create and manipulate effective conversation illustrates her conception of online communication as information transfer, a view very similar to Matthew's. The resulting form and structure of her writing also illustrates her definition of computer-mediated communication as a tool that can enhance interaction if manipulated correctly.

"How would you describe your sense of self online?"

"My sense of self . . ." Jennifer began, then after a few moments, continued, "I would say that I become very attuned to *what* is being said and *how* it is being said—particularly in a synchronous conversation and likewise attuned to how/what I am saying as part of that conversation."

I waited patiently. I knew if I could keep my hands off the keyboard, Jennifer might continue. My patience paid off a few moments later.

"I find myself thinking a lot about what is the 'right' thing to say . . . trying to make sense of and interpret the mood/attitude in addition to the words, such that I can be sensitive and focused in what I am saying in reply."

I asked, "How do you determine what the 'right' thing is? (I guess it would be hard for me . . . like when I'm interviewing, it's often difficult to determine if I'm saying/asking the 'right' thing.)"

Jennifer's reply was almost immediate. "Obviously, I have the choice to type in what I want to say to you . . . as well as how I want to say it to you . . . i.e., language choice, depth of explanation, smiling, etc."

```
Jennifer suggests, "For example, you may or may not have noted
that I insert "actions" into what I say— :) , or things like
"X explains" before launching into what I have to say, or
emphasis around certain words with asterisks,"
```

```
Jennifer continues, "things that I've found tend to humanize
the conversation."
```

```
You say, "Do you think most people do this online?"
```

```
Jennifer believes they guide both where she's going and where
the listener is going.
```

Jennifer continued, switching back to first person, ". . . and they're also useful for clarifying myself if my intent wasn't received :}"

Jennifer's prose—replete with third-person voice and what she described as "rueful grins" (that squiggly smiley face), and sophisticated sentence structures—was very clear, indeed. I felt almost silly asking her for more clarification, but I wanted her to explain further how she understood conversation to operate. "Do you think it works? I mean, do you think this thought process is crucial to effective communication online?"

"I think it's very helpful. . . . I think it demonstrates more attention to the quality of the interaction between X# of persons who are participating in the interaction."

```
Jennifer has always found it helpful to be very descriptive in
on-line environments, whether synchronous or asynchronous,
b/c it gives people more to work with...a fuller, more rounded
sense of your thoughts, feelings, environment, etc.
```

∗

Jennifer's explanations depict communication as the accurate exchange of messages, a process aided by attending carefully to the conversation and choosing words and expressions carefully to produce "higher quality interaction." But she doesn't simply say this, she enacts this definition through careful attention to the form of her online communication. Unlike most other participants with whom I've interacted online, Jennifer uses examples to illustrate what she means, she prefaces some of her statements with "Jennifer suggests" or "Jennifer continues," and she indicates pauses with ellipses and paragraph breaks. In short, the third person, carefully constructed form of her message reflects what she is trying to communicate.

Jennifer suggests that if people pay attention and think about *what* they write as well as *how* they write, the correct message is more likely to be received, and misunderstanding will be avoided. Control of the text is the key to controlling both the message and the meaning of the message.

To a certain extent, this control is possible. For instance, as I write this document, I carefully construct the form of the sentences to be as clear and accurate (true to what I want to communicate) as possible. Yet I cannot know how the reader will respond, and even "noise" does not fully explain the innumerable ways misunderstanding happens. But for Jennifer, communication is the process of creating a message and the result of transferring this message from one person to another, who receives and processes it. Presumably, understanding is possible if the messages are constructed carefully enough; and for her, it seems to work. I might say she has a limited, transmissional view of communication, and that she assumes far too much control over the context, but her online encounters appear to be successful—at least she believes they are.

For Jennifer, this communication tool is as useful and effective as any other, such as the telephone or writing letters. And within this frame, the issue of reality is not an issue at all.

"Are your online relationships real?" I asked.

Jennifer grins, thinking this is a complex question!

I laughed aloud and typed in response, "Ha! That's why I left it for last!"

Jennifer said, "It's likely no surprise that the time I spent on-line w/ my husband—esp. since it was so very formative in our relationships—was very very real. And the conversations I still have w/ friends online [friends she met offline and communicates with online] are real. My two closest female friends are online. One's in Japan, and one's in the West US. We still have heart-to-hearts online, b/c it's less expensive than the phone and in those conversations, we can achieve a very high level of understanding that compares to what we've known w/ one another face-to-face."

*

Although Jennifer described her own *experiences* online as real, this does not mean the online contexts themselves are real in the same way:

```
Jennifer thinks she's seen people give too much credence/
power to the 'reality' of their online environments...people
who've become addicted to MU*s, or who get completely involved
and agitated by things people do in (for example) that par-
ticular MU*, such that they carry it w/ them through the day.
And I've also seen people completely *ignore* their ftf/RL
existence in favor of their interaction online.
```

This statement is very consistent with Jennifer's definition of online communication as a tool. Jennifer values highly the technology that enables her to communicate with people from all over the world, and she acknowledges that some users might get caught up in their interactions with others online to the point they might come to think of it as reality. But this is very distinct from her experience. "It is other people you are interacting with, and not nebulous entities," she says. The online environment is "a great forum," but she does not experience it as a place or a way of being. A notable omission in our conversation might illustrate this best.

During our two-hour interview, as I encouraged Jennifer to talk about her online interactions and experiences, she never mentioned she was a very active, founding member of and Wizard (moderator) in an online text-based MUD. In this particular online community, characters and rooms are created around the general theme of animated cartoons, and each member of the community has an animated persona.

I learned about Jennifer's participation in the creation and maintenance of this online culture from another member of the group, Michael, who I also interviewed. When I asked Michael about his online community, he said, "I'm surprised Jennifer hasn't told you about that place . . . Wow. :) I can't imagine she would not mention the MUD. She's another of the famous people in its history!"

Jennifer's omission speaks loudly to me. It hints that Jennifer has effectively distanced herself from this still active part of her life, or that this type of interaction is like any other; entertaining enough to engage in, but not worth mentioning as a part of online experiences. Or perhaps she feels that this part of her life is very private and didn't want it to become the focus of the interview. Perhaps I make too much of it.

In any case, Jennifer did not appear to consider her online persona a relevant issue in a discussion of online communication. Her omission supports my interpretation that she conceptualizes online communication media primarily as a useful set of tools that, if controlled properly, enable effective communication with others.

✳

(Sometimes I feel so boring online. I'm in the middle of this interview, asking questions. To fill in the space between the responses, or to encourage the participant to continue, I sometimes type "yes." To vary this response, I might emote a nod, or say "yeah, I know what you mean." I feel completely bound by the text. These people talk about how great the text is, and I feel emotionally crippled by it. Oh, I realize I can express many things through the text, and I'm a pretty decent writer. But in a conversation online, it is difficult to show or establish an identity. I think it takes a very long time. Generally, when I meet new people in RL, I use a lot of sarcasm or dry humor to break the ice. But as Michael (the person I'm interviewing) just indicated, sarcasm doesn't go over really well on the Net because you can't accompany the remark with a wry grin or some other marker. I feel so one-dimensional online.

So I am stuck saying, "great!" or "cool!" or any number of other clever phrases . . .)

MIST
ONLINE SEEMS SIMPLER, I GUESS . . . IT REQUIRES LESS EFFORT AND COMMITMENT

"So what do you think of cyberspace in general?" I asked Mist.

"I think that it's an interesting metaphor. I haven't really thought about what I think of cyberspace!"

```
Mist looks thoughtful
```

After a few moments, Mist concluded, "Well, the internet and cyberspace are the same thing right now—the connections between computer networks and the 'space' created by these connections. I'm glad cyberspace is here. I hope it stays this way and doesn't get too commercialized for people to enjoy in a relaxed manner. But we gotta have user fees, ads, something so that it pays its way, right?"

"Why did you begin using the internet?" I asked. I knew Mist spent a lot of time in various communities online, or at least enough to have established a character name, "Mist."

"We got free accounts at school and I started sending email to my brother who went to school in a different city."

"Do you still use it for that reason?" I asked.

"Not to send email to him (he finished) but definitely to communicate with him, my dad, stepmom, friends, colleagues, and so forth."

I asked, "Where do you go and what do you do mostly when you're online?"

Mist said, "I primarily send email. I also look around for free stuff online. And I do some MOOing, mostly for classes."

A pretty direct answer. Matthew and Jennifer had responded similarly. I was hoping to find a question that would allow her to talk of the "space" created by the Internet. "Tell me about your most memorable experience online."

I waited a long minute for Mist's answer. "Probably while I was moderating a class a few weeks ago in a MOO. It's hard to 'moderate' in the sense that I'm used to in a physical space. So I tried some different things and was really pleased that my moderating was successful, but one of my classmates simulated a virtual rape (we were discussing that at the time) and that was pretty strange to deal with . . . so it was memorable, but not completely in a good way."

"Memorable" seems a bit of an understatement, I thought. As I waited for Mist to continue, I thought about how eerie the incident must have been. Gazing at our passing conversation on the screen, I saw other, more violent descriptions. I shuddered, remembering Julian Dibbell's (1993) account of an actual virtual rape in an online community called LambdaMOO. An image flashed through my mind of this innocent group of people Dibbell described talking together in a room on the MOO. Everyone was having a lively conversation, when suddenly Legba and Starsinger began violating themselves, each other, and others in the room, performing—without their consent or volition—unspeakable, progressively violent sexual acts. Legba and Starsinger could not control the actions of their online characters. I could almost see "Mr. Bungle," the master of this scene, laughing cruelly into his own computer screen as he wrote their performances himself, with something called a "voodoo program." I knew that the experience in Mist's class couldn't be anything like this scene, but still . . .

I waited another minute. Mist was either thinking or writing, "and I am not going to interrupt her," I chastised myself in anticipation. I sat back and took a sip of lukewarm coffee. Two minutes.

Finally, I sent the message I had composed a minute before. "How did you feel when that happened?"

After a moment, Mist replied, "Surprised. Shocked a little. Upset. And kind of resigned—the guy in question is really obnoxious in person and online, and I don't think it occurred to him that he did anything wrong. Talk about oblivion."

Again, I waited for her to tell more of the story, but she appeared to be finished talking. "I wish I could see her face," I muttered to the empty office. Curious that she doesn't seem to want to talk about this event. Perhaps it was very disconcerting .

"How did you react to the incident?" I asked.

"I think that I tried to direct us to a different topic. I think that someone chastised him. It quickly became apparent that people were upset, but we kept going. . . . The log of the event is still online if you want to read it."

I typed, "Hmmm . . . yes, I may want to do that. Sounds spooky."

Mist replied, "It wasn't too horrible—not like the Mr. Bungle thing. But it was pretty inappropriate."

Apparently Mist had read or heard about the virtual rape I was recalling earlier. Yet, I could almost see her shrugging her shoulders. I wondered if I was missing something. She seems so matter of fact, I thought to myself, perhaps I'm missing some of the nuances of her tone. I chuckled out loud. Missing the *nuances* of her nonverbals? Better to say missing *all* of her nonverbals.

I decided to leave the instance behind, although I was still curious about her reaction. "How real are your experiences online?" I asked.

Mist said, "How real . . . that's a good question. To me they seem quite real. Being online is part of my life. I send email more than I talk to people on the phone (and I stay in touch more with my friends who have email), so online is pretty real to me."

I still couldn't get over how sensible Mist seemed about experiencing an attempted virtual rape in a class she was leading. Was Mist understating her experience of the virtual rape incident? Or did she talk about everything in this mundane way? Maybe the incident really was minimal, and I was overdramatizing; . . . yet it was Mist's most memorable experience online.

"Are you still there, Annette?"

Suddenly I realized I had drifted off, distracted by my own musings. "Oh! Sorry, Mist. I'm still here. Just thinking about the rape incident." I quickly typed another question. "How would you compare communicating online with communicating IRL?"

"Well, I can communicate ok in both arenas. However, I have a lot of trouble talking about how I FEEL about things when I'm talking IRL. I can do that more easily online. I guess there's a bit of distance to being online. Online seems simpler, I guess."

That would be a distinct advantage to being online, I thought. Yet, I'm not sensing many of these expressions of feelings in our conversation thus far. Of course, I don't know what her typical level of expressiveness is, online or offline. The phrase "how I FEEL" might mean something completely different to her than it does to me.

✳

When I think back on this interview, Mist's descriptions of events and experiences were very consistent with her straightforward view of the Internet as a useful communication tool. When I asked her how real her experiences were, she said they were "very real" and went on to discuss how her online communication had, in many cases, replaced her telephone contact with friends and family. When she talked of "MOOing with multitudes," I believe she meant simply "talking with many people online." I perceived this consistency when Mist talked about her sense of self, also.

"How would you describe your sense of self online?"

"It's hard for me to assess my online self. I don't see it as being separate from my 'real' self. Of course my real self is so fragmented that I don't think I could tell if my online self was separate or different."

"What do you mean when you say your online self is not separate from your real self? And what do you mean by fragmented?" I asked.

Mist replied, "Well, I'm going through counseling right now because I suddenly got really confused about nearly everything. And apparently I hadn't been looking past the surface of my life or my self for years (if ever). So I'm trying to integrate all those unexamined things (fragments?) that have been bubbling around inside me for ages."

Mist shakes her head.

She concluded, "Boy, that's one confusing answer. I guess I feel fragmented because I'm confused. I don't think it'll get any clearer than that right now!"

✳

Although Mist engaged others in many different online contexts, these were not significantly different than interactions in any other context. Cyberspace, synonymous with the Internet, constitutes a connection of networks that facilitates various types of communication with others. Communication can be synchronous or asynchronous, but in either case it is similar to being on the telephone or writing post-it notes for someone. Online communication thus provides a context where one can be with others, but being there doesn't imply being someone or something other than yourself (any more than being on the phone does). This is very consistent with her suggestion that the real self is the real self, online or offline. These are not two different selves. Her self might be fragmented, as she suggests, but this fragmentation is not created or facilitated by the online contexts.

✳

I asked, "So tell me, what's it like to meet people online?"

"I guess that's kind of hard to answer. Do I really 'meet' anyone I don't already know? . . . not really. I guess I have 'met' people through contacting them online or them contacting me."

I wondered briefly about the quotation marks around 'meet' and 'met.' I asked, "So do you have close friendships with people you know only online?"

Mist said, "Well, I've been observing a particular list for the past several years. I feel like I'm part of that community, but I don't participate at all."

I wondered how that was possible, but then I thought of my parents. They feel like part of a town, yet they don't really participate actively in it. I asked, "Ahh . . . why do you feel like you are a part of that community?"

"I feel like I know the people who post regularly—they have definite personalities."

"How would you describe your level of commitment to this group?"

"Well, I feel like I'm part of the group in a superficial way, but at a deeper level, I know I'm not. But I've been tempted to go spy on one of their f2fGTGs."

"Hmmm . . . What tempts you?" I asked, trying to figure out what the acronym GTG meant.

```
Markham .oO (I wonder what a GTG is...)

Markham .oO(Oh. Probably Get ToGether)
```

Think bubbles are a funny trick I learned from BobZ in DU. They made me laugh when I used them, so I tried to use them as much as possible.

Mist replied, "To see if they're how I think they really are."

```
Mist nods, pleased that Markham figured out the acronym.
```

"But I really suck at being in groups, clubs, whatever. So maybe I'm better at being a part of online groups. They require less effort and less commitment, at least at the level at which I participate."

I wondered at Mist's last statement. Earlier she indicated she felt like a part of a community she had never participated in. I suppose this is possible to an extent— I can feel I am a part of something even if I don't actively participate. In physical communities others can see me, so even if I never speak, I might be considered a member. A key feature of online communities is participation, however; to be present is to participate and be responded to. As MacKinnon (1995) says, as we move into online contexts, the common phrase "I think, therefore I am," is woefully inadequate. The more appropriate phrase in cyberspace is "I am perceived, therefore I am" (p. 119). But Mist does not perceive her existence or membership in online groups to be a product of interaction. She seems to feel like she is a part of the group simply by watching the activities of the group.

As we talked, I realized Mist had reminded me that there are more important things in life than being online, even as we were in the midst of talking about being online. I had trouble reaching this conclusion, though, because her depiction of the Internet as merely a tool seemed very disjunctive with the high number and type of things she does online. Her online name threw me off as well. I thought the name "Mist" was a wonderful choice, and I anticipated a different type of conversation. (*Then I learned that Mist was really her last name—which didn't make it less beautiful, but my frame shifted immediately. All of a sudden her name became a default rather than a choice, the same as if my name were really Bambi or Fate or Gargoyle. I was puzzled by my own reaction; it's as if I expect beauty or mystery to be a put-on in cyberspace, so when it's natural, it seems deflated or somehow less exciting. Talk about privileging the hyperreal, eh?*)

Mist might not distinguish online and offline experiences in terms of degree of reality, but she does differentiate her experiences in terms of the degree of control they permit her.

"Do you feel different about yourself online than offline?" I asked.

"Online seems simpler, like I said. For some reason, when you said that, I thought about the class I'm taking right now; we have met online three times and f2f 8 times. I liked the MOO sessions better because there are several domineering guys in our class who don't really let anyone else talk. Online, they don't have much recourse other than obnoxiousness, because turntaking is different and you can only type so fast. I like that."

I laughed at the dueling images of two hands flying adroitly over one keyboard and two fingers fumbling awkwardly over another keyboard. I couldn't help commenting, "Hmmmm . . . and guys sometimes type slower for some reason."

Mist replied, "They took shop instead of typing maybe."

I nodded, still chuckling, and replied, "Yeah, and sometimes I wish I would have taken shop."

Mist demonstrated a keen awareness of one of the commonly perceived benefits of online communication: Text-based, computer-mediated communication equalizes the participants to the extent that everyone, regardless of gender, race, authority, age, etc., is limited to exchanging texts. Communicating in anonymous online settings can democratize participation, break down hierarchy, and limit stereotyping. Whether this belief is borne out in recent studies or not, in Mist's experience, online communication is a useful means of leveling the playing field among the participants in the conversation.

(*I have to keep reminding myself that these might be everyday people using the Internet to facilitate their everyday interactions. Not everyone thinks of the Internet as a "lifeline to the world" [Sheol], or a "nexus of human consciousness" [RU Sirius, editor of* **Wired**], *or a way to "meld the machine with the mind" [Anthony, a hacker interviewed by Turkle in 1984]. Yet I keep searching for the cyborg in these participants . . . it just has to be here, somewhere, doesn't it? Everyone keeps talking about cyborgs, cyberspace as the prosthetic of the mind [e.g., Landsberg, 1995], or bodies as liquid architecture [Novak, 1991]. Indeed, here's another person who is extending the capacity of her body through this technology, in the same ways she might use the telephone to extend her voice, or the radio to make her ears more receptive, or the television to extend her vision. Even so, not all people who use technology to enhance their capacities think of themselves as essentially connected to the machine.*)

A valuable feature of online communication is that it allows Mist some semblance of control over the interaction and more equal participation in mixed-gender conversations. For me, Mist's uncomplicated description and understanding of the utility of this tool also illustrates a common way of making sense of control in this context: Control is assumed to be in the hands of the person using the tool. This makes a great deal of sense to me—tools are by definition wielded by their user. If a tool was controlled by someone other than the one who benefits from the tool, that person would no longer perceive it so much as a tool but more as an instrument of control wielded like a tool by some other person. Ironically, although this assumption provides a tantalizing illusion of self-control, it also denies the agency of the Other and describes a distinctly nonrelational, unidirectional view of communication. This view might be valuable, but it also is somewhat naive.

Mist feels fragmented, as though she's "living the bit about 'he jumped onto his horse and rode madly off in all directions!'" But her discussion of computer-mediated communication leaves out any semblance of chaos, disorder, or fragmentation. In a world that is enormously complicated and fast-paced, online communication has its place, for Mist, as a tool that facilitates communication, expedites research, and allows users to participate at whatever level they feel most comfortable.

MICHAEL
THE COMMUNITY MAKES IT A PLACE

Michael, an artist with a "small army" of toys in his office, "lives" in the same Multi-User community as Jennifer and spends between two and three hours there every night.

"How would you describe your online community, the MUD?" I asked.

"Oh, it is very strong. It has survived many bad things along the way and it's still there. It's quite resilient. It's a very REAL community. We have all the problems a town would . . . or a family . . . or a group of friends, because that's what it really is."

"How would you describe your level of commitment to this group?"

Michael responded, "Very strong." Then, he added, "I hate when people deliberately try to hurt the place, and I usually let those people know my feelings on the issue, too:)"

"Do you feel like you are some *place* when you're online?" I asked.

"Oh yes! The MUD feels like a location, even if it's nothing more than a computer in California. It's definitely a real place for me. I see talking to my friends in Europe every night the same as I see talking with someone at work. There's just a little more space there . . . I've even gone MUD-hopping to see what other places are like. It's like visiting another town."

"What is it about the MUD that makes it so real for you? Are all your online experiences so real?"

"The people are so friendly, and we all share at least one interest—animation. Not all my experiences online are this real. Newsgroups definitely aren't. The web isn't. There's something about real-time chatting that gives things dimension. With real-time chatting, you're thinking on your feet. Things are active. Anything can happen. You also get to learn more about the people you're talking to."

"What do you mean by the term 'dimension'?"

"In real-time [online interactive conversation], people talk and act as they would (well most of the time) normally. They can't help but reveal more things about themselves . . . They become more than a name. They fill out as persons, so to speak."

"What makes it feel like a place?"

"Well, in the MUD, the rooms and objects there make it real. I think it must be the community that makes it a place. It's not different from a circle of friends in real life. Everyone hangs out together and such. On the MUD we just have a mask to hide behind and play behind sometimes. It's like people know it's a different world they're visiting when they log on, even though they end up chatting like we're sitting right next to them. People hide behind masks online a lot . . . but I've seen people put on 'masks' in real life too." A few moments passed, then Michael concluded, "So it's very much the same."

"How much time do you spend online?"

"Let's see . . . It used to be more. Now I'm probably down to 2-3 hours a day. About two years ago, I was on a LOT each night. :) . . . definitely 3 hours a night and probably more like 4."

"Would you spend more time online if you could?"

"Probably not. I guess you could say I realize there's a world out there that's just as or more interesting than this one. :)"

"Did you just realize that a couple years ago, when you said you stopped spending so much time online?"

"Yes, I did. The online world was just more interesting to me then. Don't get me wrong. I still love the place. But I don't want to be chained to the computer all the time, though I enjoy it."

✳

For me, Michael represents the exact center of the continuum of Tool . . . Place . . . Way of Being. His way of talking about the Net is unique among the people I interviewed. He never uses the term *tool*, or talks about using the Internet; neither does he talk about cyberspace as a way to constitute the self or a place to live one's life. The Net is a place where people can go to play with or try on different forms and identities, engage in meaningful activities with other people, and evolve as members of various communities.

I can visualize Michael at the center of a teeter-totter, feet firmly planted, looking around, laughing, and chatting with others, never noticing that, on either side of him, the teeter-totter is moving. Michael believes wholeheartedly that the Net is an actual place, and at the same time he appears to believe that anyone who goes online has an authentic self that does not change or shift as that person engages the technology.

Through this interview, I understood more how beliefs about the self might influence the ways we make sense of contexts and reality. Michael indicates a strong belief that the self is singular and authentic. No matter where the self goes, then, it performs as it would anywhere else. This straightforward conception of the performance of self influences Michael's ability to conceptualize online worlds as actual places occupied by real people. He doesn't seem to believe that people could be deceptive about who they really are, so everyone online is assumed to be enacting an authentic self. Perhaps Michael is completely unaware that people are not always what they seem, or he simply chooses to think differently and takes people at face value.

Interestingly and ironically, deception is an essential part of Michael's online community. The MUD comprises a group of people who enact animated characters. The entire community is an assortment of animated snakes, mice, tigers, humans, and so forth, and the MUD was created for role-playing with these animated characters. For Michael, who is "Mouse" in this community, these characters are not the real person, but only useful masks; the characters are an easy, nonthreatening way to get to know others.

"What's it like to meet people online?"

Michael said, "We start out very connected to the characters, role-playing."

I asked, "How do others appear to you? I mean, how do you visualize them?"

Michael replied, "We take the character names, so I personally often visualize the character, though I know there's someone else behind it. Visualizing the character makes for some interesting and funny mental pictures, too. :). You can use that character to role-play a bit, and if people are familiar with the character, they can relate to that character as they saw him or her on screen. . . . Then as people get more familiar with others on the MUD, they reveal more about themselves. The character acts as a gateway to the person inside that character. Eventually," Michael concluded, "we don't really role-play a lot. We chat a lot."

*

Putting on a mask and adopting different characteristics is an accepted and required part of the community, but it seems only an elaborate stage-setting for everyday conversation and community building dialogues. In any case, the characters are only masks. Although Michael indicates some people hide behind their masks more than others, this simply means an authentic self is hiding, not that the self is multiple. Over time and through conversation, people role-playing a character will eventually begin to fill out, because they can't help but reveal their real self, and he will come to know the "real" person.

Holding tightly to this basic assumption may allow Michael to blur the boundaries between online and offline contexts more easily, because everyone in both contexts is his or her true, singular self. They can't be otherwise.

"Tell me about your most memorable experience online."

Michael replied, "Wow . . . now let me think . . . Well, there is one that is the most bizarre experience I've had online—that's probably the moost memorable. :)"

"There was this girl, Chelsea Martin. She went by the character name Leena. She was probably the most influential person in the MUD. Well, the much-loved Leena decided she was going to move back to South Dakota to work on a farm, get away from the city. People literally wept at her going-away party online. People wanted to visit her in person, but she would never allow it.

"Soon after she left, a new character named Woofie joined the MUD. That wasn't so strange, but Woofie became a wizard there a little too quickly (forgot to tell you that Leena had been a wiz too). Anyway, one day Woofie, who I didn't like too much, said he had to talk to me and he told me that he was really Leena. . . . That Chelsea Martin was nothing more than him, Conner Moulin, roleplaying . . .

"That was a shock . . . I quickly accepted it, though. He said that he was interested in how the Net worked and how you could really be anyone online. He started as Chelsea/Leena, and pretty soon, he was trapped. Leena couldn't just go away— and it made things tricky when we started doing real-time chats and meeting others in person. But when it got to be too much, he DID do away with Leena by coming up with the 'needing to live on a farm' story. And he returned as Woofie." Michael concluded, "The weird thing to me, though, was that Leena and Woofie seemed to be two different people (they still do, in a way)."

✳

Two things occur to me after re-reading this story. First, the most memorable experience Michael—the mouse—ever had, is that someone would pretend to be something he or she is not. Second, for Michael, the strangest thing about this experience was that someone could seem to be two different people.

It seems very ironic to me that Michael would find this event "bizarre," as he puts it, particularly as a long-standing member of a community based on people adopting various animated characters as their online personae. However, the key distinction may be this: Michael playing a mouse is Michael, playing a mouse. It is okay to pretend you are a rabbit, a snake, or a mouse, because these are perceived by other members as animated characters, distinct from the real person behind the mask. Conner playing Leena was not acceptable, because the real person behind the mask was pretending to be a different gender and this pretense was not evident to the group as distinct from the real person behind the mask.

The baseline assumption that appears to be working here is that an authentic self always exists behind the mask and can be known. The basis of the MUD is role-playing, which is distinct, apparently, from the performative aspects of self. And, as Michael notes, they don't actually role-play all that much. They mostly just chat. Presumably, at these times the members are not in character.

But Conner, as Chelsea playing Leena, was always in character, never present-ing the "authentic" male self under the female mask. Conner had fooled them into believing that his real self was female, and this was too great a transgression from tradition. Many people felt betrayed, Michael concluded, and couldn't believe that someone could lie to them for so long.

∗

"Soon after I learned the truth, the rest of the MUD found out, and things turned nasty. Today Conner Moulin/Woofie/Leena/Chelsea runs his own MUD and he won't speak to me, even though I saw his side of things."

"Okay, my question is, why weren't you shocked? How did you feel about it?"

Michael responded, "I was shocked very much when I first found out . . . My chin was on the floor . . . But I was glad to have Leena back as a friend." He went on, "I didn't agree with how he/she handled things after the MUD found out, but right then I was glad to see her 'back' again."

I asked, "Did you see Leena as a gendered person before Woofie/Conner talked to you about it?"

Michael said, "Oh definitely. Everyone KNEW Leena was female. :) As Leena, Conner Martin had talked about dates, dresses, the works. He roleplayed it to the hilt."

"How did other people react? Did this event stir up the MUD quite a bit?"

"A BIG bit. People got mean, and since the MUD is usually friendly, it was pretty bad for the place. Some people left. Most people felt they had been betrayed. I think people were just so shocked that a pillar of the community was not who she seemed to be!"

*

Both here and before, Michael expressed shock and disbelief that someone could be someone other than the self they present. Michael was quickly able to accept Woofie as the former Leena, but he was very surprised when he later realized these two characters actually seemed different.

Michael presents a definite understanding that people are real, behind the mask, and that if he just interacts with them long enough, he will get to know that real person. So he is understandably stumped when one person exhibits more than one seemingly real self under the mask. Goffman (1974) questions whether there is anything but the mask. In Michael's experience, however, the masks are temporary barriers between two authentic selves; Woofie/Leena is an amazing exception to him. For Michael, then, it is possible online to know the Other as an authentic self; and in his experience, the way to know the Other is through dialogue.

Although Michael uses the term *real* to signify those events and commitments offline, he is more likely to use *real* or *RL* to signify that which is experienced. In a way, Michael's use of the term corresponds more with the dictionary definition of "real" than most of the other participants'. In the other interviews, the participants used the term *real* as if it distinguished online from real experiences, but I feel that they meant simply to distinguish online from offline experiences. However, Michael uses *RL* to actually indicate that which is experienced, and he does not distinguish between online and offline when he does so.

Let me explain, using a significant comment from our conversation as an example. When I asked Michael about the reality of his experiences, he described the Net as a visual, embodied, and spatially located place, a world. In this way, real is that which is physical, and this includes both online and offline contexts.

When I asked how his commitments to his online group compared to his commitments to his various RL communities, he refused the distinction I was trying to make between online and real life contexts: "Commitments to the MUD would always give way to RL commitments for me . . . I do, however, see commitments to the MUD people as RL commitments."

At first glance, I thought Michael was contradicting himself. On one hand, Michael seems to say that RL signifies those commitments that occur offline; they are contrasted to commitments to the online MUD. But on the other hand, Michael says that he sees his commitments to the MUD members as RL commitments. As I read over these transcripts, I realized he was differentiating between the MUD itself as a social structure, and the members of the community.

More specifically, though, he had just refused my binary distinction of RL and online. He points out that yes, commitments to his job or other RL contexts take precedence over his commitments to the MUD (as a place set aside for having fun). More importantly though, Michael carefully points out, the members of the MUD are not, as I suggest, separable from RL or *just as real* as RL. They *are* real-life friends, and this state of being is *not* connected to online or offline distinctions.

His correction of my question is a crucial point in the interview. He doesn't mean that the online world has somehow surpassed the reality of the offline world. Michael simply says that these two worlds (the MUD and offline) are contexts for authentic, meaningful experiences, to the point that one can equate them.

Michael understands reality as something concrete. He also has a sense that the self is naturally unified, stable, and strong, which might stem from his confident bearing and apparently strong sense of self. This allows him to trust that people are truly what they present themselves to be, and to know the Other's authentic self is to engage in dialogue, where the real self emerges. Interestingly, although Michael enjoys meeting his friends face-to-face, he does not discuss that physicality as a way to get to know them, but just as another place to meet and hang out with them.

Michael weaves a complex and sophisticated understanding of his online experiences as he talks about the authentic, singular self finding a new place to exist; and his discourse is quite consistent with his stated beliefs, in sharp contrast to many other participants. The Net is a place where one goes as an embodied self to interact with others. Importantly, it is not distinct from his offline life, just a different context for interaction. "It's different . . . but in so many ways it's the same . . . I have several good friends online who I would consider to be close friends—in fact, I don't really think of them as online friends much anymore. I think of them as close friends period."

Michael sits at the fulcrum of my conceptual continuum. He has a sense of balance and a good sense of humor about the whole thing. He doesn't take his online experiences lightly, but then again, he doesn't take them too seriously. Michael is also the only person I interviewed who did not appear to regard online communication as a means of control. I can only hazard a guess here, but I suspect that Michael has a strong sense of who he is, a concrete belief that others enact (or will eventually enact) their authentic self, and a seemingly unwavering faith in dialogue as a way to reach toward and know the "true" Other. These convictions allow him to focus on the relationships themselves, not the means by which they are achieved. As Michael says, "I think it's wonderful. Truly creative, every one can participate. It has definitely changed my life. I think it's given me more of an open mind about things. I've definitely met some wonderful people and had some interesting experiences. I can only imagine what the coming years hold."

*

I guess what I'm finding/doing in this study is debunking many myths about what happens to people online. I have assumed for a couple of years, based on what I've read about cyberspace, that people are essentially different online than off, that they experience a fragmenting of self through technology, or that they somehow exist in unique, multiple ways because of, or through, cyberspace technology.

What I'm finding is this: Sure, people might take on different personae online; they might become less shy, more confident. They might have more to say, or less. They might enjoy the freedom they feel when they can enact/perform different versions of themselves through technology. For the most part, however, these people are just carrying out their lives, using technology to facilitate their lives, going online to connect with others in various ways. They might experience a fragmenting of self, but as two participants noted, "I've never heard of anyone that had only one self" (Terri), and "My real self is so fragmented that I don't think I could tell if my online self was separate or different" (Mist). In other words, going online—for these people, at least—is not as wildly otherworldly as early writers led us to believe, when they said things such as:

> The design of cyberspace is, after all, the design of another life-world, a parallel universe, offering the intoxicating prospect of actually fulfilling—with a technology very nearly achieved—a dream thousands of years old: the dream of transcending the physical world, fully alive, at will, to dwell in some Beyond—to be empowered or enlightened there, alone or with others, and to return. (Benedikt, 1991, p. 131)

> The advent of the virtual announces the end of the body, the apocalypse of corporeal subjectivity. (Keeps, 1994, p. 4)

For the people I talked to, these popular portrayals of communication technology are greatly overstated. Yes, cyberspace is profound, and like any new or unfamiliar place, it takes some getting used to. But these experiences are not a part of another life-world located in some parallel universe outside the body. These experiences are simply another part of real life.

Drawing Boxes

I thought I could get beyond the dichotomy of real and virtual, especially when I heard these participants insisting there were other ways to frame experiences online. Why do many of us studying cyberspace use these terms as if they were distinct and opposite? Perhaps because technology seems to stand apart from nature. Perhaps because we have long wondered about, imagined, and—more recently—studied the merging of humans and machines. Perhaps because we fear that technology is changing us irrevocably, yet we fantasize that technology can further enhance our lives, take us away from dirt, disease, death.

The cyborg image is a fashionable way to think of humanity in movies, music videos, magazines, and so forth. As science catches up to science fiction, we come closer to actualizing the colloquial notion of the cyborg. Of course, in many ways, we're already cyborgs (see Haraway, 1991). We've augmented and extended our bodies with spectacles, prosthetics, and artificial organs. We've reconfigured our bodies to suit various perceived ideals using dyes, silicone, bleach, braces, and the surgeon's knife.

We can also talk about social groups as cyborgs because they experience themselves through the lens of the Other and are thus never centered purely in themselves (see Barker, 1984; Stone, 1991). In this case, the actual body may not be merged with a machine. Rather, Self, which is essentially connected to the body (the embodied self), is seen as a combination of human and machine (a worker whose output is scientifically managed, for example, or a woman who is seen only as a womb, a cleaning agent, a kitchen implement, or a sex toy).

As we enter the digital age full-force, when we begin to extend our bodies through the computer, this machine becomes the prosthetic for the mind as well as the body; as we extend even further, it becomes the backdrop for existence. And who can live in or through the machine? Only cyborgs. To comprehend the concept of the cyborg, we must dichotomize two other concepts, nature and technology. In vastly oversimplified terms, to understand what it means to be a cyborg, we must turn to what nature means, what technology means, and what the merging of the two means—other than the term *cyborg*. This is a ubiquitous word we throw about very casually in everyday talk, but it only hints at a concept far more difficult to comprehend.

Here, in cyborg space and in this text, the terms *real* and *virtual* reconvene as if they can help me make sense of what the merging of nature and technology means. (*And here, also, is where I attempt to rationalize why I am so drawn to the terms **real** and **virtual**, and why I tend to use them as binary distinctions.*)

When I try to understand how these people who spend so much time online make sense of their experiences, I am compelled to think of them (and myself) as a combination of human and machine. A cyborg's very essence is based on the fact that it is constituted through (and constitutes) the merging of nature (which we often perceive as authentic, genuine; in other words, real) and technology (which provides simulations of authenticity, reproductions of genuine articles; in other words, virtual). But I don't quite perceive the merging as complete. Rather, I perceive that real (natural) and virtual/not real (artificial) exist in a tension of opposites, a dialectical tension. Thus, I inevitably invoke the dichotomy/binary of real and virtual as I interpret and represent my own and others' experiences of being online.

When we compose both a conversation and ourselves in and through the exchange of texts, the selves that connect are encapsulated by the merging of mind, hand, and machine; yet this seems in many ways unreal. I "talk" without ever opening my mouth or using my vocal chords. I "LOL" whether or not my physical body is laughing out loud.

In addition to convincing myself that real and virtual are binary and opposing modes of being, I have been compelled to use online and offline as ways of distinguishing virtual from real. Again, I derive these categories from reading popular literature about cyberspace and adding those writers' thoughts to my own basic presumption that when we humans are engaging in meaningful life activities in computer-mediated contexts, we are merging with the machine, becoming cyborgs. More importantly, because I associate my own body with nature (genuine, authentic, natural) and the computer with technology (simulation, virtual, artificial), I connect the participants' bodies to their experiences in the same ways. I think of myself as online *or* offline, not both. I think of myself as typing on this keyboard, and although it feels as though I am really somewhere, I still know that the machine is connected to a fiber-optic cable and an electrical outlet; and if those mechanical devices do not function properly, my online being will cease to exist. I can see places through various windows on my screen, and sometimes I get lost in there. I still think of it in terms of "in there" and "out here," however, so I am inevitably trapped by my own worldview. Plus, my body constantly reminds me of its presence . . . mostly through physical pain.

Regardless of how it happens, I am imposing a false dichotomy on my participants. I can see that their experiences belie my categories of real/virtual, online/offline. Yet even as I try to give voice to *their* experiences, I find myself slipping back into *my* categories. By even addressing how they *do not* talk about "real" as opposed to "not real," I am still drawing a box, if only to describe what they have stepped out of, or where they are not. (*Perhaps this is the bane of research. It bothers me, but I write on.*)

Chapter 5

Stories of Places and Ways of Being

BETH
THINGS SEEM TO BE COMMUNICATED BETTER
THROUGH MY FINGERS THAN MY VOICE

"How much time per day do you spend online?" I asked.

"I don't know probably between 6-8 hours on weekdays and 16-18 hours on weekend days."

Wow, I thought. That seems like a lot of time online. I asked, "In your opinion, is that a lot of time?"

Beth seemed to consider this question a long time before answering. "I think for a lot of people it is but I enjoy my time online I like to meet people from all over."

"Would you spend more time online if you could?"

"Yes, sometimes I wish I could spend more time on the computer, depends on my mood you know. I really enjoy being here it's one of the best places I've been."

*

I had met Beth before, but this was my first official conversation with her. She is a twenty-year-old student at a university in the United States. By far, Beth was the most prolific, constantly available person I met online. She was, you will recall, the first person to call out to me in cyberspace. In effect, she took my hand and showed me the ropes. She taught me how to emote, encouraged me when I made mistakes, smiled and laughed a lot, and shared her online home with me to make my research easier. Before we had ended our first conversation, in fact, she had already volunteered for an official interview.

*

I asked, "What do you do mostly when you're online?"

"I'm usually in the MOO when i'm in my room," Beth replied, "but when I'm in the computer lab I go all over the place I have lots of bookmarks on my computer I just love to look aroud at everything and anything. I've had a lot of really interesting experiences online both in the moo and just searching around."

"How real are your experiences online?" I asked. This was a significant research question for me. Even so, I was asking it now because Beth seemed to contrast and conflate offline and online experiences simultaneously. It was odd—not what I expected.

"It's very real," she responded. "All my experiences online seem to be very real to me I mean it's a riot in here on the weekends when my roommates are not here because I while chatting am actually moving around and talking to myself and really getting into the experience of chatting. I had someone tell me today that they heard me this weekend in my room yelling at the computer and talking to myself."

"Why do you like hanging out here so much?"

"I can just be myself I can just type what commes to mind and hnot have to think about is as much. Things seem to be communicated better through my fingers then my voice."

I smiled to myself. Beth was so confident and assured. Obviously, I thought, she must be referring to content versus form here—her form was sometimes so difficult to follow, with all the fragments and misspellings. For her, "good" communication must not be defined by precision as much as it is defined by the thoughtfulness and content of the message.

Beth's next statement echoed my thoughts. "I can type what I'm feeling better then I can voice my;m feelings it just comes a little easier seeing things to answer then hearing and having to answer I like to worrk with my hands a lot."

I nodded, thinking of how much I enjoyed the luxury of seeing what someone wrote and considering what to say next without the pressure to reply immediately. "Yeah," I said, "I know what you mean. It's as if you can edit your thoughts before you let them loose, eh?"

```
Markham smiles.

Beth_ANN exclaims,"yes that's exactly what I mean!"

Beth_ANN smiles.
```

"How long have you been using the internet?" I asked.

"I started using the internet when it first came out. I first had Prodigy back I think it was about 9 years ago now it was really slow I spent alot of time there."

This comment was vaguely unsettling. If I calculated correctly, and if she was telling me truthfully how old she was and how long she'd been online (which is always a question in this disembodied space), she had been using the Internet seriously since she was eleven years old. This means many formative moments of her life have probably been spent online. No wonder it feels so comfortable for her. I was interrupted from my reverie by her next comment.

"I mostly hang out in this MOO now. I have many different online relationships lots of friends. I've also been asked out by a few people I've also had some very lengthy conversations with people about such issues as sex, relationships and other stuff I've also had a lot of virtual romances and virtual massage. I like everything about this moo. I've been on virtual dates with someone that was cool too."

I quickly typed the message, "What the heck is a virtual massage? And describe your virtual date!" Before I got a chance to send it, another message from Beth appeared.

"Some people have wanted me to have virtual sex but I've declined i'm a virgin."

I quickly pressed the send button to clear my outgoing message screen. I was anxious to follow up on this comment but stopped myself from typing another question, knowing Beth would eventually respond to the question I had just asked. Waiting also gave me a chance to consider the "real life" implications of virtual sex—would one really "lose" their virginity if they just talked about doing it? I wonder.

"A virtual massage is like a real one the person describes what their doing to your virtual body but if your really paying attention then you get the effect that it's a real one it's a mind thing though. There are a lot of romantic guys on this moo especially who will set up a whole scene of romance it's kind of cool I like to do it there's lots of things you can do to manipulate the rooms if you know the right commands."

While I tried to absorb the virtual massage comment, Beth continued, "a virtual date is a date where you meet the person in one place and they lead you around like you can go to a room that's movie theater a room that's a resturant and you just do the same thing as if you were just chatting in a room with someone kind of. It's really cool the one I went on this weekend we went to the Rain Forest and sat in one of the springs in the rain forest."

It all sounds so real, I thought. And so romantic. Virtual massage?! Yet at the same time, Beth is talking about manipulating rooms with various commands.

```
Beth_ANN smiles.
```

"How's that for an answer did you get the gist of it?" Beth asked. And then another message appeared, "Is that what you meant?"

```
Markham smiles.
```

"I think it was a great answer. Sounds like fun. Like a fun place to be."

I was stalling, arguing with myself about whether I should pursue this conversation or return to the protocol. So many things to ask her about, I thought. I sighed, wondering if all qualitative researchers have these dilemmas during interviews. I drummed my fingers on the keyboard for a moment, and then typed the next question on the interview protocol.

"Beth, are any of your online relationships particularly significant? How so?"

A long pause, then, "They are significant in different ways it really depends on the relationship and weather I bring it offline I like online relationships though becasue I like the attention I get from online relationships. But they don't rule my life I'm a very independent person. I like my online boyfriends you know in the sence that their cool to talk to. I like the one guy I talked to last night he's different and respectful unlike my offline ex-boyfriends who are downright rude and mean to me all the time from the day I met them a long time ago."

"Whether I bring it offline," I whispered aloud to myself. "Unlike my offline ex-boyfriends." What does she mean? Do they become more significant if they go offline? Or do they get worse if they go offline?

"How do your offline relationships compare with your online relationships?" I asked, then, as an afterthought, sent another message, "It sounds like your online boyfriends are nicer than the offline boyfriends."

After a long moment, Beth replied, "I don't know it's not that I'm ugly or anything it's just that guys here at school that I know are just you know after sex and beauty from the outside and not the way I am you know I don't wear make-up and I don't do alot of the girl stuff you know I'm not the stereotypical girl and I don't think the guys like that."

"What is it about the online relationships that seems better?"

"I don't know. I think it's probably the fact that they don't know you and can't see you it's just what you are typing their paying attention to and getting a mental picture from it's earsier to get to know a person here then in real life because it's not based on looks it's what's inside and how your expressing yourself I'm allways truthfull with guys here I let them know the way I really am so that they can make a realistic judgement about me in fact I don't hold anything tack in here."

Beth added, "this is a place where you can get to the real person and not have to overcome the obsticle of looks and having people judge you by your appearance instead of the real you."

∗

Throughout our conversation, Beth implies that her words—not her body—defines who she really is. The text gives Beth control over the presentation of self, whereas her physical presence only obscures or prevents the authentic presentation of self.

This makes intuitive sense to me in a culture in which we are bombarded with media images of "ideal" bodies, unattainable for the average human but nevertheless portrayed and perceived as a real goal to achieve through diet, exercise, colored contact lenses, plastic surgery, and silicone. These images become standards against which we measure ourselves, and they tend to demean us to ourselves. So even though Beth says, "It's not that I'm ugly or anything," she knows she doesn't fit the model image of Western beauty; "I don't wear make-up . . . I'm not the stereotypical girl."

These images are also standards used to judge others, which seems to be the more important point for Beth. She doesn't have a problem with her own body, she implies, but she knows that men will judge her based on her body. Hence, she seems to desire control over which elements of self get to be included as part of the first impression she gives others. Interestingly, Beth focuses exclusively on physical appearance as a major factor in first impressions; she never reflects on the fact that typing/spelling ability is also a standard used to judge people online. (*Or perhaps she understands this well, and chooses to present herself in this way. I have no way of knowing for certain.*)

∗

As we continued to talk, I wondered how Beth handled conversations offline. If she could express herself better through text, what were offline conversations like for her? For a moment, I regretted my decision to hold the interviews exclusively online.

"Beth," I said, following a thought. "How many of your online friends have you later met offline?"

"I've had a lot of people I've met online call me in fact I had one call me last night it's cool to talk and hear the voice of the person your chatting with." Beth said, adding, "Have you not met anyone you've chatted with?"

I replied, "No. what's it like?"

"it's jsut cool to hear the people's voices your chatting with and know the real personalities of the people behind the keyboard."

"what do you mean when you say *real personalities*?" I asked curiously, amazed at this turn of tables. Beth seemed to be contradicting herself. Earlier, she indicated that online (through text), she could express who she "really" was, without the obstacles of the voice or looks or other outward appearances, yet here she implies she can only know the real personality of an online friend when she has access to his or her offline presence. Strange.

Beth replied, "They can't say things you know some of the things that go on in real life atre different then in a MOO. Like the guy I was chatting with for awhile. He would say things some of the things he was typing didn't make sense to me until he called me. The voice he used was unique to what we had talked about you know what I mean?"

Well, no, I said to myself, "I don't know what you mean but I want to." I typed, "could you explain further?"

"I'm not sure there's another way to explain it. The voice of this guy was one I could get used to calling me every night. But he couldn't type some of the things he meant. it's just unique because these are people you have no clue about or what they sound like and they can't say things you know except in real life."

I could tell she was getting at something important, but I couldn't figure out how to get her to articulate it more clearly. (*Or maybe I just wasn't getting it. In fact, it wasn't until a few weeks after the interview that I was able to make sense of it.*)

I tried another route, "So how do you end up meeting these people offline. How do you decide?"

"ok, well the first guy I met was in America Online and I was just chatting with this guy and we were getting along really cool so he gave me his address and phone nmber and I gave him mine so we both signed off and he called me we talked for about 2 hrs. and then hae sent me a picture and I sent him a picture and we talked every Sunday night for about three months and we chatted online too. he was really cool I liked him we were actually going to meet in the summer but then we lost contact he got a girlfriend and it all ended.

"Then there's the two guys who I did chat with and did meet," Beth continued. "The first one that I met was just mean and the second was a flop."

"What happened with the first guy?"

Beth replied, "he was just mean to me didn't talk to me. The second guy came 45 miles and wanted to take me to McDonald's down the street he just wasn't my type he didn't shower very offten because he's really from Europe and over here going to school I just wasn't expencting what I met you know it just wasn't cool." After a few moments, Beth added, "I would consider an online relationship. it would be cool to do you know I'm one for new experiements."

＊

Beth and I talked for almost four hours that night. Later, I spent a lot of time with the interview transcript, trying to make sense of seemingly contradictory and confusing statements. Beth focused on embodiment even as she denied its significance to one's authentic self. In short, at the same time that Beth doesn't want others to see her through the bodied lens, she wants to be able to judge others using all their parts, body and voice included. Moreover, she implies that only by seeing them face-to-face can she know with certainty who they are.

It makes sense to me that offline relationships would be more meaningful for Beth, but the more crucial point she is making is that the self of the Other must be perceived offline (through the body) in order to be seen as authentic. She wants to know, in an embodied sense, who these guys really are, which directly contrasts with how she believes her self is best known by others.

I suspect this creates a dilemma for Beth. She wants to be accepted for who she is and excludes her body as a part of who she is online, but when her online relationships develop and become meaningful, she begins to realize that they are merely online. They are not satisfactory because they are exclusively online, and therefore are not as fulfilling as a real-life relationship would be. Yet when she takes the relationships offline, they don't work—perhaps because it is a different context, and a different type of relationship. In a sense, Beth is attempting to bring relationships from one context, where a certain type of dialogue has been established between two textual beings, into another context, where two bodies must establish a new, different relationship because they are different performances of selves.

As I pored over the transcripts, I concluded that, basically, Beth wants reality both ways. She want to be able to control the way others see her, to take away those elements of her self she thinks are irrelevant or will unnecessarily bias the other's perception of the self; but she wants to know others in their entirety. Beth's conception of reality seems rather solipsistic; in effect, she appears to believe that she is capable of seeing things as they really are, but others are not. She does not seem to acknowledge Other's dialogic role in the constitution of self.

Beth doesn't reflect on her inconsistencies. When I think of her in a more holistic way, I believe she wants to feel needed and appreciated; being online facilitates this connection better than being offline. In the MOO, Beth is an important member of a community, and people depend on her. I also think Beth just wants to be with others in an embodied way and be accepted and appreciated—both as a mind that thinks and communicates and exists through the fingertips and as an embodied being who should be taken for what she is, not for what she should be. It seemed that, for Beth, being with others in this "place" is more than just communicating via an electronic medium. Through the exchange of texts, a much more complex life of relationships with others is constructed—a life centered around being a part of a meaningful community.

Talking with Beth reminds me of how difficult it can be to live in a society where commercialized and idealized images often overshadow and diminish the richness of our actual embodied lives where we sometimes live in fear that we can't live up to the standards. No wonder she spends so much time online.

SHEOL
CYBERSPACE IS MY LIFELINE TO THE WORLD; I AM MANY THINGS HERE

Hi Annette, you should contact these people for interviews. They said they might be interested. Hope this helps!

genie@***.***.***

007156@**.**.***.***

Sheo005@***.***

Gargoyle@**.***.***

Gotta Run!

TTFN,

k

I don't know how Kelly does it; people just seem to open up to her. If not for Kelly's connections and my own blind luck, I'm not sure how I would have obtained participants for the study. Kelly even got me a self-proclaimed hacker, Sheo005. I had been trying to nail down an interview time with her for weeks. Maybe she's nervous about the interview, I thought, as I waited patiently for a message to appear in my

electronic inbox. She certainly seemed suspicious in her last email message, where
she wrote,

```
I am intrested in talking to:) Could you be more spesific
about what questions you will ask? Also, will you need to use
my name? Just let me know when you want to talk, and I will try
to accomidate! :)
```

```
talk to you soon!! Sheol
```

I wrote back and reassured her I would not need to know her name or address
or any other identifying information, and it took her two weeks to reply. Maybe
she's just disorganized. Other than the delayed responses, I was looking forward to
talking with Sheol. She seemed very enthusiastic.

Finally, Sheol agreed on an interview date. Early one afternoon, she emailed
me a message to "meet in IRC at 7 pm."

Well, it was a start. At least we had a time, even if I didn't exactly know the
place; "Let's meet in IRC" is almost like saying "Let's meet in Seattle." I emailed
Sheol back and asked, "Where in IRC do you want to meet?"

Three hours later, Sheol replied, "I'll be in DALnet! See you there :)"

Good, I thought. This should be easy enough to find. Finally, an interview
with a hacker! I couldn't wait.

At 6:45 P. M. EST, I logged into IRC to find DALnet. When the program showed
me the choices for places to go in IRC, I stared at the screen, dumbfounded. Aloud,
I muttered, "DALnet. Right. Twenty . . . six of them."

I quickly gathered that DALnet was a type of IRC, not a place *in* IRC. Through
DALnet, I could go to twenty-six different places, including South Wales; Bristol,
UK; Sunnydale, CA; or Espoo, FI (in EU). Randomly, I began to open various loca-
tions. Two hundred chatrooms in Bristol: #Teenworld, #Rattle_Heads, #sexpics. Okay,
I thought, maybe I should try someplace closer to home. I clicked on Sunnydale, CA.

I stared. Over 1,300 chatroom titles scrolled up on the screen; #jesus_loves_you,
#amputees, #trailertrash. I laughed out loud. "I can't believe this is happening!" I
exclaimed to myself, and opened up my email program to send a message to Sheol.

"Sheol, where are you? I'm having trouble finding you. Could you let me know
which DALnet you're on?"

Shortly, Sheol replied, "I am an avid chatter in the Le Café, if you want to
try that :)"

I went back to IRC and looked for Le Café. After about ten minutes, I wasn't too surprised that I couldn't find it. I let out my breath slowly, counted to ten, then sent another email message to Sheol. "I can't find you in DALnet and I can't find Le Café. Help! I'm feeling like a serious newbie. Maybe you should try to find me. Tell you what. I'm going to Chicago's DALnet and I'll create a room called #interview. Try to find me, okay? Yikes! Sorry I'm being so dense!"

I switched my screen back to the IRC program, typed the commands that would create a room, and waited. Ten minutes later, a character named "Xfile" appeared. I assumed this was Sheol.

```
<Annette> "Hi Xfile. Is that you Sheol?"

<Xfile> "Greetings! Yes! I am so glad that I found you!"
```

"I can't believe I got here! Should we just stay here?" I said, wondering whether Sheol would be uncomfortable outside what I perceived was her normal IRC setting.

Sheol said, "Sure. I just fixed it so people can't come into this room:)"

As I was typing a reply, more text from Sheol appeared, "This is way cool *LOL* I have never been asked for an interview before:)"

"Great!" I said, referring to the privacy of the room, which was something I didn't know how to do yet. She typed very quickly. I'd have to get used to this context and pace, I thought.

I quickly finished another message, "I guess I should tell you some official stuff before we get started. I guarantee I will never use your real or online name and I won't give any hints about who you are or where you live or anything and you can stop the interview at any time....doesn't that sound scary?! :-)"

Sheol replied enthusiastically, "I love it! I won't leave though:) You might be able to use my nick. Depends on the questions:) I love talking about the net! *LOL*"

"Cool!" I said, then added, "Okay, question #1. How much time per day do you spend online?"

"On a busy day 8-12 hours. Depends on what I'm into. I spend a lot of time on the net:) It is my life line to the world."

I loved her enthusiasm—I could almost see her bouncing up and down. As I typed my next question, I smiled. I realized I was going to enjoy this interview very much. "Would you spend more time online if you could?"

"Yes, if I could do with out sleep, I would be on all the time."

Yikes, I thought. I can't imagine ever getting to that point.

"*LOL*" I typed. "What drew you to the net?"

"No friends on campus last year. My car broke, so I could not go home on the weekends. So I found the chatlines. This year I have real life friends, but I still charish mytime with my net friends."

I asked, "what was it like at first?"

"Combersome at first, then it gets easeier:) Truth to tell, I hated chatlines the first time I was on one. Then I found one, and created an identity to fit me. I met people from all over the world, and I became an addict. I am better now I don't spend every wakeing moment on the net."

I wondered how I was ever going to follow the interview protocol. Sheol typed very rapidly and kept making intriguing comments, all of which I wanted to follow up on. So I went with my gut. "What would define an addict?"

Sheol finally paused, giving me a chance to catch my breath and take a sip of coffee. "An addict is someone who lets the net rule their lives."

"Can you give me an example?" I prompted.

"It becomes their lives . . ." Another pause, then Sheol added, "An example is: When I would wakeup, I would log in, then goto class and log in there, then after class, I would litterly run from class tomy room to login there. I would chat until 3-4 in the morning."

I replied, "Interesting. How long did you do that?"

"Over a year. Then I opened myeyes and saw what the net could be used for. Until this point all I did on the net is chat and surf."

"Why do you think addiction happens?"

Sheol waited a long moment, then answered, "On the net you can be who or what ever you want to be. That is the trap! when you want your cyberlife to be your real life. That's what happened to me. I became a very popular (I know that sounds conseeded) figuar on the line I called home. I am ruled by the right side of my brain, so I liked the idea of being that personality."

Sheol went on, "My cyber friends and I liked to roleplay . . . we went on fantastic adventurs over the net. The only limit was our imagineations. Not anything like in the real world. I am shy by nature . . . I am also a big fan of Shahspear langue. I can use that style of speaking, and not be shy about on the net:)"

Hmmm. I quickly switched to another screen, where I was working on a research journal. I typed a quick note to myself: "Interviewing Sheol—wonder to what extent Sheol separates real life from cyberlife. She seems to imply an extreme/sharp division here. Real versus not real, 'when you want your cyberlife to be your real life'. . . wow."

As Sheol and I continued to talk, I found myself sliding into an easy conversational style, completely unlike previous interviews. So many things struck me as I listened. Sheol typed very quickly and phonetically, yet she was very expressive, capturing many of the nuances of her life online in intriguing statements. In another way, perhaps related to her spelling, she seemed very young. Sheol was just so excited about this whole Internet thing.

"Sheol, what makes your online relationships so significant?"

"I have thought about this a great deal," she replied immediately. "You can tell people your darkest secrets, and not fear being judged. They can not see you, so they are speaking to you because they want to just based on what you have to say. If you have a problem, they are there for you . . . no matter what. A few of my net friends went to Georgia from New York becuase their friend was feeling suisidel (my spelling sucks!)"

"Yeah," I murmured to the screen, "it does suck, but it ain't no big thing."

I assured her, "That's okay. :-)." Then I asked, "How do your online relationships fit into your everyday life?"

"I keep them seprate as much as possible."

I asked, "Of the people you have met online, how many have you met IRL?"

"I have met two IRL. They were and are just as delightful IRL as they are on the net. I would love to meet all of my net friends."

"How old are you?" I asked, even though I knew the answer might not correspond to any traditional measure.

"I have dwelled in mortal flesh for 23 years now" Sheol replied, and then added, "I love the drmatic:)" I grinned at the screen.

"How committed do you feel to the relationships you develop online?"

Sheol replied, "define committed? as in girlfriends on the net? I have never gone that route, there is only so much you can do with a computer."

What? I read her last comment again. Girlfriends? Huh? All of a sudden, I realized I had taken many things for granted in our conversation, and with just one word many issues were becoming startlingly salient. I was surprised at myself as much as I was surprised by the statement. Why was I all of a sudden wondering about Sheol's sexual preferences? Why was this even an issue? I realized I wanted to ask a different set of questions; questions that would make her gender or sexuality an issue. Then, just as suddenly, I felt embarrassed and chagrined. It shouldn't matter, I thought. I quickly finished typing the question I had been working on, and we resumed our conversation.

Sheol went on to describe various levels of commitment with online friends and different types of communities she was a member of.

"How would you describe your sense of self or identity online?"

"I am known as Lord Sheol. Lord of the Underworld, where all souls go when one passes to the after life. This identity is many things to me. He is the hopeless romantic, the feirce defender of our rights. Out spoken on all issues. He is the philsopher, and a poet. Through him I express my religios views. He feeds the right side of my brain."

I stared confusedly at the words on the screen. Wait a second. Sheol was a girl, right? I typed several words, erased them, retyped them. Why is this such a big deal? Does it matter?

No, I tried to tell myself, none of this really matters. You're online; people gender swap all the time! But I couldn't stop thinking. I couldn't stop the questions forming in my head as I stared at the screen. I scrolled backward through the conversation. Is Sheol a female with a male character online? Is Sheol a guy? How could I interview someone for almost two hours and not know their gender?

I forced myself to type a question, "how would you compare your online identity with your RL identity/sense of self?"

"I treat Lord Sheol as a differnt personality, so I can keep this world seporate from the real one."

"How do you do that?" I asked.

"When I am at the computer, I am Lord Sheol. Or I should say when I am in cyberspace, I am Sheol. When I am away from the puter and cyberspace, then I am me. I know it sounds funny to hear someone talking and refering to himself as two people *LOL*"

"Not really, especially considering that you're sort of three people," I replied, taking note of the "himself" in the message. Sheol's a male, I decided. I took a deep breath and settled back into the interview, feeling a peculiar combination of relief and chagrin.

*

As we continued to talk, I realized I had made at least one stereotypical assumption about Sheol, or Lord Sheol, as he is properly known. When my friend Kelly originally sent me the names of possible participants, she indicated that two of them were hackers—one female and one male. In the frenzy of trying to schedule interviews, however, the names and corresponding genders got lost in my brain somewhere. So when Sheol began sending effusive email messages to me, I made the wrong connection. I assumed that anyone who was so outwardly emotional and expressive had to be female. In all my interviews to this point, I had noticed that self-proclaimed females used more emotional markers than self-proclaimed males. Women seemed to use more smiley faces, exclamation points, ellipses, and phrases like "Annette smiles" to add nonverbals to their talk. And I noticed they used more tags, such as "you know what I mean?" or "does that make sense?" Sheol was the most expressive person I had encountered yet, putting smiley faces all over the place and laughing out loud even more than I do (which is a lot). I assumed, without thinking about it too much—or perhaps guided by my understanding of gendered discourse as discussed by Herring (1993), who studies gender markers in computer-mediated communication, or Tannen (1990), who addresses gender differences in communication styles—that Sheol's use of language corresponded to Sheol's gender.

This was the wrong assumption to make.

Months after the interview, I realized something else about this and the other interviews. I did not make race or gender an issue in any of the interviews. I didn't ask anyone about their race or gender—I didn't think it was important. Yet with the appearance of a single word—*girlfriend*—in one interview, gender became an inescapable, paramount issue to me. I couldn't stop thinking about it. In effect, gender became an issue precisely because I had ignored it up to that point.

(*Interestingly, race never became an issue, perhaps because no one messed with my stereotyping presumptions. Indeed, I visualized each of the participants from my own center; in my mind's eye, they were middle-class, Caucasian, young, and attractive. I don't admire this realization, and I'd rather not own it; but my description models a normative, primarily white way of perceiving the world as if these features are the default, the center, the norm. Certainly if online characters provide descriptions of themselves, these will guide others' perceptions, but if they don't provide a description ... I'm not sure how to make sense of my own behavior, but I suspect I'm not the only one to make this mistake, online or offline.*)

Actually, the gender issue passed quickly, and Lord Sheol and I talked late into the night. He loved the idea of being interviewed and wrote voraciously about many topics. Hacking was his current pursuit, and since I was very interested in how hackers experience and make sense of technology, we spent a long time chatting about what it takes to become a hacker, what kind of community is built on the myths and secrets of hacking, and what it feels like to actually perform a hack. Sheol's understanding of the Internet emerged from an intense daily engagement with and in it. Talking with others, being with others, playing games, exploring, flirting; Sheol did all of these things simultaneously in a layered, multiplicitous world of windows.

*

"So are you Lord Sheol now, since you're at the computer?"

"Yes, and no. Truely if I were Sheol at this point in time, the flowery speech I would use:) And rearrange the things to be said like I just did. Only with thee and thous, doth and hath's. understand?"

Hmmm. I thought I might understand, so I tried it out. "Thou speaks of thyself as if here and yet not here, Sheol and yet not Sheol . . . I think you speakest well, but I am not certain understand I thee." I thought I should feel silly sending a sentence like that, but for some reason I didn't. If I really slaughtered the Shakespearean form Sheol was speaking of, I didn't think he would mind.

"The other thing about it, is you also know whom I really am. The others I speak with usally do not. They will only know me as LS." A pause, then Sheol added, "Pray tell m'lady, where hath thee learned the tounge of the well spoken?"

I replied, "oh, thouest flatters me with thy pleasant and generous nature. I speaketh only as a novice, most willing to become well spoken."

Sheol returned to the interview. "I have had to go ferther than that now. Now if I am gleaning information about gameing, or if I am speaking with someone about it, I use the name ******** [I've deleted his nickname], because I do not exsist as the UFOs do not:)"

"what do you mean, you do not exist?"

"Neah m'lady, thou hath the heart of a poet deep inside:)"

He continued, "I mean I do not exsist as ******** as the goverment tells us the UFOs do not exsist. But we all or at least I think they do exsist. I have not left any trails on the net as this name."

"Hmmm, would that be your hacker name, you mean? Is hacking what you mean when you say "gaming"? Not wanting to leave trails, I mean? And, M'lord, you are most gracious, but thou art the poet, not I. :-)" Suddenly, it felt like we had begun to dance, swirling among and into these simultaneous conversations.

"Yes, I do not even chat with this name. Hacking is the game, yes . . . And Poets we are all, just some listen to the poitry in our hearts more than others m'lady:)"

"ah... then, indeed, I would be a poet."

✳

When I first analyzed this interview, I thought it would provide support for a chapter about how computer users distinguish between the real and the virtual. Sheol consistently contrasted real life and online experiences and friends. He talked about his cyberlife as compared to real life. He mentioned his net friends as compared to his RL friends. And several times, he said he tried to keep these two lives as separate as possible.

Sheol also strongly distinguished between his online self and his Self (presumably his understanding of his authentic self). He described his self ("when I'm away from the puter I am me" or "you know whom I really am") as different and separate from Lord Sheol. He indicated that he was being "himself" (not Lord Sheol) in this interview first because if he were truly Lord Sheol, he would be using more flowery speech and second because, I knew who he really was, so he was the "real me."

Perhaps Sheol is referring to a distinction between the self we might perceive ourselves to be and the self others perceive. Or perhaps he is referring to two distinguishable, separate identities, each of whom lives a series of different experiences. Regardless, he enacts both selves simultaneously throughout the interview.

You see, he *does* use flowery speech, weaving in and out of poetic language; and even as he says he is not Lord Sheol at the moment, he had emphasized earlier that whenever he is at the computer he is Lord Sheol. In short, he attempts to separate his identities, but in actuality, all of them mesh together into "experience," just as our various roles and identities blend together to form what we perceive to be coherent lived experience (as long as we don't have multiple personalities).

As I spent more time thinking about how he talked about experiencing online technologies, I realized several things that complicate the issue of self, especially as it relates to a sense of reality: At some points, Sheol uses *real* as a convenient term that demarcates those experiences that occur offline. Meanwhile, Sheol describes *real* as a matter of degree directly related to a level of information/knowledge, particularly when speaking of other things or people exclusively in online contexts. In other words, the more he knows about something or someone, the more real it or they become. Sheol seems to distinguish his online experiences along a continuum from less to more real. Stated differently, the reality of others—and more specifically, their subjectivity—is not a static condition as much as it is a matter of degree. However, Sheol's own self seems separate from this continuum. As a hacker, he might be elusive, and as Lord Sheol, he might be poetic; but he sees his own self as singular and constant.

✳

"Are you ever afraid of being a hacker?"

Sheol asked, "You mean afriad of getting caught? or being a hacker?"

Good question. "Hmmmm . . . maybe both."

Sheol's reply came very quickly. "Getting caught, yes. That is why I have not yet tried a hack. I am learning how to hide on the net when I am finished with that, then I will do a rightios hack. Of being a hacker, yes somewhat. Power co11 corupts, and when you can get information when you want it, that is power. Power that can translate into the real world."

I asked, "How does information = power?"

"Information is the key to everything we do in life. How one weilds the information, is how we get places in life."

$$*$$

Information is power, yes. But information is power over others through knowledge. For Sheol, naming plays a vital role in this process, as does personal information that can be linked to someone's physical presence. Early in the interview, Sheol said that I knew who he "really was" because I knew his real (authentic) name and email address, which means that I could follow an information trail back to his physical body. Especially online, he emphasizes, "Your name is everything. If it does not catch the eye, or is not original, no one will ever talk with you." On the other hand, the absence of identifying marks such as online or offline names and information is crucial when hacking, because the goal is to be unnoticed, not real, nonexistent from the point of view of the other (i.e., the hackee). If Sheol wants to leave no trace of his existence, he uses a false IP (Internet Provider) address and nickname. *(To me, it seems an elaborate game of hide and seek, but that doesn't begin to describe what it means for Sheol.)*

$$*$$

"How one wields the information, is how we get places in life," Sheol said.

The whole thing seems so unimaginative, I thought. As if information can be equated with knowledge. Even so, I couldn't keep from smiling at the screen, because Sheol writes with wonderfully innocent insight. "You mean like on movies such as *The Net* or *Hackers*?" I asked. It seemed an obvious question, really, considering the central role of computers and information and power in movies like these.

"Yes. A lot of it is Hollywood show, but the things that take place in movies like *Hackers* can be done."

"Hmmm . . . do you think that someday the net will feel like it does now in movies or books?" Then, as an afterthought, I added, "(feel like or look like, I mean)."

Sheol's response was immediate "Oh yes, someday it will. I have no doubt of this."

I wondered how Sheol felt when he was moving through different online contexts, looking for information or entering forbidden systems. So many movies and films portrayed cyberspace as a three-dimensional, visual space. I knew much of it was facilitated by virtual reality programming and equipment, but even in text-only spaces, I often visualized physicality. "What does it feel like when you're hacking? Or maybe I mean more specifically, what does it *look* like to you?"

"When comeing up to a system, it looks just like irc, or a mud. It is all text and sysmbols." A pause, then Sheol continued, "Once in side it's mostly the same."

I was trying to work the conversation around to a discussion of place. I wanted to know if Sheol conceptualized any of his various online contexts as places. But I was trying not to ask leading questions. Finally, after rewording and backspacing over several messages, I gave up, and just asked the question I wanted to ask, open-ended or not. "So it doesn't feel like you're in any sort of landscape?"

Sheol replied immediately, "Nope, its all just words and symbols."

"Does cyberspace feel like a place to you?"

"Yes, somtimes it does feel like at others no."

Hmmm. Seemed inconsistent. Sometimes it's just words and symbols. But sometimes it feels like a place. I looked back at the questions. Could be the questions. Maybe landscape is not the same as place. "Oh yeah, novel insight, Annette." I said sarcastically to the screen. I sighed and wondered vaguely if I had any clue what I was trying to get at. Okay, try another question. "How about when you're in IRC? Do you visualize the other people you meet or talk with?"

Sheol said, "I thing of it as like talking withmy computer *LOL*"

I said, "Talking with your computer? Can you give me an example?"

"I think of it as the computer asking me questions right now. That way I do not have to think of it as someone else I am talking to."

That's interesting. Why would he not want to think of the other person he's talking to? What purpose did that serve? I leaned back in my chair, suddenly feeling the stiffness that came after sitting poised over a keyboard for two hours.

He added, "After I chat with someone for a few times, then they become real to me."

"So the person becomes real when you think of them as real?" I asked.

"It usually takes me some time to decide what their personality is like."

"Hmmm . . . how do you define 'real?'"

"Real is when they reach out to me. it is very hard to explain."

I asked, "Can you think of a specific instance that would help me see what you mean?"

"I guess it is when I can see a part of myself in them."

I was stumped by that statement. I was trying to think of a response when he asked, "does that help?"

I settled for my standard and uninspired, "wow." I knew I couldn't leave it at that, so I added, "It helps. It is very poetic."

<Xfile> <blushes>

*Annette smiles

I immediately added, "Oops, sorry, didn't mean to imply I was laughing at your blushing. . . . Can you describe it more? I don't quite grasp it yet."

"*LOL* that is quite all right, m'lady, all my friends laugh when I blush! Tis nothing." He went on, "When I can see a part of myself in them, they become real pepole to me. When they show feelings and compassion. A computer can not do such . . ."

Intrigued, I asked, "What of yourself must be in them for them to be real? Your real self? Your Lord Sheol self?"

"A little of both, they must be intouch with what is out there. Not be satisfied to be told no this can't be done. Ask why. To see lifes illusions and to relize that we all live in glass houses."

"Hmmm . . ." I pondered. "So what if that subject never came up? For instance, you don't know about me and those issues. Am I real?"

Sheol replied, "Yes, because I have done email with you . . . I know your real name. I know that you are a friend of Kelly's you are at perdu."

"Oh. I think I understand. There must be either a connection to the physical world, which for me there is, or . . ."

Sheol exclaimed, "Yes, that is it! Thank you:)"

I continued, "or there must be a sort of mental connection if you don't have a physical connection? Like a spiritual thing?"

"Yes! Sometimes it is very. Like I said people discuss things in cyberspace that they would not dream of telling anyone IRL." A pause, then he continued. "Some of my darkest moments were spent on the net . . . When you have no one to turn to but yourself when in the throws of depression, all kinds of things are told when someone says tell me what is wrong, maybe I can help. I have my entire furnal planned out, and on disk. None but my closest friends know that, but I feel totally comfortable to tell such things on the net."

I reflected on his statements. "You must really feel free to be yourself online."

Sheol replied, "That goes back to I am myself, but I am not. *LOL*"

✳

Sheol offers a complex and intriguing analysis of how others become more real to him. Interestingly, if others are more like the self, they are more real. This is no surprise when I consider that we all seem to act as if we occupy the center of the universe. Many scholars (e.g., Bakhtin, 1981; Holquist, 1990) contend that we require the Other to know the self; that we see ourselves through others' responses and relations with us (Bateson, 1972). Yet, mostly, we begin with implicitly self-centered assumptions: we believe *we* are real in any context, online or off, but we are uncertain whether *others* are real unless we can see or hear them (as Beth discusses), or we assume that when others are more like us, they are more real (Sheol). I suspect we all do this, to a degree. (*Of course, I know this because I think I am the center of the universe, eh?*)

Sheol indicates that, as the other becomes more like a person he would describe as himself, or when he finds a common connection between self and other, they become more real to him. In this sense, he is using real to denote authenticity and genuineness. He appears to be searching for the essence of the other, and wanting to see a reflection of his own. But until he sees himself, he will simply be talking with the computer, not an Other.

Of course, this adds another intriguing twist. As Sheol described how others progress from less to more real, he gave the computer an important degree of subjectivity in the process. Whereas most participants talked about their computers as machines or tools that facilitate the technology that helps connect them to a resource or a place, Sheol anthropomorphized the machine, giving it the role of mediator or facilitator between self and other. The computer is an entity that can serve as the proxy for Other until Sheol decides to connect to them directly (which would still be *through* the computer, but the computer's role would shift to a conduit, presumably).

This seems to provide him with a measure of control over interaction. As he describes the process, talking to the computer appears to make him more comfortable, or perhaps less attached: "That way I don't have to think of it as another person I am talking to." Sheol has mastery over the computer and its programs, and he can effectively maneuver through its technology to control other computers and/or systems. In fact, that is part of the lure of hacking for him. (*Probably much like it is for the hackers Turkle (1984) interviewed, most of whom speak of their connection with the computer in the same way.*) So if the computer is the "voice" asking him questions, or talking with him on chatlines, these interactions fall into his jurisdiction and give him a feeling of control.

Sheol lives many meaningful moments of his life online, and spends upwards of 50 percent of his time there. And if cyberspace is a significant context within which relationships and life gets carried out, it only makes sense that, in this context, things and people take on different levels of reality or, more precisely, authenticity.

As technology continues to become a bigger part of our everyday lives, our connotative meanings of "real" may change significantly. For Sheol, who has integrated online communication into many aspects of his life, the term *real* marks experiences that occur offline. Yet the qualified term—*more* real, *less* real—measures degrees of authenticity; and authenticity is measured by two things—information (which is equated to knowledge of the Other) and likeness (as in resemblance to the self's abilities to think and feel).

Although Sheol indicated a desire to control the extent to which people know him or appear real to him, he has a bigger desire to control the flow of information. His primary reason for hacking is to control where information goes, what happens to it, and who has access to it. Actually, Sheol says that everyone who seeks information should have access to it.

Control of information flow, he says, "is an awesome power that today many of us weild. The concept of hacking is much the same as being a Jedi. In the right hands, it can do much good, in the wrong hands . . ." During the interview, as he trailed off here it began to occur to me that he was any young person wanting to make a difference in the world. In a sense, he's like any of us wanting to be able to master some ability, control the output of our labor, and make things better. Sheol is very principled in this regard, and he holds tight to his convictions. (*I admire that . . . and, I guess I want a lot of us to believe we are Jedi knights who can change the world.*) "In the truest sence," Sheol says, "a hacker is some one that wants information for all. There would be no sercerts. I do not wish to break computers, I don't even want people to know I have been there."

✳

```
<Annette> ah m'lord, methinks I tire, though the time has
flown.

<Xfile> Fair thee well m'lady, and may God watch o'er thee!

<Annette> Ah, grace me with one more answer, Sheol: What do
you think about cyberspace?

<Xfile> Cyberspace is the most important thing to happen to
human kind so far. With this people can share ideas and
concepts that may not normally be thought of. Tonight I was
```

talking with a guy from Russia. That would never have been possible in years passed. It is hard to hate when you get to know people not countrys. (not that I hate the Russians)

<Annette> I know what you're getting at.

<Xfile> Here in cyberspace we can not judge on skin color, creed, religion, or looks unless we are allowed into that world.

<Xfile> The beautiful thing is: If you have a problem, someone out there knows how to help you. Weather it be just an ear to listen, or something that can be phyicly fixed.

<Annette> Ah, thy words have blessed my meager study thus far.

<Xfile> Who, my words? *LOL* Do not put to much stock in my praddle m'lady, for I am just one man:)

<Xfile> It has been fun, thank you:)

<Annette> Shall I meet thee again, m'lord, in a virtual forest of poetic exchange? Thou mayest be yet only one man, but thy words have meant much to me. Thank you!

<Annette> I mean, If I need to follow up, I'll email you, is that okay?

<Annette> LOL

<Xfile> Please do, and keep me updated on the paper:) Your soul sings to me m'lady.

<Xfile> and you would be a smashing hit on the line I go to if you would wish to meet my other friends:)

<Annette> Smashing hit? why?

<Xfile> Why thou art a charming chattest m'lady:)

<Annette> Oh, M'lord, thou makest my cheeks burn! But carpel tunnel is taking over my mind, and I must go shortly

<Xfile> What a lovely shade m'lady, thou doth bless me with thine presence:) *LOL*

<Annette> thou are a most kindly and gentle man. If thou could see me, thouest would see m'lady laughing. Good night, then.

<Xfile> Fair you well m'lady til next we meet, and may thy dreams bring you comfort:)

<Annette> bye!

<Xfile> Good night:)

<Annette> thanks, I'll probably dream of knights in cyberspace

<Annette> LOL!

<Xfile> *LOL* A knight am I?

<Annette> oh yes, m'lord, a dark knight with a deep soul and a good heart.

<Xfile> Thou hath pegged me well m'lady. Now away with you, for other wise I shall keep you til morings light:)

<Annette> yes, m'lord...

Session Close: Thu Mar 20 00:16:29 1997

TERRI
MEDIATION, AND ACCESS TO IT, IS EMPOWERMENT;
I PHYSICALLY CRAVE IT

I was surfing on the Web one night, mostly wasting valuable time, when I happened upon an intriguing online journal called *Women and Performance Quarterly*. At first, I was drawn to it by the title of Issue 17, *Sexuality and Cyberspace*. The specific article titles pulled me further in, along with fascinating graphics and eerie moving artwork. I glanced through the articles, thinking about various issues of embodiment, gender, and cyberspace. "Performing the Digital Body—A Ghost Story," by Theresa M. Senft; "Turing, My Love," by Matthew Ehrlich; "On Space, Sex, and Stalkers," by Pamela Gilbert. The next time I looked up, two hours had passed.

I was fascinated, needless to say, and on impulse I wrote an email message to the guest editor, Theresa M. Senft, complimenting her on this wonderful collection of essays and asking her if she would like to participate in my study. Several weeks passed, and I assumed the absence of a reply meant, "No, thanks." Actually, Terri wanted to say "Yes, of course!" but, as she explained later, she had experienced a systems crash. We eventually found a space in our schedules to talk in my and Beth's room at Diversity University.

```
Terri says, "Okay. How shall we start?"

You say, "well, let me give you some official sounding pre-
interview stuff:"

Terri exclaims, "okie dokie!"

You say, "I guarantee that I will not ever reveal your ad-
dress/name/location. I also guarantee that I will delete any
references that might give a reader clues about where you
live, who you are, or where you work."

You ask, "You can disconnect from this interview at any time
and I will not bother you again. Do you mind if I archive this
conversation for later analysis and possible publication?"

Terri says, "sounds good. but you also have my permission to
use my identiity for anything I say. I'm fine being on record;
record away."

You exclaim, "Thanks. And can I just say that I have been
looking very forward to meeting you. You are a fantastic
writer!"

Terri exclaims, "you are such a sweetie. If you tell me I am
rich and thin, too, we can get married!"

Markham laughs!
```

Terri works for Prodigy, an online service provider, where she writes a column called "Baud Behavior." She's also a doctoral candidate at New York University's Department of Performance Studies; a prolific writer in various online arenas; a guest editor of *Women and Performance Quarterly*; a reviewer for the feminist journal *SIGNS*; an active member of the WELL and ECHO, two of the best-known communities online; and a dominatrix in another online service. To put herself through college, she worked as a phone-sex operator. (*Incidentally, she's also a wonderful, open, and engaging person. I feel lucky to have met her.*)

Of all the people I interviewed, Terri was the most candid about her experiences in both online and offline contexts. When I asked her again recently if she wanted me to use her real name, she responded immediately, "I have this weird belief that since the Net is a space of writing, people should 'own their own words.' Unless, of course, they request you grant them anonymity. But I have no anonymity, for I am a brazen hussy."

Terri is also highly reflexive about her identity and performance of self in various contexts, which makes sense given her research interests in feminist theory, performance studies, and technology. In addition to talking with me in a formal interview, Terri gave me access to several essays she had written or participated in as well as to her website. Some of the conversation below is supplemented by these resources, all of which are included in the bibliography.

✳

"What does the Internet mean to you?"

Terri said, "I'm assuming you don't want a technical answer here, let me think." After a moment, her answer appeared on my screen. "Truthfully? The internet gave me guts. It allowed me to write people I had never met to ask them to read my book. It allowed me to realize my dream of NEVER wearing pantyhose to a job. It has helped me understand that I can move anywhere and still be connected to my friends and lovers. I know the phone can do those things too, but the phone means very very different things to me than the net."

I asked, "What about the net makes it so unique or different (say, from the phone, or face-to-face conversation)?"

Terri replied, "I really believe that online experiences (for me) are similar to offline, with this one major exception—online life has a paper trail. I try to capture every long conversation I have online. I find myself reading over what just happened. I like that feeling. I wish I was videotaping my offline life for examination. It would save me therapy bills! haah!"

Markham laughs!

"Can you imagine?" Terri asked.

"Yes. I can imagine how quickly I'd end up in therapy trying to examine and analyze my every move . . . yikes!!!"

Immediately, Terri responded, "I'm already there, so for me, it would be like mother's little helper, I swear."

I laughed aloud. "The image cracks me up! You know, it would be the basis of a great novel called *Terri's Little Helper.*"

"Yeah," Terri said, "It could be directed in the film version by woody allen, starring some nutty young chick . . ."

※

When the interview began, I assumed we would be talking about Terri's online experiences as they *related to* her regular life. I soon realized we were actually talking about Terri's life, period. For Terri, life online is not a reflection of, a reproduction or, or a simulation of real life or even offline life. Online and offline are two different modalities in which living one's life just happens. Roughly, one is based in text and the other is based in the body. But these distinctions blur significantly for Terri, not just because she spends a great deal of time online, but also, as she says, because "cybernetics is a condition, not a life-style choice. If you are disabled, use a sex toy, utilize telephone messaging services, are chemically dependent in any way, if you have sent e-mail or keyed a bank ATM lately, then you are, yourself, a cyborg—a body containing both organic and technological components."

As well as collapsing many of the distinctions between technology and humans to talk about identity, Terri also focuses on identity as the effects of ongoing performances rather than as a stable state. She writes, "There has been a recent impulse . . . that suggests that online life is the ideal spot to experiment with hypothetical identity-making. This line of thought . . . carries a wrong assumption that only an online textual body is performative, whereas a biological body at the end of the terminal is stable. . . . Online or off it, identity and gender are complicated performances" (Senft, 1997, p. 7. Terri elaborates on these issues in her other writings.)

Not only is Terri's computer a natural extension of her body, her connections with others through the computer are a normal, meaningful part of her everyday life. After all, if we perform identity, gender, sexuality, and community, it doesn't make much sense to privilege one particular performance over another. As she describes her various online roles, I realize that issues of technology and the body inevitably infiltrate every aspect of her life. Put differently, when she is online, Terri is neither living in words nor trying to escape the idea of the body to be with others in some existential way. Rather, Terri performs embodiment through the text, in a visceral way.

"When my mother died, I found it difficult to talk to people—on the phone, in person, anywhere. That was when I got introduced to a cybersex community called Cyberoticom, where I was Jane Doe. Jane Doe, on cyberoticom, was this spoiled little rich girl, something I never was. She would do any kind of wild thing sexually, as long as there were yummy gifts at the end."

The first time she went online, Terri recalls, she had an explicitly sexual encounter before the night was over. In her online community, she freely shares stories of her various sexual performances online: "I go back to Echo to report my AOL sex antics . . . My favorite part of the experience is when I climax on line, typing 'yesssssssssss' and everyone claps. . . . I think I'd really like it if after my real-life orgasms, I got an applause track played."

I asked, "How would you describe your self online?"

Terri paused a moment, then said, "Well, it depends on where online. Like, I am different here than I would be in a spazzy fun conference on Echo, or who I would be as a NYC 'outsider' on the San Francisco based WELL, or how I would be when I am posting to an academic listserv, cuz Gawd knows who reads those things."

I grinned, knowing exactly what she meant. I sometimes felt strange writing in vastly different voices to different audiences.

Terri added, "And I am definitely different now than when I am running the 'Obey Me' room at America Online, working as an online dominatrix. All of these are 'me,' you know?"

"Wow," I said, in my usual unimaginative way. "I'm sure I'd get confused. But I know what you mean. I enact these same sorts of multiple roles all day, every day . . . online and offline."

"Yeah." Terri agreed, "It's like we expect to be a singular being, and every moment of our life, we're proven wrong. When I first joined Echo, I was advised to be 'myself,' and I couldn't really figure out what on earth that was. Was I supposed to be a graduate student, a sex worker, a bisexual woman, a family cancer survivor, a person who suffered from depression, or what? In time, I have learned to 'be' all of those things online, but there is a time and a place for each of these manifestations of personality."

A moment later, Terri concluded, "I don't think I've ever met anyone who had 'one self.'"

"I agree," I said, "But here's another question I've been grappling with. We all live multiple manifestations of personality, as you say. But sometimes the mediated (computer) contexts make me seem almost distinct from my self at times. I'm not being clear, I'm sure. I guess I'm asking: Do you think your sense of self as a person online is fundamentally distinct from your sense of self offline?"

"Hmmmmm. I feel far more vulnerable offline. That is the most honest way I can describe it. Sometimes vulnerability is great! Sometimes it's crippling, and I like muting it when necessary."

"What do you mean, muting it?"

"Going online to mute the vulnerability I feel offline. At this point in my life, I'll suppress expressing stuff if it makes 'me' uncomfortable. But at the same time, I'm not ashamed of my life, you know? And because I am physically separated from other people online, I have no trouble revealing all kinds of other things about myself, within the text."

"On the other hand, one thing I conceal online is my physical presence: my body, my home, my voice, my health."

Markham nods

"Terri," I asked, following a thought, "Why do you feel vulnerable offline?"

There was a long pause, and then Terri replied, "Everyone has their own story about this. Mine goes like this—I was a textbook abused child, which is to say I was beaten and yelled at repeatedly through childhood. To cope I learned to speak quickly and well. As a result, I am damn near overbearing in person. I experience the phone as a very visceral thing, grain of the voice and all that. Probably why I like and understand phone sex so much. But things feel too raw on the phone for me sometimes, I crave mediation, physically crave it."

Terri continued, "I crave mediation because of the abuse I suffered for years in the name of 'familial immediacy.' I didn't even get to have a lock on my bedroom door as a child. For me, mediation, and access to it, is empowerment. So being online allows me to choose my level of immediacy. It gives me the power to mediate my own presence."

"How so?" I prompted.

"My thoughts are here, on this screen, and for now, that is enough. You can't hear if I am sobbing, or if I am off my medication, or anything. This makes me feel safe for now."

Interesting, I thought to myself. When I think of "safe" I think of being anonymous, part of the crowd, not singled out. But Terri doesn't seem to be referring to this kind of safe. She is referring to separating the presence of others from herself physically.

Terri verified my thoughts a moment later, "I don't think 'real' need be synonymous with 'available for anyone, all times and in all ways.' Women have been synonymous with the body and immediate presence for all history, look where it gets us. No thanks. I far prefer choosing my level of immediacy."

✳

As we continued to talk about the performance of self in online contexts, I realized Terri was talking about control in a very different sense than the other participants. I had met many other users who said they felt empowered by the Internet because it gave them more of a voice, it made them more confident, or it allowed them to talk to people they might not otherwise feel comfortable talking with. I assumed that Terri was talking about power in much the same way. However, for Terri, empowerment means she can control directly the *form* and *degree* of the connection. Through online communication, Terri can limit the level of intimacy, and control the extent to which relationships are mediated.

This makes sense. Any of us who are raised without privacy or power might physically crave it as well. And like Terri, while sitting at our terminals with the capacity to make or break walls between self and other at will, we might feel "tremendously powerful."

Interestingly, Terri does not worry about the online presentation of self. She does not attempt to control her online appearance or persona, but allows it to emerge spontaneously, through conversational interactions with others. Yet at the same time that Terri does not try to control the presencing of self, she does seek to control the absence of self, as well as the presence and absence of others.

In other words, Terri wants to be able to disconnect from Other whenever she chooses to. Of course, this is more possible online than off because it is easier to shut off the computer and instantly rid yourself of the other's presence (or "mute" the other, as Terri says), than to walk away from a physical person, or to try to lock a door with no locks to keep abusive family members away. This measure of control is at least part of the reason she prefers to exist online.

Online or offline, our selves are constructed throught multiple performances and responses to those performances. We can imagine that some of our performances are more authentic or meaningful than others; we might like to erase certain performances, repeat others, create new patterns. As I talked with Terri, though, it occurred to me that she doesn't seem to suppress or privilege any performances of her self, online or offline. They are all meaningful components of existence. As she says, "they are all me, you know?"

However, Terri consciously separates the contexts in which the performances take place, whether these contexts are online or offline. This is a crucial move; for her, understanding self as it is performed in one context can help her perform in other contexts. As Terri notes, she often gets too comfortable in one context or the other, which makes her realize she needs to find more balance:

"Two months ago, I would have said that I am most comfortable with the virtual version of me. Now, I am realizing that when I am more comfortable with myself online than off, this is a sign that I am retreating from the flesh, if that makes any sense. In some ways, online life is too comfortable for me.

"This is not necessarily a bad thing: online life has taught me all kinds of new ways to re-imagine myself in the physical world. But now, I am trying to use my physical experiences (vulnerability, sexuality, mortality and the like) to broaden my online persona, and I have to say that it is a much more difficult project, at least for me."

Terri appears to have accepted online and offline experiences as part of the performance of everyday life. Although they might be different experiences, and each mode of experience may offer different advantages, technology is as natural as any other means of expressing and enacting identity. In effect, Terri is not only rejecting my question "Is it real?" but she is simultaneously rejecting a traditional way of thinking about how identity gets constructed in the first place. And in most of her discourse, everything about "being" is inevitably also about performance.

I think it is important to note that Terri was one of the few people I met online who actually acknowledged that being online is not such a great thing; rather, it marks an impossible attempt to escape the body.

You say, "Do you think 12 hours online per day is a lot?"

Terri says, "Yes, I do! I am beginning to feel like the online equivalent of a stockbrocker with his shoulder permanently disfigured (cuz he's the one with the phone all the time and holds it up to his ear with his shoulder)."

You ask, "Good imagery....I wonder what appendage is disfigured (disfigured for you, that is)?"

Terri says, "my posture has completely fallen apart in the last few years due to hunching over the screen. I am also displeased by the arrival of what can only be called Computer Butt."

Markham grins understandingly

Terri asks, "I am hoping its a phase, you know?"

You ask, "the computer butt or the being online so much?"

Terri exclaims, "hahaha both!"

Terri says, "like, we fell in love with online stuff and

binged on it, and soon we'll realize that we simply MUST exercise and such in order to live full healthy lives."

You ask, "would you spend more or less time online if you could?"

Terri says, "sitting at the terminal, with so much going on, makes me feel tremendously powerful. I could give a shit about large-scale corporate power, but now I see its seductiveness for people like my brother (who works for an investment house)"

Terri says, "But, no, I wouldn't spend less time online. Instead, I would figure out how to spend *more* time exercising, singing...physical things that DON'T require other people."

You ask, "What do you mean, physical things that don't require other people?"

Terri says, "Well, because so much of my life is connected to being online all the time, and because of grad school, I feel like I have MORE than enough human contact, you know. What I DON'T create is time to be alone, NOT in a book, NOT in a conversation, NOT writing, but doing something like running, or singing, or (gads) meditating..."

Markham grins, thinking of her own life

Terri says, "It just doesn't take much for life to turn into a version of "Codependent No More," you know? It gets wearisome."

I knew what she was talking about, especially when I looked at my own life of breathing filtered air and always walking on concrete. Perhaps after one incorporates technology to such an extensive degree, one feels the urge to get connected to the planet again. We get plugged in, we think it's everything, and then we need to get offline to live healthy lives because our backs are sore, our butts have grown soft, and our posture is atrocious. Our eyes hurt from the glare of the screen, we suffer repetitive stress syndrome in our hands and wrists, and we lack vital nutrients because we spend all our time inside, sitting at the computer, forgetting that we need to nourish our bodies.

So Terri is currently somewhere in New England, painting houses for a living. She'll do a few things online, but for the most part, she's getting connected in a different way.

SHERIE
ELOQUENCE MAKES ME BEAUTIFUL ONLINE

"Oh, there you are, Sherie! I'm glad you found me. Did you have any trouble getting here?"

  "no. it was no trouble."

  "I can't believe I'm finally chatting with you . . . busy semester . . ."

  "yes, i'm busy also."

  "So, I'm doing a study of people who might consider themselves heavy users of the internet."

  "yes"

  "I suppose we should get started. Here's some up front stuff to ease your mind about anonymity. I guarantee I will never reveal your address/name/location."

  "ok"

  "do you mind if I archive this conversation for later analysis?"

  "i don't mind."

  Oh, and you can disconnect from this interview at any time and I will never bother you again :-)"

Annette smiles.

  "ok"

  "okay, one secondo . . . I have to make sure the log function is working. Can you hang on a minute while I figure it out?"

  "ok"

Annette grimaces.

  "sorry, Sherie, I'm still pretty new at this. I'm still trying to see if the log is on or off . . . sorry for the delay."

  "that's okay"

I was feeling embarrassed. This was supposed to be my interview space, and here I was blocking on a command I'd performed countless times before. I knew I shouldn't be so nervous, but Sherie was a big deal in the community where I had lurked for over a year. Of all the people I was interviewing, I knew for sure that Sherie spent a lot of time contemplating what it meant to be online. I knew she would have great stories to tell, and now I was wasting time. I suppose I was also feeling anxious because she seemed in a hurry. Her responses appeared almost immediately after I sent my own messages. Compared to hers, my typing was slow as molasses.

Finally, I figured out that the log function was on and working. "aah . . . got it. Okay, do you have any questions before we begin?"

"i'll ask later."

I quickly typed the first question. Sherie seemed hurried, her statements clipped. She probably wanted to get on to the good stuff.

"How much time do you spend online?" I asked.

"that depends on the day of the week really. i'm not really sure . . ."

"could you estimate per week time?"

"i'm not sure i can. i spend several hours online during a weekend, maybe two hours each evening. maybe half hour in the morning . . . i'm not sure i can quantify it"

"okay. In your opinion, do you spend 'a lot' of time online?"

"yes"

"would you spend more time online if you could?"

"probably. i used to spend more time online. i do spend more time online during school breaks."

Her responses were so short. I felt like the conversation might be boring for Sherie, so I jumped down to my favorite question. Whenever I asked the participants to tell me about their most memorable experience online, I got at least one very long story, and sometimes several vignettes. I could always count on this question if I needed to walk down the hall to heat up my coffee.

"Tell me about your most memorable experience online."

"gee, i don't know, so many. some are personal. some aren't."

"great!" I replied, "choose any—all. talk all you want!"

"well, most seem to have something to do with the community i belong to. everything from personal relationships to flesh meets to flame wars . . ."

I waited. I was pretty sure the ellipses meant she was thinking. Given my tendency to blurt out questions, after several interviews I had trained myself to wait for the answers. It took drastic measures to keep silent. Mostly, I was forced to remove my hands from the keyboard and trap them between my thighs and the chair. It worked.

I waited longer than for any of the other interviews. She must be writing a lot. Sixty-five seconds, two minutes. Finally, her message appeared, "are you there?"

"oh! yes, I'm here!" I said, quickly adding, "I'm sorry, I thought you were thinking . . . . I have a tendency to ask questions too quickly, and always interrupt people."

I wondered what she was thinking. Maybe I asked the wrong question. I thought a moment, then typed, "is it too hard to pick just one experience to talk about? if you want, we can go in a different direction . . ."

Immediately, she replied "ok."

I added, "and maybe weave back to it."

Annette smiles.

"ok"

Okay, I thought. I can live with that. Onward and upward, as Beth would say. "tell me, what is it like to meet people online?"

Sherie replied, "meet online people online or meet online people offline?"

"oh. meet online people online. sorry."

"very textual. very discursive and rhetorical. also poetic. That's why i love it."

Beautiful turn of phrase, but something about it didn't fit. I leaned back in my chair, stretching my arms above my head to work out some of the kinks in my back. I couldn't make sense of her statement. She's talking about what it's like to meet online people online, and we've just met online, and this conversation didn't seem particularly discursive or poetic. I resisted a grimace. "Patience," I muttered. I just needed to figure out how to ask the right questions. Everyone could be reached, but not necessarily in the same way.

"how does online communication differ from offline communication?" I asked.

"the emphasis on words and writing as the determining factor of the communication, which is great for those of us who are most comfortable in writing."

"what do you mean?"

"i can speak out of my thinking, and let my thinking speak for me."

"How would you describe your sense of self in the internet?"

"i get to express myself as a writer, in writing, more than in any other aspect of my life. my net sense of self is myself in language."

"is the self you get to express in the net different than the self you express in RL?" I asked.

"yes and no."

"What do you mean?" I prompted.

"my net self is less inhibited than my offline persona, more expressive."

"How so?"

"i choose to exist as myself in language online. i don't try to come up with other personae, so it feels more like being me than i sometimes feel offline. offline one often finds oneself in certain social roles that one must maintain; student, teacher, family member, etc."

"this might not be a fair question, but do you like yourself better online?"

"yes"

I waited, but again, as throughout most of our conversation, a single word marked the beginning and end of Sherie's response.

"because you don't feel as trapped?" I suggested.

"yes"

"What do you mean when you say 'myself in language'?" I asked, trying a different route. The conversation was beginning to go somewhere, and I didn't want to lose the moment by staying with a question she didn't want to respond to.

"my health isn't the best and i don't like my appearance all that much, and so i don't like myself in flesh all that much. i think myself in language is more communicative of who i am." Then Sherie added, "and because i'm a good writer. eloquence makes me beautiful online."

I was feeling strangely ambivalent toward Sherie, even as she was beginning to open up. Perhaps it had taken too long to get to this point; after so many "yes," "no," and "ok," responses to my questions, I just didn't believe she was particularly eloquent. At least not in this conversation. I was irritated by Sherie, who answered all my questions with monosyllabic responses. I was intrigued by Sherie, who hinted at poetry with the turn of a phrase like, "eloquence makes me beautiful online." I was intimidated by Sherie, who had volunteered to be interviewed but didn't seem to like my questions or want to waste any letters talking with me. I felt sorry for Sherie, who didn't like her body and seemed to seek refuge in a textual, fleshless world.

Trapped by the flesh. Living through language. Existing through technology.

I wonder if Sherie hates her embodied self? Or if she simply doesn't care for embodied beings?

Curious, I asked, "Do you have an 'embodied' self online?"

"i'm not sure. i've been looking for the meaning of embodied. a lot of my writing has dealt with just this question and i don't know the answer yet."

"It sounds like interesting stuff. What are your thoughts so far?"

Sherie responded, "you would have to read a lot of my writing to begin to know what i think."

I paused, wondering how to respond to a comment like that, then typed, simply, "yes." As I hit the send button, I said aloud to no one in particular, "That's it, I'm done."

I'd had enough. I was only halfway through the interview and had been prodding and pushing Sherie for almost two hours, trying to be a good interviewer. I thought she was shy. I assumed I was asking the wrong questions, that she would open up if I could get my interviewing act together. The moment I read her last comment, I realized I was wrong to keep talking with her for so long only to come to this point. Whether she meant to be rude or not, I felt patronized and demeaned. I only wanted to end the interview as quickly as possible and never talk to her again.

"Okay. last question. what does the concept of being online mean to you?"

"it means existing in pure language."

"do you have anything else you'd like to add about your experiences in various online contexts?"

"in cyberspace, one dwells in language. and through language."

Ironic. *Now* she's beautiful.

*

Like everyone else I interviewed, Sherie believes the Internet allows her to communicate with others in different ways than she otherwise might. But whereas most people talk about their online experiences as means of extending the communicative capacity of their physical, embodied selves, Sherie talks of the Internet both as a context where she can avoid her embodied self and as a way of being through the text. Sherie feels trapped by her body, and by the influence it has on her presentation of self.

The appeal of existing through technology, particularly the text, is that it enables Sherie to choose those aspects of her self that perform, and to enact the self through pure poetic expression. Control of the performance of text through both form and content, then, is control of the presentation of self. Whether her performed self is the same self that others perceive is an unanswered question, but this does not seem an important detail for Sherie. Living through language seems to be satisfaction in itself for her.

Not surprisingly, Sherie departs from those participants who maintain that they are essentially the same people online and offline. For her, the online and offline selves are both real, and they are distinct entities. Her online self, for instance, exists in and through textual expression. In contrast, her offline self is based in and trapped by the body and its various roles.

As Sherie explains, the self in language and the self in body, both as they are presented and experienced, "are equivalent," but "not the same." The self in language can express itself directly from mind to text, but the self in body must be mediated by "looks or race or social standing or whatever."

HOW DOES A RESEARCHER ANALYZE SOMETHING
SHE DOES NOT UNDERSTAND?

For months, I tried to make sense of my conversation with Sherie without success. I could not understand why she was so insistent that she was a textual, poetic, eloquent being. I got very little of that during the interview. I now believe that my interview with Sherie is an excellent example of two people who speak different languages, but who think they speak the same language, trying to have a conversation. The entire interaction illustrates a very complicated process of trying to come to know the Other through the exchange of text.

Several notable things happen through my interaction with Sherie. First, she implies that although she lives through language, the text *is* the relationship. For her, this is a significant part of being through technology, and she spends a lot of time (in her online communities) talking about the expression of self through the text and her eloquence and beauty through her textual being.

However, I have to take her word for this, because the interview does not support her claim. In seemingly direct conflict with her statements that she is more expressive through writing, and that she fits into her online community because she writes with poetic grace and form, I experienced Sherie's discourse as truncated, brusque, nonexpressive, shallow.

I thought a lot about the contradictions in the form and content of this interview, and agonized over the transcripts, trying to interpret her actions. Did she find the interaction distasteful? Were my questions unclear or trivial, thus leading to dead-end answers? Did I ask closed-ended questions? At first, I thought Sherie was arrogant, placing herself above and beyond the simplistic questions I asked. Later, when I wrote an early version of this analysis, I thought she was simply self-centered; perhaps bored with the entire interview, perhaps sick from allergies. Now I have reached a third conclusion.

I originally felt that Sherie thought of cyberspace as a place to go to attempt to escape the body. She indicated that, in a world where the body is only a barrier between souls, online communication is profoundly real and a much more meaningful way both to express the self and to know others. I still believe this to be true. But, and this is the crucial point, I have also come to the conclusion that Sherie found it difficult to extract herself from *being* through the poetry of the text, to *reflect* on what it means to be in textual conversation with me. In this way, Sherie embodies the text but cannot express it, only live it. She cannot metacommunicate its meaning to others. Let me try to explain how I arrived at this conclusion.

Sherie rejects my binary distinctions and seems put off by my questions

I was intrigued, both during and after our conversation, that even as Sherie talked about her self as distinctly online or offline, and implied that the online self reflected more accurately who she was, she persistently rejected my efforts to categorize her experiences as offline/online.

"What happened at your first flesh meet?"

"we arranged to meet at a restaurant."

"How was it?" I asked. Meeting your online community for the first time in the flesh. How exciting! How strange!

"it was very nice. we had lunch. talked. walked to a nearby park."

That was it? No, that couldn't be it. Must be the form of my question. I drummed the tops of the keyboard, a nervous habit that sometimes seems to help me think more clearly—or at least reminds me I need to be typing so I can see what I'm thinking. I asked, "Did it feel at all strange to meet your online friends finally in the flesh?"

"yes"

"How so?"

"it was odd. i was interested to see what the people looked like. it's hard to remember."

Hmm. Hard to remember. I imagined it would be hard to forget. "Did it seem as 'discursive,' like you mentioned earlier?"

"as online?" Sherie asked, then answered herself, "no. for one thing, you can't talk as much when you're eating."

As her interest in that topic seemed to dwindle, I asked her about a specific relationship she had taken from online to offline. I was interested in the distinctions between these two contexts, and tended to polarize them in my questions. "How does your offline relationship with him compare to your online relationship?"

"it's hard to compare"

"Could you give me an example that might help me understand?"

"there aren't really the distinctions made between on the net, on the phone, and in the room aspects of the relationship." This seemed an odd response to me. She had stated earlier that she felt more like herself when she's online. Surely, I thought, the context would influence the relationship. Sherie added, "when you say online and offline, i don't know how you categorize our phone relationship for instance, if that's a part of online or offline."

Still bent on understanding the *difference* between her online and offline relationships, and still stuck in my binary terminology, I said, "Oh, I see. Do you consider your phone relationship 'online'?"

Sherie refused the distinction once more, with the rejoinder, "i guess i consider it 'on the phone.'"

In the same way, I asked Sherie how "real" her experiences in the Internet were.

She replied, "how real are experiences off the Internet? . . .they're equivalent. they're not the same, but I'm still emotionally and intellectually invested in them, physically too even."

"What do you mean?" I asked.

"i get as emotionally upset and physically stressed over a flame war as i do over a conflict that i'm a part of."

Again, Sherie rejected my efforts to separate online and offline experiences into real/not real distinctions. Instead of talking about whether experiences are real or not (they are all real), or focusing on the media through which the self (selves) and relationships are enacted, Sherie seemed to focus on the fact that selves or relationships exist, regardless of the context.

"email is different from talk which is different from cuseeme," she pointed out, "and it's all one relationship." (*CU-SeeMe is a video conferencing package developed by Cornell University. Basically, it is a series of small video cameras attached to the tops of many computers that allow users to see each other; it was very popular at the time of the study.*)

Sherie seems to focus on the text as the being, not being through the text

After re-reading her transcripts several times, I began to realize our differences. Whereas I focused on online technologies as a way to establish relationships, Sherie conceptualized online technology as the relationship itself. (*It's important to note here that my interpretation of Sherie's understanding of cyberspace is limited by my own frame of reference. And while I struggle to get out of my own frame to describe hers, I conceptualize online technologies primarily as a place, and have difficulty comprehending and representing online contexts as "ways of being."*)

In our conversation, Sherie described meeting people online as "very textual. very discursive and rhetorical. also poetic. that's why i love it." In online contexts, you develop relationships through the text, "you're attracted to the words and the thoughts that are reflected in the words."

Living a relationship in and through the text is, at baseline, a continuous interweaving dialogue of texts. Most of the participants talked about meeting people and establishing or strengthening those relationships *through* online discussions, but for Sherie, the discussion *is* the relationship. This gradually became clear to me as she talked about relationships, but not because she was describing it in a complete or even rudimentary way. The only direct reference she actually made was to describe relationship development as: "a feeling of excitement at having found such a mentally stimulating discussion . . . the intelligence, the soul, the depth of reading."

I wonder if she's onto something I don't quite grasp, namely, living as text rather than reflecting on—via text—life through the text. (*In a way, trying to make sense of Sherie's answers reminds me of trying to comprehend Tyler's (1986) discussion that postmodern ethnography should be pure evocation. I kept trying to figure out what he meant by taking notes on his text, analyzing closely his statements. Finally, at 4:00 A.M., as I was falling asleep over the book, I had a flash of insight and comprehension. He was arguing that ethnography should be evocative, and to make his point, his discussion was not straightforward, logical, or traditional. Rather, it was evocative, and until I stopped looking straight at it, I couldn't see what he meant.*)

Sometimes, absence makes you notice what might otherwise be present

I learned of texts as relationship only through a striking absence of any conversational connectedness during the exchange of messages I had with Sherie. She answered me in fragments and was reluctant to elaborate on those sound bytes. Sometimes her response would be an even more vague or general statement, which struck me as a very odd way to respond. This pattern went on and on and on, yet Sherie described herself as eloquent online, someone who feels more comfortable writing than speaking, less inhibited, more expressive. How does one interpret the contradiction between Sherie's words and her words about her words?

Well, I could say she's a boring person. To look at our conversation, one would never suspect that Sherie lived an eloquent life through and as the text. But perhaps the form of the interview or my style of questioning did not allow her either to get away from the text completely and talk about it (as would have been possible face-to-face), or to express herself in poetic abstraction. (*Perhaps she did the best she could. Perhaps if she looked at this transcript, she would shrug her virtual shoulders and say, "oh, that day…yes, i was feeling fragmented and decentered," or perhaps, "oh, i remember, what an absolutely anti-narrative mood i was in." Or perhaps she had a headache.*)

At the end of the interview, when she said, "you would have to read a lot of my writing to begin to know what i think," I was extremely put off. But now I think this may have been a key to understanding Sherie's connection with the text. In her online community, Sherie has a reputation for communicating in very poetic free-flowing forms. She expresses herself in abstractions, using allusion and fragments, and she considers this, the text, to be her self.

So here I appear and start asking her to describe herself, using a linear, traditional interview protocol format. How can she describe herself without enacting her self, since self exists through the form and content of the text? I suspect she did not feel like herself at all during this interview. I didn't give her the choice to speak in abstract artistic expression; I was asking direct questions that requested traditional answers. Perhaps for Sherie, this was impossible.

Sherie talks of being a decentered self, but this also implies flight from a center

Throughout our conversation, Sherie indicates that online and offline contexts are equivalent, and that they can both contribute to individual and relational development. Through her descriptions of her self, however, it is clear that she values online contexts more highly; online, self can flourish as a mind with others, without the complicating bonds of the flesh.

Online, the body is a text controlled by the user. It can be nonexistent or present, but most people online realize that the body is a description and enactment that may or may not correspond with the actual physical body attached to the Other (of course, I am referring only to text-based spaces here). Offline, the body is less changeable, thus it plays a more concretized role in addressing others. Sherie feels defined—and confined—by her body offline, because her body is used by others to make judgments about who she is. In the physical world offline, the interplay of texts that form a sense of self-identity is complex; multiple contextual factors centered in embodied existence work simultaneously as we encounter and engage others. We cannot archive the scene for later, more careful analysis. Our offline identities are constructed dialogically and in ways we cannot always control. In short, "we are not," as Terri (the previous participant) notes, "simply the sum of our posts."

Sherie doesn't like her appearance. She calls her body "flesh." Face-to-face meetings are "flesh meets." In a sense, Sherie's use of this term and evident migration from her body into the text reflects a utopian dream of transcending the body. In this sort of transcendence, there is no room for the body. It's mere flesh, just meat. It interferes with the authentic self, which for Sherie is exhibited by the mind giving voice to thought through the text, the thought speaking for her self as text. In this idealized space, she believes she can control the depiction of self, and define one's own boundaries.

IN SUM . . .

During this study, I spent hours and days sitting in my office chair, engaging contexts created primarily through words, accomplishing conversations through the exchange of messages. In many ways, because I felt so isolated from my own body during this time, I felt compelled to think of cyberspace as essentially disembodied. Yet, as I sat silently, alone in front of my computer, I watched people, including myself, compose themselves through word choices, sentence structures, graphic accents, typos, and eloquent phrases. Responding to responses, we wove dialogic understandings of each other, sometimes connecting, sometimes deciding it was best to move on.

All we have in text-based Internet spaces are texts. The multiple effects of our texts, like the effects of our behaviors and actions in the physical world, cannot be known. We just guess and try to communicate the best we can in each particular situation. For instance, the participants wrote to me, I sketched images in my mind about their appearance, age, race, etc., using templates I derived from my own life experiences. I have no way of knowing whether my (non)imagination matched their physicality, but this is not so important. In text-based spaces, self is constructed through dialogue and thus is more embodied by the text than by the body. To complicate this physical uncertainty, I also could have no way of assessing the "truth" of their texts. After a few weeks of second-guessing the honesty of their words, I realized that, online or offline, all of us make sense of our experiences and tell the stories of our lives in self-centered and self-understood ways. Truth is an elusive term in any context; however, because truth is always tentative online, it doesn't make sense to dwell on it too much. It's really more about faith and acceptance.

Studies of online communication should include the texts of people who constitute these social spaces. This medium offers unique ways of expressing the self and constructing social reality. The *process* of building relationships and social structures, though, is thoroughly dialogic; online cultures exist because people interact with each other through writing, over time. Just as the text cannot capture the nuance of the voice, the voice cannot capture the nuance of the text. Because of this, researchers (*myself included at the top of the list*) must be willing to study online contexts in their own contexts, without trying to impose alternative categories, false dichotomies, a priori assumptions and templates. And of course, once the researcher is *willing* to discard these, she must be *able* to do so, which is a much more difficult task of rearranging one's frame of reference, I'm afraid.

Real is that which is experienced or that which is known

I learned from talking to these people that being is not related to some abstract concept like "real" or "virtual." Life is much too complex for that. They did not question the reality of their experiences. Instead, they took for granted that being online is as real as being offline—all experience is real. These are their real lives, not some simulation. Even when these participants distinguish sharply between that which is real and that which is otherwise, their descriptions remain solidly grounded in their experiences.

In Matthew's case, for instance, real means nothing more or less than being offline. He does not describe online living as different than being offline. Online only means you have accessed more information. For Jennifer, going online is real in the sense that other people's texts are really there, and a person's text is a substitute for their voice or bodily presence. Mist also experiences her Internet experiences as real, but at the same time, she does not let them interfere with "more meaningful contexts." For Mist, there are real and more (meaningfully) real aspects of experience.

Beth considers all experiences real, online and offline. For her, authenticity of self is a reality represented in text. But when it comes to knowing Other, the text is not enough; it is not a sufficient means of knowing what is *really* real. For Sheol, life online is as meaningful as life offline, perhaps more so. The realities of online life are a matter of degree; different contexts online express different levels of reality.

Terri doesn't ponder the issue of reality. She's more concerned with how technology and the body are implicated in determining what is real. Online or offline, every aspect of self and being is an effect of performance. Hence, the reality of self and other is not a useful categorization tool because it is a shifting activity, not a given state.

For Sherie, the text represents more than just a means to create identity and self; the text is the very embodiment of self. Online and offline realities are separate, very different aspects of reality.

A person's experience of computer-mediated contexts may be startling, profound, and unique. However, this does not necessarily mean online experiences are more or less real than other life experiences. In this technological age, if we want to use the term *reality* as a useful descriptive category, it must be reconsidered and expanded to encompass multiple experiences that may or may not be connected to the physical world. In addition, we need to remain grounded in our explanations of cyberspace. Online, self, others, and social realities are constructed through the exchange of texts, which can occasion a euphoria that we can transcend the social realities our physical bodies occupy. This is a tantalizing but exaggerated perspective.

The potential to experiment with experiences and self-expression can be a refreshing escape from the pressures of living in societies that mostly constrain us; but as most of these users articulate, the reality of online life cannot be separated from offline life, no matter how much we might wish it could be. Kept in perspective, however, both are valuable contexts for experiencing life.

Framing experience as a Tool . . . Place . . . Way of Being

When I first decided to put these people in categories along a continuum from less- to more-connected to online experiences and technologies, I didn't really think the continuum was progressive, where people moved along it from one end toward the other; I anticipated that people would shift around on the continuum as they shifted through contexts. I made this presumption, of course, because it reflected my own experience at the outset of the study. However, as I continue to talk with people about their online experiences, I am realizing that the continuum is marked by significant differences in vocabulary and ways of describing and talking about self, other, and experiences.

For example, those participants who consider the Internet primarily as a *tool* (Matthew, Jennifer, and Mist) all used the term *information* as an important way of making sense of online communication. Michael, who considers the Net a real place, never mentioned the word, but he talked of going there, hanging out, chatting, spending time. On the other hand, of those participants who frame cyberspace as a place to live or a way of being (Sheol, Beth, Terri, and Sherie), only Sheol made a point to talk about information and that was due mainly to his life goal to control information as a hacker. Thus, for those who experience the Internet more ontologically, their online relationships constitute the most meaningful aspect of their experiences.

Perhaps I picked up on certain vocabularies because I had placed them in these categories, but I don't really think so. Only now—as I tied these interviews together—did I begin to notice any trend among their discourses. Interestingly, I sensed a connection between the way people framed their online experiences and their understanding of their sense of self through the body. Most participants who consider the Internet to be a place or a way of being talked about issues of embodiment. This makes sense, because the more connected one feels to online experiences, the more those feelings loop back to the embodied self. To go to the Internet simply to access information is to envision it as a tool, not a place; but to go to be with others implies a place to be, and this necessarily implicates a sense of embodiment.

For instance, the three women who frame their experiences as a place, or a way of being, seem simultaneously to deny and privilege the body. For Beth, cyberspace offers a way to keep men away from her body so they don't try to judge her self based on her bodily presence. For Sherie, the body is flesh, and even if it cannot be escaped, it can be avoided; yet, ironically, throughout the interview, the body was central to the discussion. For Terri, the self is not questionable and the body itself is not the problem. Rather, it is others' access to her body that she worries about. Like Beth, Terri wants to control the extent to which people can touch her, but for different reasons. Beth wants to remain a virgin; Terri never wants to be abused again. These women have found some measure of success in achieving their goals through their online lives, but they are plagued by the embodied self. Terri understands this and is trying not to run away from her embodied self. She understands that ultimately there is no way to escape embodiment so she is working to accept, not deny, the fact of her bodied existence.

For Matthew, Jennifer, and Mist, the embodied or disembodied self is not a salient distinction or subject of discussion because online technologies are tools, not places. Technology facilitates research and enables one to communicate farther. Going online means turning on the computer, just as one would pick up the phone. They know of other people who experience cyberspace as more of a place, but they consider these people extreme.

Michael considers the Internet a place where he can get to know others and expand his community of friends. He is stable in his physical understanding of the world, however; embodiment online is the same as embodiment offline. Armed with this conviction, Michael can actively participate in a community where every member wears an animated mask. He believes that, under each mask, he will find the authentic and true person. Online and offline places may look and operate differently, but they are both places where real people go to get to know one another.

Through online communication, self can control bodies

Online technologies extend our physical capacities in many ways and offer the potential for greater control over the flow of information and the presentation of self. When we connect to the Internet, we can access seemingly endless amounts of information. We can search through many types of online groups and lurk to see what they say and do before we decide to participate. As Matthew notes, the Internet allows us to communicate with colleagues, friends, and family in bits and pieces during our spare time, writing and editing messages we might send now, later, or never. As an augmentation of the self that is situated outside the body, online communication technology offers a powerful means of control over the text, over the performance of self through the text, and control over Others' capacities as well. In general, the participants in this study expressed through our conversations a desire and tendency to control the contexts through which they live their lives.

Key to the process of controlling the context is separation from the physical body. With the body comes a host of uncontrollable aspects of the context. For Matthew and Mist, the voice just talks, and they can't edit the words that come out of the head in face-to-face conversations nearly as well as they can in the textual environment of cyberspace. For Jennifer, seeing the conversation allows her to be more attuned to it, more able to adjust it (and adjust to it). In this way, she can more effectively control the course of conversation and the relationship that emerges from it.

Beth and Sherie do not feel the need to control the text. Each just lets her texts speak her thoughts directly, but they both emphasize that online communication allows them to present certain aspects of the self and omit others, specifically those related to bodied being. In this way, Beth's and Sherie's physical distance from the text is vital to sustaining a belief that a more authentic self can be presented online.

For Sheol, as well, physical separation from the context is a vital means of control. Sheol is not trying to omit his body because he feels it interferes with the authentic expression of self, however. Rather, he wants to control successfully the flow of information as it passes through the network, which requires the absence of presence; indeed, it potentially keeps him out of jail.

In contrast, Terri considers her body to be precious. It is a part of her self that no one is allowed to approach without expressed permission, and online communication provides an essential means of controlling the access others have to her body. When Terri craves solitude, separation of the body from online contexts enables her to shut down the connection whenever she chooses to be free of even the disembodied presence of the Other.

For all these people, control is primarily perceived both as an outcome (product) of the self's communicative efforts and as a performative act (process) that can be directed toward the self or Other. If the body is physically separated from the context, as it is online, the extent to which the other can control self is diminished. Hence, the other isn't something to worry about. (*Until something happens to make you question that assumption, like getting hacked, or being stalked, or having another online persona control your physical ability to control your online character [see Julian Dibbell, 1996].*) For these users, control is unidirectional. Control is wielded by the user of the tool, the one writing the text, the one writing the script for the performance—a distinctly non-interactive, non-transactional view of communication.

This notion of control is somewhat illusory. Online, we begin to exist as a persona when others respond to us; being, in this sense, is relational and dialogic.

As Laing (1969) explains, our identity cannot be completely abstracted from our identity-for-others, our identity-for-ourselves, the identities we attribute to others, the identities we think they attribute to us, what we think they think we think they think, and so on (p. 86). We thus might believe we control the presentation of self through vivid descriptions, careful editing, and constant self-monitoring, but we are always relating with others in this ongoing construction of self—others whose responses are not always calculable. Even so, these participants believe they have a high degree of control, which seems to satisfy them. Perhaps the illusion of control is sufficient.

Interestingly, for all these participants, the body is still the center of being, whether they want to believe this or not. Whether they talk explicitly of their bodies, or choose to flee the reality of their bodies, their experiences still are located in the place where they live the most visceral parts of their lives, the body. No matter how much Sherie wants to talk of "being the text," her words make it clear that her point of reference is her embodied experience. Her body still plays a central role. For others less anxious to de-center the self, the body and its senses and feelings are crucial ways to verify the authenticity of the online Other. Sheol, for instance, knows his online experiences are real because they are very emotional, and when significant things happen online, he feels the emotion in the body, which lends credence or authenticity to his experience. And even though Jennifer accepted Brian's proposal of marriage before they ever met face-to-face, meeting each other as physical bodies was the crucial next step, without which marriage would have been impossible for them.

Everywhere I went online, I saw the body as a privileged site for experience. It is, after all, where we live as breathing organisms. As these persons continue to experience their lives (as mediated through computers), they are shifting the grounds of their own being; or at least I am shifting the grounds of my own being, which makes me suspect they are as well.

The question I am trying to answer is not "What is virtuality, as compared to reality?" Perhaps it is not even "What is real?" Perhaps I am asking, "What does it mean to be? And how—if at all—is virtuality altering our understanding of being?" These people may not be resolving these questions in definitive ways, but they are playing out different possibilities knowingly and unknowingly, getting answers in various ways and in various contexts.

We now have the technological capacity to interact and exist in multiple contexts at the same time. Because our experience of this technology is new, we are only just beginning to ask ourselves how we can accomplish these multiple modes of experience or ways of being and what the possibilities and consequences may be. A professor down the hall says online communication seems a more interactive form of the novel. Beth says everyone should have this technology, especially older people, so they can connect with others even as their bodies force them to stay in a confined physical place. Sheol says it has changed his life "forevermore." Mist says she can't imagine what the world would be like without it. Gargoyle, a programmer I met, says it is the most significant thing ever to happen to humans. My online friend Scooter says it is consuming, and all of us will have to be completely online before we realize what it's doing to us.

The more I talk about these issues with others, online and offline, the more mundane the entire question seems to become . . . after all, we exist. Things change. New contexts emerge, and with each new context, we struggle to frame our experiences of it in meaningful, self-reflective ways.

This one seems just another part of life, another place to "grow old with others," as my friend Bill likes to say.

Silence

I'm struck by how silent the Internet is. I can hear the humming of the computer, typically white noise, but noticeable tonight for some reason. I haven't talked to many people today, but at the same time I've talked to many people. My jaw is sore, as it is when I spend a lot of time being quiet. Very silent. I am trying to write about what it feels like to be in a conversation with someone online. She is typing and I am typing, and there is nothing but the sound of my fingers hitting the keys. It can be musical to a degree, I suppose, but nothing like the lyrical lilt of voices.

I feel lonely.

Yet, even as I sit in a deadly silent and lethargic state of thinking and writing, I am witnessing and participating in several group discussions. The conversation in one of these groups has been growing more and more vehement; in any physical context, this party would be considered a cacophonous screaming match. Even here, though, people's words seem loud. I actually started the whole thing several days ago with an offhand comment that "I would walk out on any professor who tried to make me watch an overly violent film, for whatever supposed educational value." My name has long since disappeared from the topic; other participants and topics have become more relevant. Now they are talking about yelling. One participant insists on writing in all capital letters, arguing that HE IS NOT YELLING AT ALL; ONLY TRYING TO DISTINGUISH HIS TEXT FROM OTHERS. I can't help thinking that he is yelling, conditioned as I am to netiquette these days.

People not engaged in the conversation have begun to ask the participants to please stop their bickering. "Thank god for the delete key," one member notes, "so that I don't have to listen to this pissing contest." Interesting description. I have been reading the conversation, and while I sometimes hear voices in my own head, I rarely hear the participants pissing (or see them, for that matter).

And now, tonight, after an entire day of going places, seeing things, being with others online, I am struck by the silence here in my office. Not a sound. Not a whisper. Not a shimmer of a voice, a quake of an emotion. All of it silence. And this silence deadens the air in my office. I feel the weight of the silence pressing on me through the hissing/humming of the machine.

I see a square face framed in materiality. Across the face, figures dance. A prominent upright stick blinks constantly. An hourglass tells me to be patient. I press buttons on the keyboard below the face and the face changes, slowly, shifting to another countenance. I sometimes see people and objects, brightly colored, leading me on. Other times, I just see text appearing on the screen, put there by me or others.

They say this is surfing, and perhaps that accounts for that white noise; yet it feels more like jumping from place to place—Sherry Turkle's home page, Sandy Stone's home page, then to a British publishing company, a zine (online magazine) called "Bust" that features articles on how to act and appear more French. I hopped from location to location on the Web, looking at various articles, wondering why certain places led to others. For example, Terri pointed me to an article she had written for a zine called "Stim." When I got there, I didn't find the article by Terri. Instead, the outline of a woman's thigh stenciled against a pink and cream latticed background filled my screen. Stuck in her garter against all this pinkness was a calling card on which the word *Stim* was printed. As I scrolled down, I revealed the rest of her shapely leg, right down to her high heels. I could choose from "map," "archives," "interact." At the very bottom of the screen, the word *BUST* was flashing in orange and yellow. I clicked on this word, and my browser surfed to another zine, with an article by Courtney Love. I browsed around this site for awhile, found little of interest, and went back to "Stim," wondering where the article by Terri was located and what this place was all about. I don't even know what Stim stands for.

Several hours passed while I searched various places on the Web, making connections based on what caught my eye and seemed interesting, moving from one place to the next, and only sometimes retracing my steps. Sometimes running; sometimes pausing to examine something more closely. I ran across some Hubble Telescope computerized photos of nebulas. The Lagoon Nebula was breathtaking, although my computer took ages to reveal the photo (what seems like ages now, of course, would have seemed lightning-fast five years ago). I stayed with the Hubble Telescope for a long time, waiting for other photos to appear. I couldn't figure out whether the pictures were real, whatever that means. I wondered if these were the real colors of the most beautiful natural phenomenon I had ever seen. If not, I wondered, what did a nebula look like, really? And what would the sky look like if you lived in the middle of the nebula? I realized how insignificant and vain and self-centered we humans are. Then I left the Lagoon Nebula in all its glory and hopped to the next link in a randomly ordered web of information.

This silent and invisible hopping/surfing goes on for hours. The silent turn-taking weaves a community. I shout to Beth when I learn to catch a Frisbee. Terri types "yesssssss!!!!" when she has an online orgasm, and sometimes gets "applause." Is this the tribal dance? Am I sitting on the edge of the dancers' circle watching a bizarre ritualistic ceremony? Am I the observer? Or by simply collecting these experiences, am I inventing the entire enterprise—in which case I can't really be considered a researcher as much as an innovator, a writer of new worlds.

Chapter 6

Reflecting

I went online to study a new and rapidly evolving cultural context. In doing so, I became part of a transitory and unique network of connections among people, information, games, places, and communities. My choices and communicative actions during the course of this study were instrumental in constructing a unique and individually experienced context that became the basis of this ethnography, the object of study. By interviewing many users online and analyzing the conversations we had, as well as my own movements through this process, I created a space within which to witness the construction of meaning—theirs, mine, and yours—through textual interactions. I wrote this book to offer a set of possibilities for how I made sense of my experiences in this individually negotiated online context, how the people I met make sense of their experiences in their individually constructed lives in online contexts, and how you, the reader, make sense of these experiences in relation to your own.

I did not intend for this study to emerge as it did. It assumed this shape through me and my experiences and what I learned from the people I met online. If I did it again, knowing what I do now, it would take on a different shape, I'm sure. I touched, for a moment, the edge of an emergent, ever-changing set of communication practices that comprises temporary and shifting relationships, communities, organizations, and cultures. I have shared the particular ways I made sense of all of it. Now, I want to close with some general remarks about online communication, my goals in this study, the project itself, and the future.

THOUGHTS ABOUT ONLINE COMMUNICATION

My understanding of what it means to be online is growing more conservative as each day passes. I am struck by the normalcy of my conversations with others, in the interviews and online. I am amazed that I don't find more weird stuff and more exotic transmutations of the body and mind online.

I see and interact with many people who seem to be experimenting with identity. Although many of the people I talk with feel more comfortable with themselves online than offline, I am beginning to realize that this is really not a big revelation, or even a fundamental shift in the way people feel about themselves. I remember a composition teacher telling me the following rule: If you don't want to face the reaction of the other person, or if you want to choose your words carefully, or if you want to speak without interruption, use the written versus spoken word. If you want to minimize the reaction, but don't want to offend with the distance of a letter, use the phone. If you want close contact and are willing to be vulnerable, say it face-to-face.

We have long known that we can choose various communication media to suit the purpose of the communication. It makes perfect sense to me that these participants would say they are more confident online, or that they feel they have a protective barrier online, or that they feel more powerful online, or that they feel more distant from their loved ones online. Of course. But feeling different in these various contexts does not *necessarily* mean the self is transformed, or even different.

In other words, we academics who write about the transcendence of the body, the fragmentation of identity in cyberspace, the hyperreal, etc., may be making too much of the entire phenomenon. I am completely complicitous in this endeavor, of course. I have longed to meet people online who would represent the epitome of fragmented identity, the decentered self, the addict. I have wandered through MUDs of every sort, looking for—and finding—cybersex, gender play, flame wars, and creatures of every description.

I've seen a lot of text. I've flirted and role-played different personalities. I've talked to addicts, who seem pretty normal other than the fact that they spend most of their day online. I certainly think my life is different than before this project began, but I don't want to overstate the case. Talking with these users has taught me something very meaningful: People *know* they are not really transcending their physical world; their body is the place where they live. They might like to forget it; they might like to escape the confines of a less-than-ideal physical context; they might like to play with various roles and encasements and personalities. Some of these online identities and experiences may be more real than others, but these users do not live under the illusion that one place is more real than the other. All the people I have met, anyway, know that there comes a time when the computer must be shut down and the needs of the body must be met. Terri put it well when she answered my question "How do you feel when you're online?" "Um, depends what I am working on or who I am talking to. Sometimes blown away. Sometimes bored. Sometimes angry. I often have to pee."

THOUGHTS ABOUT MY GOALS

Several goals inspired this study. First, I wanted to present the voices of some of the users of, or dwellers in, cyberspace. When I started this project, many writers were theorizing about online technologies, but few presented the words of the people upon whose experiences their theories are based, and many did not base their theories on peoples' experiences at all. Yet the words of those people who are engaging and living through online communication contexts are invaluable for theorizing about what it *means* to be online, because these are the people who construct its meaning through their engagement with and in it. They speak eloquently of their own experiences, and through careful consideration of their words, we can see personalized ontologies being articulated, selves being realized, and relationships, communities, and worlds being organized into ever-solidified frames of meaning.

Second, I sought to destabilize some of our entrenched notions of the concept of reality. That concept is embedded in our everyday language as authenticity and truth connected to physicality and the senses that operate in a physical world. But for the people whom I interviewed, *real* is a slippery term. For these users, having experiences in virtual spaces of the imagination does not mean that reality has disappeared into some mirror or vacuum. The term just encompasses more than it used to, and its meaning shifts as the self moves from context to context. Frankly, as I try to get closer to it—to understand it—the term *real* continues to slip away, as if it is becoming unfamiliar; and my understanding of self, being, and reality is being steadily transformed, blurred, or perhaps disfigured.

Third, I wanted to speak to the issue of communication technology and control, to address some of the ways we have convinced ourselves that technology is the magic key to controlling our lives. It doesn't surprise me that, as the pace and stress of everyday life increases, we crave control over ourselves and our environment. Scooter told me, "All our lives are out of control. We're spinning in this whirlpool, getting sucked toward the next something. I don't know what. Meanwhile we're drowning in information." A colleague mentioned the other day that he wished he could slide a faster information processer into his forehead to keep up with everything. A decade ago, my mother wrote a short story in which my father replaced his aging body with a machine because it would be so much easier to troubleshoot and maintain as he got older.

We crave control, and at the same time, we don't want to give anything up. We want control over the body, its shape, its abilities, its aging processes. And even as we are completely overwhelmed by information—as it swirls ever more maddeningly around us, obliterating us in a black-on-white blizzard of red tape, forms, messages, email, and volumes and volumes and volumes of data—we want to consume it.

Ideally, interfacing with the computer speeds up information processing, expands our own capacity to remember, and extends our reach to unimaginable distances around the globe. And perhaps more importantly, it increases our desire to consume. Here, in print, saying this seems silly; but think of this: Every few months, a new personal computer outpaces the reigning leader in terms of speed, capacity, and so forth. We race out to buy it, only to replace it in a year or two with another, faster system. To what end? To consume. And to hope, with all that consumption, that we are somehow assimilating information that will in some way help us better control our lives. Whether our capacity is equal to our desire is unknown—I suspect it is not, and eventually we will have to face up to this illusion of control. Yet, for the moment, these participants feel better able to control certain aspects of their lives through technology.

Fourth, I wanted to explore some of the ways people who use, live in, or exist through online communication contexts frame their understanding of their experiences. We give online communication a variety of labels to help us define what it means: Information Superhighway, Worldwide Web, Internet, Cyberspace, Electronic Frontier, and the like. As Sheol aptly notes, "without a name you don't exist, no one will talk to you." All of these alternative names are vying for our attention, wanting us to make them real. Current definitions of online communication will influence significantly the way people think about, respond to, and interact with it. In this book, I have presented some definitions from within. These participants are struggling to make sense of their online worlds discursively, recursively, dialogically.

They speak of the Internet as a communication medium, a conduit that transmits information from one place to another, a means of keeping in touch with friends in faraway places, a way to avoid face-to-face contact with the people just upstairs. They also frame cyberspace as a place created and sustained mostly through the exchange of texts, a place to meet and talk with others. Still others describe this technology as a way of being with others as a textual being, creating and expressing the soul in abstraction through language.

Whether as a tool or a place or a way of being, these participant use cyberspace, go there, or exist in the text to achieve a sense of freedom and control. Some feel that they are more vocal or are allowed a voice. Some receive more desirable attention online than they can in physical spaces. Some escape the scrutinizing, persistent gaze that follows them in bodied spaces. Some reconstruct their bodies to please the self, or to please others. Some call it home.

People's perceptions of computer-mediated communication shift and change depending on what they're doing. This makes intuitive sense; people experience cyberspace as they experience life—it's not that profoundly different. Just like all life experiences, sometimes they are more meaningful than at other times. All of this must be made sense of, and so the frames used to define online experiences will continue to evolve.

My final goal in this study was to explore the project itself, the process of coming to know others online through ethnographic inquiry. I have begun a search to understand how people make sense of a technology that occupies a great deal of their time, but it is apparent that this project is in many ways a model of itself. For example, I am trying to understand how people carry on conversations, relationships, and sometimes their lives through the exchange of texts. And to learn about it, I am carrying on conversations, building relationships, and living much of my life through the exchange of texts as well. The resulting texts, which were created dialogically online, became my objects of analysis. It's almost like living on a Möbius strip, a never-ending recursive loop of sense-making, which makes it difficult to separate the researcher from the researched, the product from the process. I went online to find a cultural context to study. I ended up creating one of countless cultural contexts through my own choices, movements, and encounters.

I do not mean to overemphasize my role in this process, but I am also wary of underemphasizing it, as too many scholars do. To adequately make sense of the final product (this document), it is necessary to understand where I (the researcher and the co-creator of this context) began, how I gradually made sense of the context, why I made the choices I did, and how I struggled through the process of creating this product. The process of organizing online communication happened as this project progressed. Hence, the project itself is a necessary element in the ethnographic report.

THOUGHTS ABOUT THE PROJECT

Why did I do this study? To understand *them* or to understand *the place* or to understand the *nature of research* or to understand *me*?

June 2, 1997; approximately 3:00 a.m.: Tonight, everything I have ever known seems to be relevant; it all seems connected. Memories flow by like IRC texts scrolling up on the screen, capturing my attention for an instant and then drifting out of sight, to be replaced by another moment in some time and space other than here and now. But it's not really the same experience. When I watch an IRC screen, the texts are more removed from me unless I know the participants and feel a connection to the conversation. In IRC, when I shut my eyes, I can shut the voices off in my head, though images and words will continue to scroll for a few moments, like when you shut your eyes tightly after staring at a beautiful spring scene and then see it vaguely against the back of your eyelids.

✳

It is more difficult to turn off the memories that scroll through my brain at 3:00 A.M. when I'm trying to sleep; but if I concentrate, I can make something else take the place of a persistent thought. You see, there are so many things that need thinking about, so much of life past to remember, so much of life future to contemplate. Books I've read, the book I'm writing, family troubles, summer, bills, wars, comets, suicides, my brother, bad dreams, song lyrics—all drifting back just when I think they've finally disappeared. We've always been this way, we humans. We have the capacity to think, so we do. I'm learning, however, as I entertain and engage this ethnography, that the result of all this thinking—the product of the process, if you will—is a complex, reflexive, and mostly nonlinear narrative.

This ethnography is situated in time, yes. It is taking place over a period of months, and has been stewing for several years. I am not certain, in fact, when it began. Does my understanding of the way people engage and live with technology begin when I start to interpret the texts of my conversations with them? Or does it begin when I start talking with them? Or did it begin when I was a child, sitting on the hard wooden floor of the local library, pulling science fiction books off the shelves, drifting to other times and places, imagining other ways of being and knowing?

I understand the need to narrativize. I understand the need to attempt to understand other cultures. I know that ethnography provides a valuable means of understanding the depths and particulars of human experiences. But for the life of me, I can't figure out what my own ethnographic project wants to be. I want to know the Other, and I want to know what cyberspace means to those who dwell there, because I believe it will provide valuable information about human interactions and interfaces with technology. But at the same time, before I can know Other, I must know myself. Perhaps this ethnography is about myself. For me, this seems a self-centered stance. Is this one of those self-reflexive postmodern explorations of subjectivity, interpretation of the self's impossibility through stream of consciousness, where self is both subject and object, observer and observed, self and other? Good mental exercise. Useful. Is that what this is?

Perhaps that's all there is.

Oh, Annette, it isn't that simple; you see, there is more than just you here.

Everything is in dialogue with everything else. And through conversations, self and reality are co-created and sustained. Commands become emotions. Keyboard strokes become created texts that mingle and weave an intricate pattern of being. Cyberspace is a mosaic, a random organization of moments embedded in text and lived through the body/mind to create a narrative in retrospect. Mapping this mosaic into a narrative gives me relief from the apparent meaninglessness of dislocated conversations, disembodied presence, disjunctive arrival and departure from Others' moments. This shimmering mirror-like nothingness becomes a meaningful world of relationships as it is molded into patterns. I create a narrative because I need stories to live by. I need a history, a way of understanding the present.

This book will be the history of this project, the retelling of the year I was thirty-two years old. It is my future memory. It tells a story that will never be relived, yet will never end. It means everything to me now; I can't imagine not knowing every moment of its creation. Soon, though, it will begin to change, and with every re-reading, become more unfamiliar.

THOUGHTS ABOUT THE FUTURE

We are at a juncture of the technological age where we have the potential to move more of our everyday lives to various information spaces. I have learned a lot since I began this study. I am not so much the neophyte I once was, although I am now confronting other boundaries. As interactive interface technologies become more accessible, communicating face-to-face via the computer becomes a virtual reality (pun intended). Particularly in the United States, we are caught in a technological whirlwind that threatens to overtake other sensibilities. I am told in almost any magazine I pick up that if I want to be connected, I need to get connected; and although I am completely aware of the hazards of overreliance on technology, I have bought into it. It is almost impossible to escape the onslaught of messages persuading us to get in line to go online.

My mother is thinking of using the Internet to help her build the family genealogy. I have almost convinced my colleague Bill that he needs to update his computer abilities; I already got him to go online to research buying a car. On my own computer, I can go to any number of university libraries, and I have a personalized navigator to help me get around in the Web. I have put the course I currently teach online using an in-house networking program. This year, I'll teach a course completely online, never meeting some of my students face-to-face. I communicate with thousands of people using email, sometimes when they are sitting in the office across the hall and both our doors are open. I have programs that allow me to interact more easily with online groups and communities. I have programs to transfer files from place to place, which is also useful for transferring additional helpful programs to my computer. I have programs to help me construct and update my home page on the Web. Sure, these are all useful projects to spend time on, but I spend more time in front of my computer screen than I would like to talk about.

Technology usefully aids us in the everyday accomplishment of life. I don't need to mention the computer, the telephone, the pager, the answering machine, the fax and copy machines, global positioning systems, or the hundreds of thousands of technological devices we use almost without thinking to make our lives easier. But as many scholars have articulated, technology shapes us into something different when we come to rely on it. As we enter another phase of technological development, it behooves us to think about the potential of technology, not only to connect us, but to isolate us, tame us, and decenter our selves away from our bodies.

As it continues to become more sophisticated, more accessible, and less expensive, people are using technology to mediate greater—and I think more significant—elements of their lives, and this comes with a mixture of curses and blessings, like anything else. I spoke with a woman who is separated from her husband because they hold jobs in distant cities; they have homes separated by half of the United States. I told her I was critical of online technology, and she was aghast. She couldn't imagine life without interactive email and interactive video conferencing, which allow her and her husband to communicate several times a day. She said technology greatly enhanced her relationship with her husband. It was great to be able to see his face, see him in his office, and feel like she was really with him.

I understood how she felt and couldn't imagine being apart from someone I was married to; but at the same time, I couldn't believe what I was hearing. I asked her if she ever questioned the fact that technology enabled her to believe it was *acceptable* to be separated from her husband permanently. There was a long silence, and then she told me, "No," she had never thought of it that way. I told her I was critical of technology, not because it connects us to others and it feels like we're really there, but because it beguiles us to think it's okay to be connected to others *only* or *mostly* in that way.

I heard about a twelve-year-old American boy who saved a Finnish student's life online. He said a Finnish woman appeared in this chatroom in IRC one night, asking for help. She was locked in a computer lab, she said, and was having a severe asthma attack. Most of the people in the chatroom thought she was joking around and paid little attention to her, or played along with the joke. But for some reason, the boy said, it began to feel more real, so he decided to do something about it. With the help of local police and long-distance operators, rescuers in Finland found the woman and took her to the hospital. She lived because she was able to connect to a vast network of people interacting with each other digitally.

Sheol told me during our interview that the Internet is a place where you will always find someone who is willing to listen and help you with whatever troubles you, whether it's a research question, an asthma attack, or your own life. "Some of my darkest moments have been spent on the net. . . . My net friends drove from NY to Georgia because another net friend sounded suicidal." Terri told me that while she was online, her friends talked her through a few scary moments when she had quit her medication and was swinging into a massive depression.

The Internet is a great dance we do to shape an imagined dimension of startlingly live reality. What you do there is only limited by your ability to create texts, to respond to others' texts, and to be creative. It can be a place to go to find others to connect with; yet even as powerful as words can be, our relations with others online are also constrained by the network that controls a significant part of the connection.

The Internet is deceptive that way, and as I've mentioned before, beguiling in that it makes us believe we have found something good enough. It is a Band-Aid for some, a prosthetic for others. But as good as it feels, as real as it is—cybersex, a virtual massage, living through language, controlling the self—I believe these pleasures cannot suffice in a world that must still be lived through the body in the physical dimension.

Even for those who have found like-minded and -bodied people through the Internet (in support groups, particularly), an online hug can satisfy for only so long.

(*I spent two weeks alone, in my office or at home. Sometimes I went for more than twenty-four hours without speaking to another human, not counting talking to myself or the screen, of course. Today, for the first time in eight days, a dear friend hugged me. Immediately, tears came to my eyes because it felt so good. It felt so wonderful to be touched by a real somebody. I felt alive.*)

At some point, we need physical encounters with others; we need to be touched. Terri knows this, even when she is most integrated with the system. She knows that when it feels too good online it means she is trying to escape the body. So she returns to the body sometimes, to live there and learn to be happy there. At the moment, she has moved out of the city and is feeling the grass tickle her toes, getting connected to another pulsing, vibrant, planetary network.

I guess, in the end, I don't have many answers. I think the Internet is both blown completely out of proportion and completely underestimated regarding its capacity to change us and our world. I don't think it will take away our humanity, but I think it has the capacity to take us away from a grounded, bound-to-the-earth sort of understanding of what it means to live a full and healthy life. This has been happening for decades, of course, ever since we got into cars, started speeding down highways, and stopped noticing the glorious details of the planet as we race past them to get somewhere. Some would probably say it began even earlier. As much as technology connects us, it also isolates us, with or without online forms of communication. This has serious implications for traditional notions of community, family, and the environment, but it isn't the technology that does it to us. We engage it. We live it. We use it. We choose.

Afterword

I just went to the MOO and logged on in the usual way, by typing "connect markham ********" (the *s are my password). After a short pause, the screen told me I was home, but it didn't look like Hut X. So I typed "look," a command that would show me the description of where I currently stood in the MOO. The same, absolutely incorrect description scrolled up the screen:

```
Room 1703 (Hut X)

As always, the room you wake up in is filled with sunlight,
but the decor has changed. Low beige sectionals circle the
room, someone has moved in a coffee table and a gaggle of
rubber plants of varying heights. The carpeting is pale beige
too; everything is in shades of neutral here. What does it
mean?

The imagination fills the interstices. Wander out. Look around.
As long as you stay in the hotel, you are in transit.

Exits include: [Hallway] to 2nd Floor Hallway

vigo (asleep) is standing here.
```

I felt confused and disoriented. Who was Vigo? Whenever I came to the MOO, Beth would be here, and if she wasn't online, the MOO would tell me she was asleep. But now, no matter how many times I typed "look" to verify my location, Beth's name did not appear. I typed "@who" to see if she had moved somewhere else, but couldn't find her.

I didn't know what to think. I just stood there, (or sat here), and stared at the furniture. It was beige. Beige. The description told me I was in transition. It seemed to say that this place wasn't really my home. I typed "sit," and the screen replied, "Markham lays on the bed."

I felt a little forlorn, and lonely. I didn't know where Beth was, or why she wasn't here, or why the room had changed. Clearly, this was no longer her home. It wasn't like anything she would say at all. After a few moments, I remembered Beth had told me in one of our earlier conversations that another person had let her have this place. The original owner had taken it back, apparently, and now that she was gone, I felt like a squatter.

I didn't really have anyplace to go, but I started walking anyway. I just typed "out" and hit the enter button, which took me out into the hallway. I guess I was feeling a little dejected, because I just kept typing "out," "out," "out," "out," "out." Scenes flashed by on the screen as I typed this word. "Out" is a default movement command that you can use if you don't know what direction you want or need to go. Enough "outs" will take you back to the orientation center, the place where you began. The Birdcage elevator, the Grand Lobby, the conference center, the street, down the street, Free Speech Alley. The pretzel stand flashed on my screen for a moment, then the park bench. I didn't even pause. "out," "out," "out," "out." Finally, a message appeared that repeated itself whenever I typed "out":

```
You can't get much more out than this.. Maybe you should try
picking a direction to go. (type 'ways' for a list)

You can't get much more out than this.. Maybe you should try
picking a direction to go. (type 'ways' for a list)

You can't get much more out than this.. Maybe you should try
picking a direction to go. (type 'ways' for a list)
```

I typed "@quit," and pressed the enter key. And then the screen went blank.

References Cited

Argyle, K.
   1996 Life after death. In *Cultures of Internet: Virtual spaces, real histories, living bodies,* edited by R. Shields. Thousand Oaks, Calif.: Sage.

Ashmore, M.
   1989 *The reflexive thesis: Wrighting sociology of scientific knowledge.* Chicago: University of Chicago Press.

Bakhtin, M. M.
   1981 *The dialogic imagination.* Austin: University of Texas Press.

Barker, F.
   1984 *The tremulous private body: Essays in subjection.* London: Methuen.

Bateson, G.
   1972 *Steps to an ecology of mind.* New York: Ballantine.

Baudrillard, J.
   1988 *The ecstasy of communication.* Translated by B. Schutze and C. Schutze. New York: Semiotext(e).

Baym, N.
   1995 The emergence of community in computer-mediated communication. In *Cybersociety: Computer-mediated communication and community,* edited by S. G. Jones. Thousand Oaks, Calif.: Sage.

Benedikt, M.
   1991. *Cyberspace: First steps.* Cambridge, Mass: MIT Press.

Bromberg, H.
  1996 Are MUDs communities? Identity, belonging, and consciousness in virtual
      worlds. In *Cultures of Internet: Virtual spaces, real histories, living bodies*, edited by
      R. Shields. Thousand Oaks, Calif.: Sage.

Cherny, L. & Weise, E.
  1996 *Wired women: Gender and new realities in cyberspace*. Seattle: Seal Press.

Clark, N.
  1995 Rear-View Mirrorshades: The Recursive Generation of the Cyberbody. In
      Cyberspace/Cyberbodies/Cyberpunk: Cultures of technological embodiment, edited
      by M. Featherstone & R. Burrows. Thousand Oaks, Calif.: Sage.

Dibbell, J.
  1993 A rape in Cyberspace; or how an evil clown, a Haitian trickster spirit, two
      wizards, and a cast of dozens turned a database into a society. *Village Voice*
      (December 21): 36–42.

Fisher, W. R.
  1984 Narration as a human communication paradigm: The case of public moral
      argument. *Communication Monographs* 51:1–22.

Geertz, C.
  1973 *The interpretation of cultures*. New York: Basic Books.

Gibson, W.
  1986 *Neuromancer*. London: Grafton.

Goffman, E.
  1974 *Frame analysis: An essay on the organization of experience*. New York: Harper
      and Row.

Grumet, M. R.
  1991 The politics of personal knowledge. In *Stories lives tell: Narrative and dialogue
      in education*, edited by C. Witherell and N. Noddings. New York: Columbia
      University Teachers College Press.

Haraway, D.
  1991 *Simians, cyborgs, and women: The reinvention of nature*. New York: Routledge.

Herring, S.
  1993 Gender and democracy in computer-mediated communication. *Electronic
      Journal of Communication/La Revue Electronique de Communication* 3(2):1–17.

Holquist, M.
   1990 *Dialogism: Bakhtin and his world.* London: Routledge Press.

Jameson, F.
   1991 *Postmodernism, or the cultural logic of late capitalism.* Durham, N. C.: Duke University Press.

Jones, S. G., ed.
   1995 *Cybersociety: computer-mediated communication and community.* Thousand Oaks, Calif.: Sage.

Keeps, C. J.
   1993 Knocking on heaven's door: Leibbniz, Baudrillard and virtual reality. Ejournal 3, n.p. Available via anonymous ftp: EJOUNAL@albany.bitnet (accessed March 1994).

Laing, R. D.
   1969 *Self and others.* New York: Pantheon.

Lakoff, G. & Johnson, M.
   1981 *Metaphors we live by.* Chicago: University of Chicago Press.

Landsberg, A.
   1995 Prosthetic memory: Total recall and Blade Runner. In *Cyberspace/Cyberbodies/Cyberpunk: Cultures of technological embodiment,* edited by M. Featherstone & R. Burrows. Thousand Oaks, Calif.: Sage.

Ludlow, P.
   1995 *High noon on the electronic frontier: Conceptual issues in cyberspace.* Cambridge: MIT Press.

MacKinnon, R. C.
   1995 *Searching for the Leviathan in usenet. Cybersociety: Computer-mediated communication and community,* edited by S. G. Jones. Thousand Oaks, Calif.: Sage.

MacKinnon, R. C.
   1998 The social construction of rape in cyberspace. In *Network and Netplay: Virtual Groups on the Internet,* edited by F. Sudweeks, S. Rafaeli, & M McLaughlin. Menlo Park, Calif.: AAAI Press. [cited from the online/ascii version. Retrieved March 1997 from the World Wide Web: http://www.actlab.utexas.edu/~spartan/texts/rape.html]

Novak, M.
    1991 Liquid architectures in cyberspace. In *Cyberspace: First steps*, edited by M. Benedikt. Cambridge, Mass.: MIT Press.

Reid, E.
    1995 Virtual worlds: Culture and imagination. In *Cybersociety: Computer-mediated communication and community*, edited by S. G. Jones. Thousand Oaks, Calif.: Sage.

Rheingold, H.
    1991 *Virtual reality*. New York: Touchstone.
    1993 *The virtual community: Homesteading on the electronic frontier*. Reading, Mass: Addison-Wesley.

Robins, K.
    1995 Cyberspace and the world we live. In *Cyberspace/Cyberbodies/Cyberpunk: Cultures of technological embodiment*, edited by M. Featherstone and R. Burrows. Thousand Oaks, Calif.: Sage.

Senft, T. M.
    1996a Of Women and Dogs. [Online]. Retrieved April 1998 from the Worldwide Web: http://www.echonyc.com/~janedoe/writing/womendogs.html
    1996b My first time. [Online]. Retrieved from the Worldwide Web April 1998: http://www.echonyc.com/~janedoe/baudbehavior/index.html
    1997 Introduction: performing the digital body—a ghost story. Women and Performance Quarterly [Online Journal] 17. Retrieved May 1997 from the Worldwide Web: http://www.echonyc.com/~women/Issue17/

Senft, T. M. & Horn, S.
    1996 An Interview. [Online]. Retrieved from the Worldwide Web April 1998: http://www.echonyc.com/~janedoe/writing/grandinterview.html

Shields, R., ed.
    1996 *Cultures of Internet: virtual spaces, real histories, living bodies*. Thousand Oaks, Calif.: Sage.

Slouka, M.
    1995 *War of the worlds*. New York: Basic Books.

Sproull, L. & Keisler, S.
    1991 *Connections: New ways of working in the networked organization*. Cambridge: MIT Press.

Stone, R. A.
  1991 Will the real body please stand up?: Boundary stories about virtual cultures. In *Cyberspace: First steps*, edited by M. Benedikt. Cambridge, Mass.: MIT Press.

Tannen, D.
  1990 *You just don't understand: Women and men in conversation.* New York: Morrow Press.

Terkel, S.
  1974 *Working: people talk about what they do all day and how they feel about what they do.* New York: New Press.
  1984 *"The good war": An oral history of World War Two.* New York: Pantheon Books.
  1992 *Race: How Blacks and Whites think and feel about the American obsession.* New York: New Press.

Turkle, S.
  1984 *The second self: Computers and the human spirit.* New York: Simon and Schuster.
  1995 *Life on the screen: Identity in the age of the Internet.* New York: Simon and Schuster.

Tyler, S.
  1986 Post-modern ethnography: From document of the occult to occult document. In *Writing culture*, edited by J. Clifford and G. E. Marcus. Berkeley: University of California Press.

Van Maanen, J.
  1988 *Tales of the field.* Chicago: University of Chicago Press.
  1995 *Representation in ethnography.* Thousand Oaks, Calif.: Sage.

Weick, K. E.
  1979 *The social psychology of organizing.* 2d edition. Reading, Mass.: Addison-Wesley.

Wolf, M.
  1992 *A thrice told tale: Feminism, postmodernism, and ethnographic responsibility.* Stanford: Stanford University Press.

Woolley, B.
  1992 *Virtual worlds.* Oxford: Blackwell.

Index

"andrewm," 29–30, 31–4
anonymity online, 43

"Bambi" (Annette Markham), 10, 35–6, 120–3
"Ben," 106–14
"Beth." *See* "Beth_ANN."
"Beth_ANN" ("Beth," "Ellen"), 10, 42, 43–7, 49, 50–2, 53, 54, 59, 72–6, 87–8, 89–114, 169–76, 211, 212–3, 214, 216, 219, 233, 234
biorhythms, 53
"BobZ," 44–7, 50, 154

chatrooms, 18, 41, 58
"Cheryl" ("Diamond_Guest"), 44–6
"Cindy T's Emissary," 39–40
client program, 64
communication
    asynchronous, 56, 153
    computer-mediated (CMC), 8, 13, 18, 20, 21, 63, 78, 79, 85, 87, 88, 138, 155, 182, 225
    informality of, 57, 146
    nonverbal, 48–9, 71–2, 182
    online, 21, 73, 79, 80
        as cultural context, 20
    as self, 208, 209
    as supplement to face-to-face, 144, 227
    as tool, 20, 54, 80, 147, 148, 155–56
    synchronous, 62, 153
    traditional vocabularies in, 119
    virtual, 17
communication and information transmission, blurring of, 64–65, 213–14
connection through technology, 227–30
continuum (*tool* to *place* to *way of being*), 10, 20, 85, 87, 88, 114, 125, 157, 162, 212
cyberpunk novels, 52, 83
cybersex, 30, 36, 222, 229
cyberspace, 7, 8, 9, 18, 21, 23, 24, 54, 79, 82, 210–2, 227
    as evolving cultural form, 17, 115, 145
    as place, 10, 20, 52, 86, 87, 113, 137, 156, 158, 176, 181, 185, 186, 189, 205, 212–3, 224, 229
    as tool, 10, 20, 87, 88, 137, 138, 140, 212–3, 224
    as way of being, 10, 20, 86, 87, 189, 212–3, 224
    definition of, 17
    sense of freedom in, 57, 187, 202, 224
cyborg, 86, 165, 194

"Diamond_Guest," 44–6. *See also* "Cheryl."
Diversity University (DU), 10, 37, 38, 40,
    67, 88, 126
DominO, 139
DU, 41, 49, 50, 54, 55, 59, 113, 154. *See also*
    Diversity University.

email, 54, 64, 140, 141–2, 181, 191, 194,
    207, 228
embodiment, 17, 20, 23, 24, 35, 57, 58, 59,
    79, 128, 136, 139, 162, 175, 176, 191,
    194, 203, 204, 212, 213, 215
    ambivalence about, 8, 48, 60, 113
    text as embodied self, 211
emote commands, 48, 71, 141, 149, 169
emotion, expressing online, 76, 217
"Esra Franko," 29–30
ethics online, 36–37
ethnography, 7, 8, 9, 11, 18, 19, 20, 25, 54,
    61–2, 63, 65, 77, 83, 126, 128, 221,
    225, 226
    postmodern, 208, 226

flaming, 24, 56, 57, 222

"Gargoyle," 54, 56, 69–70, 176, 216
gender
    perceived importance of, 182, 213
    perceptions of, 43, 180, 191
    playing with, 159, 160, 181, 222
global society, 12
going online, fear of, 25, 56

hyperreal, 118, 154
    definition of, 116

information, as power, 185, 212, 214
Internet (Net), 15, 21, 61, 63, 210, 211,
    229–30
    addiction to, 179, 222
    as tool, 20, 80, 86, 137, 154, 224, 227
    empowerment through, 197
Internet Relay Chat, 30, 34–5, 40. *See also*
    IRC.
IRC (Internet Relay Chat), 9, 10, 40, 41, 53,
    54, 56, 63, 67, 74, 99, 177, 186, 225–
    6, 228–9
isolation through technology, 230

"Jennifer," 87, 124, 140–9, 150, 211, 212,
    214, 215

"Kelly," 68, 176, 181, 187

LambdaMOO, 35, 150. *See also* MOO.
"Lord Sheol." *See* "Sheol."
Louise. *See* "Moonstone_Guest."
lurking, 24

"Matthew," 87, 129–40, 141, 150, 211, 212,
    213, 214
"Michael," 87, 148, 149, 156–8
"Mist," 87, 149–56, 163, 211, 212, 214, 216
MOO, 9, 10, 37, 38, 41, 43, 45, 47, 49, 53,
    54, 56, 58, 63, 64, 67, 68, 74, 89, 113,
    129, 130, 136, 137, 139, 150, 152,
    155, 170, 174, 175, 233
"Moonstone_Guest" (Louise), 55–6
MUD, 9, 49, 67, 139, 143, 148, 156–7, 158,
    160, 161, 186, 222. *See also* Multi-
    User Dimension.
multi-task, 50
Multi-User Dimension, 18, 35, 37, 140,
    141. *See also* MUD.

Net. *See* Internet.
NetMeeting, 26, 30, 35, 67

Object-Oriented, 37. *See also* MOO.
"Obsidian_Guest" ("Matthew"), 129–32
online relationships, 18, 141–4, 180, 212,
    225, 229
Other, 11, 25, 124, 156, 165, 209, 215, 227
    controlling, 124, 188, 197, 214
    knowing, 83, 115, 161, 162, 175, 189,
        205, 211, 226
    making sense of, 82, 188

"pejay," 120–3
power of naming, 35, 36, 40, 43, 224

Rawlins, William K., 12, 14
real life (RL), 72, 115, 136, 137, 161
real time, 26, 30, 31, 42, 63
real, definition of, 116
real/hyperreal, blurring of distinction, 118
real/not real, binary distinctions of, 116–7,
    120, 162, 206–7
real/virtual, blurring of distinction, 117,
    135–6, 157, 166, 187, 194, 197, 211,
    223
reality
    comparisons with virtuality, 30, 39, 52–
        3, 78–9, 115, 117, 119, 153, 157, 163,
        165, 174, 179, 183, 215
    of online experiences, 18, 25, 40, 62,
        147–8, 170
    of time, 53
    postmodern theories on, 116–9
referent versus sign, 119
research
    interpretive dilemmas, 119, 126, 166–7,
        172
    limitations of, 126
    organization of, 82–3
    separating process from product, 128,
        225

    separating researcher from researched,
        114, 207, 225
research methods
    interpretive, 80–2, 208
    interview protocol, 77–8, 79, 82, 89
    interview techniques, 74–8
    nonlinear nature of, 77–8, 83
    qualitative, 61–2, 72, 81, 126

"Scooter," 15–6, 216, 223
self
    co-creating the self, 227
    confidence of self online, 80, 135, 222
    control of self online, 20, 86, 123–25,
        154, 155, 196, 214, 215, 224, 229
    controlling the self of the other online,
        150, 195, 214, 222
    creating the self online, 8, 16, 26, 37,
        114, 159, 163, 184, 194, 210, 225
    expression of self online, 86, 149, 152
    presentation of self online, 22, 48, 79,
        123–25, 173, 197, 204, 213, 215
    protection of self online, 26, 214, 222
    sense of self online, 79, 114, 139, 145,
        165, 195, 202, 212
"Sheol" ("Lord Sheol," "Xfile"), 35, 76–7,
    83, 87–8, 155, 176–91, 211, 212, 214,
    215, 216, 224, 229
"Sherie," 65–8, 87–8, 115, 139, 200–4, 205–
    9, 211, 212, 214, 215
silence of the Internet, 11, 76, 217–9
space, sense of dislocated, 42
SPAM, 109, 110

teleport, 42, 43, 114
telepresence, 17
"Terri," 87–8, 163, 192–9, 209, 211, 212,
    214, 218, 219, 222, 229
threads, 24

time
    miscalculating time for interviewing, 75,
        175, 177
    passage of, 15, 59, 113, 136
    perception of, 57

Usenet group, 140

virtual community, 7, 86, 150, 176
    and level of commitment, 154

virtual life, 16
virtual spaces, 9, 18
virtual, definition of, 116

Web. *See* Worldwide Web.
Worldwide Web (WWW, Web), 41, 49, 53,
    218, 228
WWW. *See* Worldwide Web.

"Xfile." *See* "Sheol."

Index of Authors Cited

Argyle, K., 17
Ashmore, M., 78

Bakhtin, M. M., 188
Barker, E., 165
Bateson, G., 188
Baudrillard, J., 79, 88, 116
Baym, N., 88
Benedikt, M., 79, 88, 116, 163
Bromberg, H., 88

Cherny, L. & Weise, E., 88
Clark, N., 88

Dibbell, J., 150, 214

Fisher, W. R., 21

Geertz, C., 82
Gibson, W., 79
Goffman, E., 161
Grumet, M. R., 21, 78

Haraway, D., 165
Herring, S., 182
Holquist, M., 188

Jameson, F., 79
Jones, S. G., ed., 54, 88

Keeps, C. J., 117, 163

Laing, R. D., 215
Lakoff, G. & Johnson, M., 114
Landsberg, A., 155
Ludlow, P., 88

MacKinnon, R. C., 117, 154

Novak, M., 155

Reid, E., 88
Rheingold, H., 18, 79, 88, 116, 117–8
Robins, K., 88

Senft, T. M., 88, 191
Shields, R., ed., 88
Slouka, M., 79
Sproull, L. & Keisler, S., 88
Stone, R. A., 79, 88, 165

Tannen, D., 182
Terkel, S., 31, 62

Turkle, S., 79, 88, 134, 155, 188, 218
Tyler, S., 208

Van Maanen, J., 78, 126

Wolf, M., 78
Woolley, B., 79

About the Author

Annette N. Markham is assistant professor of communication studies at Virginia Polytechnic Institute and State University, where she teaches courses in organizational communication, argumentation and critical thinking, ethnographic research methods, and information technology and organizational life. She received her Ph.D. from Purdue University, where she achieved a Bruce Kendall Award for Excellence in Teaching and was designated an Alan H. Monroe Graduate Scholar for life. She recently published a critical ethnography of strategic ambiguity and workplace control in *Management Communication Quarterly* and is continuing her studies of communication and subjectivity in cyberspace.